CAMBRIDGE STUDIES
ANGLO-SAXON ENGLAND
29

# LITERARY APPROPRIATIONS OF THE
# ANGLO-SAXONS FROM THE
# THIRTEENTH TO THE TWENTIETH CENTURY

# CAMBRIDGE STUDIES IN
# ANGLO-SAXON ENGLAND

FOUNDING GENERAL EDITORS
## MICHAEL LAPIDGE AND SIMON KEYNES
CURRENT GENERAL EDITORS
## SIMON KEYNES AND ANDY ORCHARD

*Volumes published*

Milton's commonplace book (Trinity College, Cambridge, R.3.4, page 38), reproduced by permission of the Master and Fellows

# LITERARY APPROPRIATIONS OF THE ANGLO-SAXONS FROM THE THIRTEENTH TO THE TWENTIETH CENTURY

EDITED BY

DONALD SCRAGG AND CAROLE WEINBERG

*University of Manchester*

CAMBRIDGE
UNIVERSITY PRESS

CAMBRIDGE UNIVERSITY PRESS
Cambridge, New York, Melbourne, Madrid, Cape Town, Singapore, São Paulo

Cambridge University Press
The Edinburgh Building, Cambridge CB2 2RU, UK

Published in the United States of America by Cambridge University Press, New York

www.cambridge.org
Information on this title: www.cambridge.org/9780521632157

First published 2000
This digitally printed first paperback version 2006

*A catalogue record for this publication is available from the British Library*

*Library of Congress Cataloguing in Publication data*

Literary Appropriations of the Anglo-Saxons from the Thirteenth to the Twentieth
Century / edited by Donald Scragg and Carole Weinberg.
p. cm. – (Cambridge studies in Anglo-Saxon England: 29)
Includes bibliographical references and index.
ISBN 0 521 63215 3 (hardback)
1. English literature–History and criticism.
2. Anglo-Saxons in literature.
3. English literature–Middle English, 1100–1500–History and criticism.
4. Great Britain–History–Anglo-Saxon period, 449–1066–Historiography.
5. Civilization, Anglo-Saxon, in literature.
6. Medievalism–Great Britain–History.
I. Scragg, D. G. II. Weinberg, Carole. III. Series.
PR151.A53L57 2000
820.9′358–dc21 99–34241 CIP

ISBN-13 978-0-521-63215-7 hardback
ISBN-10 0-521-63215-3 hardback

ISBN-13 978-0-521-03117-2 paperback
ISBN-10 0-521-03117-6 paperback

# Contents

## Contents

# Contributors

JULIA BRIGGS, *De Montfort University, Leicester*
DANIEL DONOGHUE, *Harvard University*
JOHN FRANKIS, *University of Newcastle*
JILL FREDERICK, *Moorhead State University, Minnesota*
EDWARD B. IRVING, JR, *formerly of the University of Pennsylvania*
SARAH MITCHELL, *University of York*
JACQUELINE PEARSON, *University of Manchester*
LYNDA PRATT, *Queen's University of Belfast*
ANDREW SANDERS, *Durham University*
DONALD SCRAGG, *University of Manchester*
LEAH SCRAGG, *University of Manchester*
T. A. SHIPPEY, *St Louis University*
CAROLE WEINBERG, *University of Manchester*

# Acknowledgements

A collaborative volume needs input from numerous hands, and only a few of those who contributed to its final form are acknowledged here. We are grateful to many colleagues in the English Department at the University of Manchester who helped in the organization of the third G. L. Brook Symposium, especially to Gale Owen-Crocker who made many of the administrative arrangements, and to Maxine Powell who acted as Conference Secretary. We also wish to acknowledge help from Maxine and from Julie Saunders in the preparation of the typescript of this volume.

The contributors were forbearing in responding to requests for re-writing and to a great many queries. They have also been very patient during the long gestation period of the book. Michael Lapidge was most supportive of the volume when it was first proposed for the Series, and Sarah Stanton helped us put it together and made a great many useful suggestions. We owe them both many thanks.

DGS
SCW

# Abbreviations

# Introduction
# The Anglo-Saxons: fact and fiction

## DONALD SCRAGG

The essays in this book are based on papers presented at the third G. L. Brook Symposium held at the University of Manchester in 1995. They show ways in which the history of the Anglo-Saxon period has been manipulated to satisfy the agendas of poets, dramatists and writers of imaginative prose works – even briefly by composers of film scripts and lyricists – ranging in date from a little over one hundred years after the Norman Conquest to the present day. Although there has been much scholarly interest in recent decades in the agendas of antiquarians, linguists, and political and ecclesiastical historians writing about this period, those of creative artists have been largely ignored.[1] The subject is a topical one. It is notable that although nationalism is in vogue at the present time, evidenced by the break-up of eastern Europe, the conflict in former Yugoslavia, tribal antagonism in Africa and even devolution in the United Kingdom, the English today are very unclear about their own cultural identity and their history, as Tom Shippey's essay at the end of this book makes clear. It has not always been so, and the preceding essays examine some of the attitudes towards the first 'English' men and women

[1] Some of the essays in *Anglo-Saxon Scholarship: The First Three Centuries*, ed. C. T. Berkhout and M. McC. Gatch (Boston, 1982), glance fleetingly at the work of creative artists, and recently V. B. Richmond, in 'Historical Novels to Teach Anglo-Saxonism', *Anglo-Saxonism and the Construction of Social Identity*, ed. A. J. Frantzen and John D. Niles (Gainsville, Fla., 1997), pp. 173–201, looks at juvenile historical fiction in Victorian and Edwardian England, published after the essays in the present book were written. For pictorial and sculptural art, there is a useful bibliography in *Alfred the Great: Asser's 'Life of King Alfred'*, trans. with an introduction by S. Keynes and M. Lapidge (Harmondsworth, 1983), pp. 218–19, note 77, and cf. also the entry by Simon Keynes in *Blackwell Encyclopaedia of Anglo-Saxon England*, ed. M. Lapidge, J. Blair, S. Keynes and D. Scragg (Oxford, 1999), s.v. *Anglo-Saxonism*.

1

in literary works of different periods and the cultural concepts that such attitudes embody. Literature in English is this book's primary target, although some essays refer to material in French or Latin to locate their subject's topics in an appropriate framework. The purpose of this introductory chapter is to contextualize what follows, first by giving a brief history of the Anglo-Saxon period,[2] and second by adding further evidence of the incidence of the Anglo-Saxons in fiction to the more detailed analyses of the individual essays.

The term 'Anglo-Saxon' was first used in the pre-Conquest period as a means of distinguishing the English Saxons from their continental neighbours.[3] Since the nineteenth century scholars have used the term to denote the Germanic peoples who invaded Britain in post-Roman times in the second half of the fifth century. They replaced the existing Celtic and Romano-Celtic political structures with a series of kingdoms throughout southern Britain in most of the area now known as England and in part of modern Scotland south of the Firth of Forth. Their common defining characteristic was that they all spoke varieties of the ancestor of modern English, although for some centuries the political reality was that they consisted of warring groups, the success of each of which lay in the strength of character of their kings. The principal kingdoms were, from north to south, Northumbria (sometimes divided into Bernicia in the north and Deira in the south), Mercia (broadly the midlands area), East Anglia, Essex, Kent, Sussex and Wessex. One by one, these kingdoms were converted to Christianity, initially by missionaries sent by Pope Gregory the Great to Kent at the end of the sixth century and by Irish monks from Iona in western Scotland during the early seventh. The earliest significant Christian kings were Æthelberht of Kent (d. 616), and Edwin (616–633) and his nephew Oswald (634–642), both of Northumbria. It was Gregory

---

[2] Since I am here simplifying the historical background for the benefit of those without specialist knowledge of the period, I offer no supporting evidence. For a fuller account of the whole period, see F. M. Stenton, *Anglo-Saxon England*, 3rd edn. (Oxford, 1971), or *Blackwell Encyclopaedia*, ed. Lapidge et al.

[3] According to the *OED*, the modern use dates from William Camden, *Britannia* (1586–1607), who uses *Anglo-Saxones*, *Anglo-Saxonicus* in Latin and *Saxon* in the vernacular. His translator (Holland, 1610) adapted the Latin as *Anglo-Saxon*, i.e. English Saxons rather than continental ones, and this gradually displaced the earlier term *English Saxon*. But the term is much older; cf. *Blackwell Encyclopaedia* ed. Lapidge, et al., s.v. *Anglo-Saxons, kingdom of*, and see below, p. 232.

who first referred to the whole English-speaking conglomerate as a single unit. His term, *Anglorum gens* 'race of the English', was taken up by Bede in the title of the best known of his voluminous writings, *Historia ecclesiastica gentis Anglorum*, a work which was completed in 731.

Unification of the English under a single ruler came about partly by accident, brought about by a new wave of foreign invasion, and partly from policy. This story begins with King Alfred the Great who had inherited the combined kingdom of Wessex and Kent (roughly all the lands south of the Thames) in 871, but attacks by Vikings (known to the Anglo-Saxons as Danes, wherever they came from) against all the English kingdoms became increasingly frequent during the second half of the ninth century, and by the time Alfred came to the throne, Wessex and Mercia were the only Anglo-Saxon kingdoms not in Danish hands. The main focus of Alfred's reign (he died in 899) was firstly to secure his own realm and secondly to extend his control into other areas. His work was continued by his son and successor Edward the Elder (899–924) and his grandson Athelstan[4] (924–939), with the result that most of the areas formerly existing as independent (or at least semi-independent) Anglo-Saxon kingdoms gradually came under a single rule. By the time of Athelstan's death, not only were the modern boundaries of England more or less fixed but the king had some degree of suzerainty over much of the British Isles and had links through marriage into many of the influential families of Europe. Politically, England was born.

The new polity had, however, a difficult childhood. The successors of Athelstan, his brothers Edmund and Eadred, lost control of Northumbria for short periods, and his nephews Eadwig (Edwy) and Edgar divided the kingdom between them once again in 957, Eadwig ruling Wessex and Edgar Mercia. Two years later Eadwig died and Edgar succeeded to the whole, but most of the long reign of his son Æthelred the Unready (978–1016) was disrupted by renewed attacks by the Danes led by their king, Swein. Æthelred was even forced into exile in 1013 and returned only when Swein died the following year. On Æthelred's death, war once again swept the country, with Æthelred's son Edmund Ironside leading the English and Swein's son Cnut (Canute) leading the Danes. The battle

---

[4] I use the forms of the Anglo-Saxon names which are found most frequently in the texts under consideration, even though this leads to inconsistency in the representation of the Old English ligature *æ*.

of *Assandun* in October 1016 was won by the Danes, and Edmund subsequently ruled only Wessex and Kent, with Cnut as king of Mercia and the north. Edmund's death six weeks later left Cnut in control of the whole country, but a disputed succession after his death in 1035 once more aggravated the Wessex/Mercia split, and this issue was not finally resolved until Æthelred's last surviving son, Edward the Confessor, was brought back from exile in Normandy, to succeed in 1042. From the last years of Cnut, the country had been governed under the king by earls belonging to three major aristocratic families, Siward (of Shakespeare's *Macbeth*) in Northumbria, Leofric (married to Godgifu, modern Godiva) in Mercia, and Godwine in Wessex, together with the latter's powerful sons, notably Harold in East Anglia who succeeded to Godwine's earldom in 1052. Edward died without heir in January 1066, and a final disputed succession led to the Battle of Hastings, with Harold at the head of the English forces, on 14 October of that year. The Anglo-Saxon period may be said to have ended with the Norman Conquest.

The concept of 'Englishness' in vernacular literature is closely linked with the developing political power of the house of Wessex. Late in the ninth century, at the end of the 880s and early in the 890s, the pious King Alfred, believing that the attacks of the Danes were God's punishment for the sins of his people, devised a far-reaching revival of Christian teaching and learning, at the heart of which was to be a series of vernacular translations of Latin works which he deemed most necessary for all men to know. Amongst these was almost certainly a translation of Bede's *Historia*, where *Anglorum gens* was rendered as *Angelcynn* 'English people'. The same word appears at the same time in the *Anglo-Saxon Chronicle*, which, given the propagandist tone of its Alfredian annals, was almost certainly inspired by the Wessex court. *Angelcynn* occurs once more in the prefatory letter which the king himself appended to his own translation of Gregory's *Cura pastoralis*. By the late 880s, the West Saxons were inculcating the idea of Alfred as king of the English, and Bede's precedent was a useful one. In other words, the idea of the 'English people' was being promoted amongst the reading public (potentially the ecclesiastical and lay aristocracy) at just the time that 'England' as a political structure was becoming a reality.

From King Alfred's day until the Norman Conquest, a variety of works in the vernacular display a consciousness of national identity and the 'foreignness' of other ethnic groups. The succession of annalists who compiled the *Anglo-Saxon Chronicle*, for example, although they remain conscious of differences between West Saxons, Mercians and Northumbrians, refer to themselves collectively as the English, differentiated from Danes, Welsh (or British), Scots, and, increasingly in the annals for Edward the Confessor's reign, the French. The poem *The Battle of Brunanburh*,[5] which survives in four versions of the *Chronicle* and which is the subject of the late Ted Irving's essay below, looks back at its close to the whole span of Anglo-Saxon history from the coming of the settlers in the fifth century. The poem, first recorded in a manuscript dating from the middle of the tenth century, records the battle of 937 in which King Athelstan won a resounding victory against a combined force of Vikings from Dublin, Strathclyde Welsh and Scots. It clearly exhibits the fact that by the second quarter of that century, Englishmen were aware of their collective history, of their conquest of the previous occupants of the land, the Celts, and of their relationships with their neighbours. In short, this is a literary work with a clear sense of national identity.

How far that sense of an English nation survived the Norman Conquest in the minds of creative writers, and to what extent national identity was associated with the Anglo-Saxons (as against other settlers in England), is the subject of many of the essays in this book. In the nature of things, coverage is far from complete; a single volume of essays can hardly do justice to such a wide subject, some parts of which have, in any case, been touched on elsewhere.[6] Although there is relatively little evidence of national consciousness in the literature of the later Middle Ages, the situation changes dramatically with the Renaissance, with intense antiquarian and growing literary interest in the Anglo-Saxon period. Though in the early eighteenth century, the sense of 'Anglo-Saxonism' was unsettled by the union with Scotland, from the middle of that century the Anglo-Saxons were looked upon increasingly as the founding fathers of the nation. Similarly, writers in the nineteenth century looked for the roots of Britain's pride in Empire in its Anglo-Saxon past. In contrast, and perhaps in part because of an anti-imperialist reaction, the twentieth

---

[5] A paper was given at the Brook Symposium by Patrizia Lendinara on the poem, with a history of the later reputation of King Athelstan in Latin and Norse chronicles and his association with the hero of French romance (later also found in Middle English), Guy of Warwick.

[6] Notes to many of the essays draw attention to such other discussion as has been published.

century has less sense of the Anglo-Saxons and their heritage than any other period of our history. It is this contemporary stance, above all else, that gives the subject its immediate interest.

The concern of the rest of this introductory essay is to construct links between the items that follow and to fill the gaps between them.[7] To begin with the immediate post-Conquest period, Carole Weinberg's essay on Laȝamon's *Brut*, which is the earliest repository of Arthurian material in English, naturally distinguishes between the Saxons, the enemy, and the Celts, the upholders of chivalric values. Yet the essay suggests also a wheel-of-fortune motif in the poem: the rise and fall of the Celts, the rise and fall of the Saxons, and the rise of the Normans. There is consciousness of the Anglo-Saxons as a people here, but since Laȝamon was writing only a century and a half after the Conquest, that is to be expected. The later medieval period shows little awareness of pre-Conquest England, although some of the major kings of the period continue to attract attention. The collection of proverbial sayings which appears in the early thirteenth-century text *The Proverbs of Alured* indicates the compiler's sense that Alfred would be recognized as a significant English writer, but the early fourteenth-century verse romance *Athelston*,[8] which is theoretically about the eponymous king, merely uses tenth-century names for nostalgic effect. The impetus behind *Athelston* is not unlike that which motivates the clerical author of the roughly contemporary *Chronicle of 'Robert of Gloucester'*: a desire for the harmony and piety of an earlier period, as Sarah Mitchell's essay shows. In 'Robert', however, there is also some sense of 'Englishness', reflected, according to Jill Frederick, in the *South English Legendary* of the same period, where there is much more

---

[7] For much of what follows I drew on the resources of the Huntingdon Library, San Marino, California. I am most grateful to the Librarian and his staff for their assistance and for access to the collections. In all cases books are published in London unless otherwise stated.

I make no claims to completeness in what follows, but undoubtedly the list of references to the Anglo-Saxons in fiction is longer here than any previously published. Other titles, especially many nineteenth-century children's books which tell the adventures of fictional Anglo-Saxon heroes, will be found in *Anglo-Saxon England: Being a Catalogue of the Shaun Tyas Library*, published by the Merrion Book Co. of Wickmere House, Wickmere, Norfolk, England (n.d.). I owe this reference to Nicholas Howe.

[8] Elaine Treharne presented a paper at the Brook Symposium on *Athelston* which has now been published as 'Romanticizing the Past in the Middle English *Athelston*', *RES* 50 (1999), pp. 1–26.

interest in Anglo-Saxon saints than in Roman or British ones. John Frankis looks briefly at both of these works, but his principal interest is the Anglo-Norman verse historian Nicholas Trevet, and the use of his work as a source by Gower in the *Confessio Amantis* and by Chaucer in the *Man of Law's Tale*. Though Trevet, writing not long after the *Chronicle of 'Robert of Gloucester'* and the *Legendary* were composed, is patently very interested in the Anglo-Saxon period as the time when England became Christian, both Gower and Chaucer neglect this nationalist interest. Clearly, few authors of the Middle Ages had any interest in the Anglo-Saxon period, and the subject held no attraction for major writers.

However a new consciousness of an Anglo-Saxon heritage appears in the sixteenth century with the growth of the sense of the nation state. The work of Stephen Hawes (1474–1523), although backward looking in many respects, nonetheless exhibits that new spirit. *The Example of Virtue*, written according to its conclusion in the nineteenth year of the reign of Henry VII (1485–1507), acknowledges its debt to Gower, Chaucer and Lydgate, but unlike their works it has a strong sense of national identity. It concludes with the marriage of Righteousness and Cleanness, the bride led to the marriage feast by St Edmund, the ninth-century king of East Anglia martyred by the Danes, and by St Edward, eleventh-century king and confessor. This is reminiscent of the *South English Legendary*, with its particular awareness of early English saints. One of the most enduring books of the Renaissance was *A Mirror for Magistrates*, a poetic anthology of moral tales by various hands which, in mode and purpose, is in direct descent from Lydgate's *The Fall of Princes*. In Lydgate, the lives of a series of ill-fated historical figures are expounded for didactic intent, almost all the tales being of continental origin. Only one English figure is included, St Edmund, and since Lydgate himself was a monk of Bury St Edmunds, his inclusion is perhaps hardly surprising. The *Mirror for Magistrates* was originally published in 1559 with a limited selection of illustrative personages, none of whom derives from the early medieval period, but it reappeared in a series of expanded versions during the next half century or so, and the later accretions included more and more Anglo-Saxon subjects. The edition of 1578 by Thomas Blener Hasset added brief verses on King Sigeberht, on the Lady Ebbe's efforts to save her virginity against marauding Vikings in 870, on Æthelred the Unready and on Harold Godwineson. Further additions in 1610 by Richard Niccols included three eleventh-century figures: Edmund Ironside, Alfred, the brother of

Edward the Confessor, and Earl Godwine. The popularity of the book may be judged by the frequency of its editions and expansions. Its publication span is almost co-terminous with the popularity of the history play, which may be dated from John Bale's *King John* of 1538. Since both the *Mirror* poets and the many dramatists who wrote history plays drew on the chroniclers Hall, Holinshed and Stow, the question of influence here is problematic, but it may well be that each fuelled the historical interest of the other. Certainly, although the moralizing thrust of the *Mirror* poets is very different from the dramatists' use of history, both poets and dramatists function in the same way: they appropriate figures from earlier periods (including the Anglo-Saxon one) to comment on their own age.

Despite the history play's interest in English (and Scottish) subjects, few dealing with the Anglo-Saxons have come down to us. Leah Scragg's essay below lists the remnant still extant (as well as others which we know to have been written) before concentrating her attention on one late sixteenth-century play, the anonymous *Edmund Ironside*. In the following essay, Julia Briggs writes about an early seventeenth-century play by Thomas Middleton, *Hengist, King of Kent*, which, unusually, takes as its subject the period of the Anglo-Saxon invasion.[9] These two plays initiate a long tradition of dramatists' interest in characters and topics drawn from Anglo-Saxon history, a tradition which, as I shall show, extends into the twentieth century. John Milton's commonplace book, a page of which is reproduced as the frontispiece of this volume, lists almost thirty possible Anglo-Saxon subjects for plays that he contemplated writing, a list compiled some time after the appearance of *Comus* in 1634. Furthermore, following the synopsis of a play on King Alfred he noted: 'A Heroicall Poem may be founded somwhere in Alfreds reigne, especially at his issuing out of Edelingsey on the Danes, whose actions are wel like those of Ulysses.' Any possibility that these or any other plays written by Milton might ever have been performed was pre-empted by the very Puritans whose cause he served and who closed the public theatres in 1642. But detailed examination of adjoining pages of the commonplace book shows that the reason for his failure to write the plays – or even a

---

[9] One of the eighteenth-century William Henry Ireland forgeries is a play 'by Shakespeare' entitled *Vortigern*, played once in London in 1796 and revived at the Bridewell Theatre in 1997.

heroic poem on Alfred – lay elsewhere, for in them we can see the conception and growth in dramatic form of *Paradise Lost*. All that remains of Milton's view of Anglo-Saxon England is in the last three books of his *History of Britain* (1670),[10] which cover the period from the fifth century to 1066, and which, though more discursive than many of the chronicles and distinctly partisan, are heavily indebted to the twelfth-century chronicler William of Malmesbury. Writings of antiquarians and historians are outside the scope of this book,[11] but poets and dramatists were undoubtedly influenced by them and in some cases drew their material from them, and I shall touch on some examples of such work later. Milton's writings, both the *History* and the play topics, were widely read subsequently, and I intend to show his influence in later centuries both in the theatre and in verse.

When the theatres reopened after the Restoration, playwrights turned again to the chronicles for material, and Anglo-Saxon subjects, although rare, were not wholly neglected. Edward Ravenscroft's tragi-comedy *King Edgar and Alfreda* (published in 1677, although the Prologue claims that it was written 'at least Ten Years ago') is among the earliest, a tale of love and jealousy, interspersed with songs and dances, with the Anglo-Saxons transformed into Restoration gallants. Like so many others considered below, the play has little to do with history, as the Epilogue admits:

> Nor let the Critick that is deeply read
> In *Baker*, *Stow*, and *Holinshead*,
> Cry Dam-me, the Poet is mistaken here,
> . . .
> They writ a Chronicle, but he a Play.

---

[10] Written probably during the 1650s and published in 1670. See volume V of *John Milton, the Complete Prose Works*, gen. ed. D. M. Wolfe, 8 vols. (New Haven, Conn., 1953–1982).

[11] They have been extensively studied. See, for example, *Anglo-Saxon Scholarship: the First Three Centuries*, ed. Berkhout and Gatch, and its sequel currently in preparation; and some of the essays in *Anglo-Saxonism and the Construction of Social Identity*, ed. Frantzen and Niles, esp. S. C. Hagerdorn's 'Received Wisdom: the Reception History of Alfred's Preface to the *Pastoral Care*'. Readers might also consult A. Frantzen, *The Desire for Origins: New Language, Old English, and Teaching the Tradition* (New Brunswick, N.J., 1990), and, for transatlantic views of the Anglo-Saxons, María José Mora and María José Gómez-Calderón, 'The Study of Old English in America (1776–1850): National Uses of the Saxon Past', *Journal of English and Germanic Philology* 97 (1998), pp. 322–36.

The following year Thomas Rymer published *Edgar, or the English Monarch*, with masques and balls intertwined in a 'Heroick Tragedy', which, much to the author's chagrin, was never staged. Rymer's agenda is clear from his dedication to Charles II (the Advertisement maintains that the dramatist has 'chiefly sought occasions to extoll the *English* Monarchy'), and in his hands inevitably Edgar is a worthy king. Other dramatists treated Edgar less well. In the next century Aaron Hill staged his first play, *Elfrid or The Fair Inconstant*, at Drury Lane in 1710 (revived in 1723 and again, renamed *Athelwold*, in 1731), while William Mason, the minor poet who is also known for his drama *Caractacus*, published *Elfrida*, a dramatic poem in the style of Greek tragedy in 1752. *Elfrida* was revised for the stage in a version published in 1779 and republished in 1796. Although all four plays treat the subject differently, each takes the same incident from the life of King Edgar, his marriage in 964 to Ælfthryth, the widow of Æthelwold, who held the major earldom of East Anglia from 956 until his death in 962 and who was Edgar's foster brother. Ælfthryth became a powerful figure at court during the brief reign of her stepson Edward the Martyr (975–978) and during the minority of her son Æthelred the Unready. Unsurprisingly the Anglo-Norman chroniclers wove a great many tales around such an unusually significant woman. In the plays noted above, the plot invariably turns upon Æthelwold, constructed as trusted friend and counsellor, secretly marrying Ælfthryth whom he had been entrusted to woo on behalf of the king. The situation lends itself to subsequent betrayals – by Æthelwold, Edgar or Ælfthryth herself.

Stage success followed by revival suggests that, although these plays are no longer seen or read, at least two of them were popular in their own day. They reflect an interest not in the historical characters themselves but in a situation which leant itself to dramatization. Milton had seen the possibilities of this love triangle many years earlier. No. 26 in his list of play subjects reads:

Edgar slaying Ethelwold for false play in woing wherin may be set out his pride, lust, which he thought to close by favouring monks and building monasteries. also the disposition of woman in Elfrida toward her husband.

The tradition was revived later. The philosopher William Henry Smith, who trained for the law under Sharon Turner, wrote *Athelwold* (performed 1843, published 1846), while two female writers, both better known as

10

minor novelists, also turned to the theme – Amélie Rives in *Athelwold* (1893) and Edna St Vincent Millay in *The King's Henchman* (1927). The second of these two depends heavily on the first, and they are also linked in that both were published in New York.

Another cluster of eighteenth-century plays figure King Alfred. Again, all are concerned with a single historical event, his conflict with the Danes and the victory at Edington (878), with the accompanying legends of the medieval and later chronicle tradition – exile as a lone wanderer in the Somerset marshes, burning the cakes, and visiting the Danish camp disguised as a minstrel. The earliest of this group is the poet James Thomson's re-writing of David Mallet's masque *Alfred* in 1740, with music by Thomas Arne, which is remembered today for its concluding song, known by the opening of its refrain, *Rule, Britannia*. The others are *Alfred the Great: Deliverer of his Country* (anon. 1753, by 'the author of *The Friendly Rivals*'); John Home's *Alfred* (published in Dublin, 1777); *The Patriot King or Alfred and Elvida* (1788) by Alexander Bicknell (who was also author of a life of the king); *Alfred, an Historical Tragedy* (printed in Sheffield, 1789), attributed to Ebenezer Rhodes, part of which is dependent on the French work by d'Arnaud; and *The Battle of Edington or British Liberty* (1796), which its author John Penn dedicated to William Pitt. In *Rule, Britannia* and indeed throughout the tradition, Alfred is a focus for eighteenth-century patriotism, a point reinforced by the titles of many of the plays, and made explicit by such comments as Bicknell's in his Advertisement stating that his piece was written in 1778 since: 'at that time Britain was threatened with an invasion from the united powers of France and Spain.' In similar vein is a play on a different Anglo-Saxon subject, Richard Cumberland's first tragedy *The Battle of Hastings* (1777), a tale of medieval knights composed in pseudo-Shakespearian blank verse complete with false archaisms which seemingly did not detract from the popularity of the piece. A few lines are worth quoting as representative of the majority of verse tragedies of the period. In Act V Northumberland (*sic*) says to the king:

> To horse, dread sir; brace on your beaver strait,
> Caparison with speed, and meet the sun,
> Who thron'd and beaming on the upland edge,
> Stands in his fiery wane with glowing wheels
> And panting coursers to behold a scene,
> Worth his diurnal round.

More tellingly in terms of the author's agenda is Edwin's assertion that:

> When we're call'd to arms
> For England's safety, private feuds should cease,
> And every son unite in her defence.           Act II, scene i

The *London Magazine* for January 1778, misquoting the lines as 'all private feuds should cease when England's glory is at stake', reported that this 'was so sensibly felt by the audience that a repetition was called for'.

Coupled with the nationalistic fervour of the Alfred plays is the desire to strengthen the union between England and Scotland forged in 1707. Although at first sight the use of the term 'Britannia' in Thomson and the references to the Anglo-Saxons as 'Britons' in Rhodes and elsewhere suggests confusion or lack of historical awareness, in at least one case it is clear that the blurring of periods is the product of a conscious decision. In Penn's piece, where *British* is in the subtitle, Alfred ends as king of Britain (including Scotland) even though the author in his 'Argument' recognizes that this does not accord with historical fact. He is deliberately representing an ideal here, rather than what he knew the historical situation to be.

In the eighteenth century, Anglo-Saxon attitudes were occasionally expressed in other kinds of literary modes. In James Thomson's verse world history *Liberty* (1734–1736), the virile Anglo-Saxon overrunning of demoralized post-Roman Britain is the first stage in the development of that quintessential English civilization which is seen as a pattern for the world. Thomson's Anglo-Saxons established laws and good governance; their kings were 'prudently confined' (line 696) as, by implication, he wishes the constitutional monarchs of the Hanoverian dynasty to be; and their valour was esteemed:

> And tho' more polished times the martial Creed
> Disown, yet still the fearless habit lives.           (683–4)

This last theme is an old one, which can be traced back to the the 1578 issue of *Mirror for Magistrates*: 'It is the best with forren foes to fight' (p. 245). Patriotism, it would appear, is an intrinsic part of the Anglo-Saxon heritage.

The eighteenth century also saw the appearance of a series of poems on King Alfred. Lynda Pratt in her essay below deals with two from the turn of the century that present Alfred as the central character of a national epic, and she deals in detail with the political context. Other poems adopt a different approach. The earliest is Sir Richard Blackmore's *Alfred* (1723), described on the title page as an epic poem in twelve books. It begins, in true epic style: 'I Sing the Man, who left fair Albion's Shore', and indeed Alfred does leave Britain (*sic*) to visit 'foreign nations' in order to improve his mind, not, as one might expect of the period of composition, for the Grand Tour, but on the sort of Odyssey seemingly envisaged by Milton. His journeys are largely confined to Mediterranean nations, where he engages in foreign wars, restores and defends monarchs, acts as peace-maker, and indulges in sight-seeing, but apart from a brief encounter with Pope Leo his wanderings have nothing to do with history, or even with the Anglo-Saxons, until in Book XII he returns home on his brother's death to become king.[12]

Rather more in tune with its own age is Robert Holmes's *Alfred, an Ode* (1778) which has Alfred, after his victory over the Danes, musing from a vantage point above Oxford (the author was a Fellow of New College and the poem was published by the Clarendon Press). The piece is heavily annotated to explain historical and classical allusions, and was clearly intended to be seen as a modern classic. Its spirit is summed up in the concluding lines:

> Hail, British Alfred, patriot king,
> Great Father of thy people, Hail!

A similar sense of cultural continuity is evident in Joseph Sympson's *Science Revived or The Vision of Alfred* (1802),[13] a poem in eight books tracing the growth of scientific knowledge. Alfred is seen here as the progenitor and guiding light of a Britain destined to become the best of all possible civilized worlds. Other early nineteenth-century poets and playwrights, before novelists took up the subject (see the essay below by Andrew Sanders), also extolled the virtues of the Anglo-Saxons, in particular King Alfred once again. In 1822 Wordsworth published a chronological sequence of twenty sonnets on Anglo-Saxon figures and themes,[14] ranging

---

[12] See also Lynda Pratt's essay below, at pp. 140–1.

[13] Chronologically the Anglo-Saxon interests of Thomas Chatterton fit here, on which see Jacqueline Pearson's essay below, at p. 123, and note 3.

[14] The sonnets were published as *Ecclesiastical Sketches* in 1822 and later renamed the Ecclesiastical Sonnets.

from Gregory's decision to send his mission, in a story ultimately derived from Bede:

> A bright-haired company of youthful slaves        Sonnet I.xiii

through Edwin, 'the pious Alfred . . . Mirror of Princes',[15] Edgar, Edward the Confessor, concluding with the Conquest:

> The Saxons, overpowered
> By wrong triumphant through its own excess.        Sonnet I.xxxii

For Wordsworth, as for many in the period following the publication of Sharon Turner's mammoth *History of the Anglo-Saxons*,[16] the Normans destroyed a civilization greater than their own.

The longest poem of this period is *Alfred*, a 'romance in rhyme' by R. Payne Knight (1823). It is one of the last works of a poet who, like William Mason, author of *Elfrida*, is of the picturesque school, and because it is far from his best, it has been largely overlooked by modern critics. But the verse is generally competently handled, although it has to be said that Knight does occasionally nod, as when Alfred's bride-to-be Elsintha kills, Judith-style, her would-be ravisher:

> Terror and pride unwonted strength impart, –
> I raised the steel, and plunged it in his heart!
> In purple torrents gush'd life's ebbing tide –
> He groan'd! he gasp'd! he gnash'd his teeth, and died!        (p. 76)

Alfred's characterization owes something to the chivalric tradition in that, as an embodiment of all that is good, he observes, or is involved in, a series of romantic episodes. There is little semblance of historicity. Nonetheless, like Wordsworth, Knight is indebted to the view of the Anglo-Saxons promulgated by Sharon Turner. His poem concludes with the recognition that the Danes will attack again after Alfred's day, and that the Normans will come to rule, but that ultimately '[Heaven will] fix in adamant great ALFRED's laws' (p. 335).

References to Alfred as a lawmaker appear in fiction from the medieval period through to the Victorians. Laȝamon, following his sources Geoffrey of Monmouth and Wace, maintains that Alfred merely translated Celtic law into English (*Brut*, lines 3143–54), in an obvious attempt to counter

---

[15] The phrase is Milton's.

[16] Sharon Turner, *History of the Anglo-Saxons*, 4 vols. (London, 1799–1805).

14

the prevailing view. By the Renaissance, when the soubriquet 'the Great' earlier given to Alfred became widespread, contrary voices had been silenced. The seventeenth-century lawyer Robert Powell wrote two works which are still extant: *The Life of Alfred* (1634), which is much more than a life because it draws an extended (and often ingenious) parallel between Alfred and King Charles I, styled 'the British Alfred', and *A Treatise of the Antiquity, Authority, Uses and Jurisdiction of the Ancient Courts of Leet* (1643), 'derived from the institution of Moses, and the first Imitation of him in the island of Great Britaine by King Alfred'. The Anglo-Saxons' influence on the law in Thomson's *Liberty* was referred to above. It is from the end of the eighteenth century, however, that Alfred – and occasionally the Anglo-Saxons in general – are seen as bringing order and stability to England through the imposition of law. John O'Keeffe's *Alfred or The Magic Banner* (performed 1796, printed in his collected works 1798) has Alfred decree trial by jury at the end of the play,[17] and this is echoed in the last scene of *Alfred the Great or The Patriot King* (1831) by James Sheridan Knowles. As the nineteenth century progressed, so the drama reflected the widespread admiration of Alfred that we find in other literature (on which see Lynda Pratt's essay) as well as the pictorial and sculptural arts,[18] hence *Alfred the Great* (1811) by Mrs J. S. Faucit, *Alfred, A Patriotic Play* (1858) by Martin F. Tupper, and an anonymous *Alfred* performed in 1861. The mood is best summed up in the dedication to Viscount Stratford de Redcliffe's *Alfred the Great at Athelney* (1876). Dedications throughout the history of printed drama are informative; they may show where the dramatist stands politically, or if the work supports the establishment (for example, more than one Anglo-Saxon play is dedicated to a reigning monarch). *Alfred the Great at Athelney*, a play about 'our greatest Saxon king', is handsomely printed as befitted the author's rank. The dedication, to Albert the Prince Consort, who had died of typhoid in 1861, contains the following lines:

> Oh! had thy star prevail'd o'er Fate's decree,
> Another Alfred would have lived in thee!

In view of the reverence in which Albert was held in the period following his death, it is hard to imagine a higher tribute to Alfred.

---

[17] For other examples of the Anglo-Saxons' assumed inauguration of trial by jury, see the references below, p. 221.

[18] See note 1 above.

In the light of Alfred's standing in the popular imagination, it is difficult to understand how he became the hero of a comic opera, unless his appearance in this context is adducible to his prominence in the theatrical tradition. *The Magic Banner* by John O'Keeffe, a prolific writer of comic operas, is one of the forty or more of the author's works in the genre that survive. (Another is *Peeping Tom of Coventry*, which features Harold Godwineson and has a small part for Leofric of Mercia, with one line for his wife Godgifa; this piece is also printed in the 1798 collected works and was played at least as late as 1837.) Only the dialogue of *The Magic Banner* has come down to us, revealing it to be a species of 'Comedy of Errors' involving farce, cross-dressing, and endless punning and word-play. Alfred is anything but the patriot, and the 'historical' element is reduced to references to battles off-stage and the king as a minstrel in the Danish camp. An interesting contrast is Isaac Pocock's *Alfred the Great or The Enchanted Standard* (1827), advertised as a musical drama, and acknowledged by its author as 'founded partly' on O'Keeffe's play. In fact, although Pocock takes the character of Gog the cowherd and a little of his foolery from O'Keeffe, his plot is wholly different, and one can only suppose that the dependence lay in the music. In Pocock, Alfred is once again the king found in the chronicles, and O'Keeffe's Alfred may be regarded as an exception.

O'Keeffe and Pocock are not the only dramatists to place Alfred in either a musical or a visually elaborate setting. Both features are intrinsic to works produced for the Victorian stage. Tupper's *Alfred, A Patriotic Play* recommends an overture containing 'exclusively English and national music . . . including Rule Britannia . . . ending with God save the Queen' and 'the like music between the Acts'. Even Lord Redcliffe's *Alfred the Great at Athelney* is interspersed with songs. Spectacular scenes include Alfred and his Saxons creeping armed into the Danish camp at the end of Act IV of Tupper's play, which concludes with: 'all being overpowered, a picturesque military tableau'. The play was performed in 1858 and presumably reflects a high degree of Victorian patriotic feeling.

In the nineteenth century, interest in the Anglo-Saxons in general, and King Alfred in particular, reached a height greater than at any other period since the Norman Conquest. Some texts lie on the border between history and fiction, notably those by writers whose principal output is in the latter class. Of particular interest here is *Alfred the Great*, a life of the king published in 1871 by the novelist Thomas Hughes, author of *Tom*

16

*Brown's School Days* (1857). Hughes's agenda, like that of Milton's *History*, is strictly political (Hughes was a Member of Parliament) even though the work is addressed to 'ordinary English readers' (p. 5) and was published in Macmillan's Sunday Library for Household Reading. From the time of Milton onwards, it would seem that Alfred eclipsed almost all other Anglo-Saxon kings as a literary subject, the other figures that appear being few (and insignificant) by comparison. Edgar, in the series of plays mentioned above, has little relevance to the historical king at all, while Edmund Ironside is the subject of one of three plays by the novelist and prolific poet Jane West (*Edmund surnamed Ironside*, 1791), but there is no record of any other interest in this period in this king. Chief among the monarchs who do achieve a slightly higher profile is Athelstan. The tenth-century poem *The Battle of Brunanburh*, which recounts Athelstan's victory of 937, was the basis of a poem by Tennyson (the subject of Ted Irving's essay below), and of a slightly earlier 'dramatic chronicle' by George Darley: *Ethelston or The Battle of Brunanburh* (1841). In his Preface, Darley writes of his intention to use the play as one stone in building a

cairn, or rude national monument, on some eminence of our Poetic Mountain, to a few amongst the many Heroes of our race, sleeping even yet with no memorial there, or one hidden beneath the moss of ages.

For Darley, it seems, Athelstan was a sleeping hero. William Mason's *Elfrida* alludes to the king in rather different terms when Elfrida's father, Orgar, says of another character in Act IV, scene iv:

> and he shall fall
> As did the traytor Oswald, whose false tongue
> Defam'd me to King Athelstan.

The same character swears 'by Offa's shade', assuming knowledge of an eighth-century king of Mercia on the part of a contemporary audience. Although this reference was removed in later versions of the work, the reference to Athelstan was allowed to stand. It would appear that eighteenth- and nineteenth-century dramatists expected their audiences to have a greater awareness of the name and reputation of Athelstan than could be envisaged today.

An earlier play entitled *Athelstan* (1756), by Dr John Brown, which was played at Drury Lane with Garrick in the title role, is not in fact about King Athelstan but a rebel Saxon earl of the same name engaged in

(unspecified) wars against the Danes. Even earlier is George Jeffrey's
*Edwin, a Tragedy* (1724) with an eponymous hero who is 'King of
Britain'. Two lines in the Prologue suggest the reason for the choice of
Anglo-Saxon subjects here and elsewhere:

> A British Bard with British Tale this Night
> Shall raise your Pity, Terror and Delight.

The lines are surely in direct line from the opening of the Prologue to
Aaron Hill's *Elfrid*, performed from 1710 to 1731

> To Night our Author tells an *English* Story
> And brings your Ancestors to Life before ye;
> Heroes, whose innate Worth descends to you.

The Anglo-Saxons, despite confusion over the 'British/English' termi-
nology which is widely attested in the period, are identified as 'ancestors'.
It is noteworthy, however, that audience admiration is not always directed
to them alone. Jane West's *Edmund* has Cnut acting in as heroic a manner
as Edmund himself, while Darley's *Ethelston* displays equal esteem for the
Danes (especially as poets) because they too are part of our heritage. The
integration of the Normans into the national identity had to wait,
however, until the prose writers of the nineteenth century, who are
considered in Andrew Sanders's essay below.

A last group of plays concerns the ill-fated love affair between
Athelstan's nephew, King Eadwig, known in the dramatic tradition as
Edwy (thought by Milton and others to be an abbreviated form of Edwin)
and his cousin Ælfgifu. At least five such plays survive: Thomas
Warwick's *Edwy* (1784), Frances Burney's *Edwy and Elgiva* (1788), which
is considered in detail in Jacqueline Pearson's essay below, Revd Thomas
Sedwick Whalley's *Edwy and Edilda* (1800), Charles Jared Ingersol's *Edwy
and Elgiva* (1801, published in Philadelphia), and Henry Taylor's *Edwin
the Fair* (1842). The historical reality, Eadwig's beautiful appearance
(acknowledged by his contemporaries), his division of his kingdom half-
way through his reign in favour of his younger brother Edgar, and the
brevity of the reign itself, cut short by his early death (he died before he
was twenty) were the stuff of romance, especially when allied to the
unfortunate history of his marriage to his cousin Ælfgifu. The tenth-
century story that he left his coronation feast to engage in dalliance with
a noble lady and her daughter, only to be forcibly dragged back by

Dunstan, the powerful abbot of Glastonbury (later archbishop of Canterbury), is advanced to explain the undoubted dislike between the two men, though its first appearance in Dunstan's biography, written soon after the archbishop's death in 988, suggests that it is far from an unbiased account. The daughter of the tale was the Ælfgifu whom the king subsequently married, and, though we will never know the truth of what happened, we can be certain that the enmity itself is a historical fact. The king secured Dunstan's exile for a while, and the church enforced Eadwig's divorce a year before the king's death. Given Eadwig's youth, it seems likely that he and Ælfgifu were pawns in a wider political game, with the marriage and exile showing the king's party (or his mother-in-law's) initially in the ascendency and Dunstan's return and the divorce indicating a reversal in their fortunes.

The plays depict a love affair made tragic by the intervention of Dunstan, who is portrayed wholly unsympathetically, very much in line with the anti-clerical tone of much late eighteenth- and early nineteenth-century literature. Ælfgifu is usually, but not always, Eadwig's queen, though in some cases Dunstan prevents the marriage. All the playwrights consciously take liberties with historical fact, usually to enable the lovers to die in each other's arms, though Warwick goes further and has Dunstan stabbed to death at the altar (whereas he in fact survived for a further thirty years). The popularity of the subject in the half-century of these plays is related, as Jacqueline Pearson notes,[19] to its appearance in literature for women, but there are two other sources through which it may have gained currency: Taylor's Preface to *Edwin the Fair*, while acknowledging that 'Sharon Turner's learned and elaborate work has done much to make the Anglo-Saxon times better known' states that in the case of 'the tale of Edwy and Elgiva', it 'had been current in the nursery long before it came to be studied as an historical question'. This in itself might be sufficient to explain the repeated use of the story on the popular stage. The earliest play in the series, however, points to another factor influential in shaping the stage tradition. The frontispiece of Warwick's *Edwy* quotes the synopsis of a play on 'Edwin' from what is described as 'Milton's Subjects for the English Drama'. Indeed, so many of the plays – and some of the poems – of the late eighteenth and early nineteenth centuries coincide in subject matter with Milton's list in his

---

[19]  See below, p. 130 note 22.

commonplace book (Alfred, Athelstan, Edgar, Edmund Ironside, Harold, as well as Edwin/Edwy) that it seems highly likely that the long hand of the epic poet had a significant influence on the drama of the later period.[20]

In style, however, and sometimes in theme, the majority of the plays (especially the tragedies by minor dramatists) that have been dealt with here, from the Restoration right through to the nineteenth century, are heavily influenced by Shakespeare. One passage already quoted above suggests verbal indebtedness in Richard Cumberland's *The Battle of Hastings*. Throughout the tradition a constantly recurring theme is the responsibilities, duties and cares of kingship, concepts in essence more pertinent to the sixteenth century where they originate than the historical period to which they are assigned, but which are given resonance by the changing political situations from the Restoration, through the Glorious Revolution to the arrival of the Hanoverians, and finally the events of the French Revolution. The terms in which the theme is expressed throughout are distinctly Shakespearian, from the assertion of Rymer's Edgar, who represents Charles II, that: 'The Regall State no reall Friendship knows' (II.vii), to the regret of Cumberland's Harold, in a play staged two years before the French Revolution: 'I'm loaded hard with cares, / For I'm a King' (Act II). Edwin's last words in *Edwin the Fair*: 'I pray you, Sirs, . . . there . . . there' (V.xv) show that even in 1842, although the king dies, Shakespeare lives.

The principal nineteenth-century prose works with Anglo-Saxon links are discussed in Andrew Sanders's essay on the novels below, and by Daniel Donoghue and T. A. Shippey who consider other aspects of nineteenth-century fiction, and move the discussion forward into the twentieth century as well.[21] To bring this survey up to date, I will add only that the Anglo-Saxons have not as yet proved very fertile ground for

---

[20] The commonplace book was not published until W. A. Wright's *Facsimile of the Manuscript of Milton's Minor Poems* (Cambridge, 1899), but various editions of Milton in the eighteenth century made use of the manuscript, and knowledge of it was therefore presumably fairly widespread.

[21] Among recent studies of the influence of Anglo-Saxon on modern poets should be noted N. Howe, 'Praise and Lament: the Afterlife of Old English Poetry in Auden, Hill, and Gunn', *Words and Works: Studies in Medieval English Language and Literature in Honour of Fred C. Robinson*, ed. P. S. Baker and N. Howe (Toronto, 1998), pp. 293–310.

the current vogue for light, specifically detective, fiction set in medieval times, although A. E. Marston's *Domesday Books* series comes chronologically close to it.[22] The latest work of this class to be published as this book goes to press is (appropriately) Julian Rathbone's *The Last English King* (1997), which is currently being turned into a screenplay. Films involving the Anglo-Saxons are very rare indeed (in contrast with those involving Vikings). 'Alfred the Great' (1969, director Clive Donner), with David Hemmings oddly cast as an introverted Alfred and Michael York as a refined yet rather more successful Guthrum, brings this survey to a close.[23]

This chapter has traced a process of flux in writers' perspectives on the Anglo-Saxons across the centuries. Although in the later medieval period authors showed little consciousness of Anglo-Saxon England as a definable and significant stage in the nation's history, Renaissance dramatists followed the interest in the period established by churchmen and chroniclers. In the later seventeenth and eighteenth centuries, interest was largely confined to those whose work has now all but disappeared from view. But in the nineteenth century the Anglo-Saxons truly came into their own, enjoying a standing and cultural significance higher than at any time before or since. And this prominence is particularly associated with that most notable of Anglo-Saxon kings 'whose actions are wel like those of Ulysses'.[24]

---

[22] T. A. Shippey's essay below considers other historical novels of the twentieth century. A few more are listed in B. Mitchell, *An Invitation to Old English and Anglo-Saxon England* (Oxford, 1995), pp. 359–60.

[23] Interest in the Anglo-Saxon period may be about to take an upturn, with the appearance in 1999 of a cartoon version of the poem *Beowulf*, and with publication of a new translation by Seamus Heaney. More important to this study is a play newly written for Shakespeare's Globe, the first to be produced especially for that theatre (first performance scheduled for 6 August 1999): *Augustine's Oak* by Peter Oswald, which tells the story of Augustine's mission in 597 to convert the Anglo-Saxons.

[24] I am grateful to Simon Keynes for reading this essay and saving me from some stupid errors. Any that remain are my own responsibility.

# Victor and victim: a view of the Anglo-Saxon past in Laȝamon's *Brut*

## CAROLE WEINBERG

The purpose of Laȝamon, parish priest of Areley-Kings towards the end of the twelfth and/or beginning of the thirteenth century, in writing the *Brut* was – as he tells us himself – to recount *wat heo ihoten weoren and wonene heo comen, / þa Englene londe ærest ahten* 'what they were called and whence they came who first possessed the land of England' (8–9).[1] And while his engagement with the past history of the English is evident, his creative imagination was clearly fired by the content of his main source, Wace's *Roman de Brut*, a mid-twelfth-century verse history which slotted the Anglo-Saxons into an even earlier period of insular history, a reading of the past in which the Britons held sovereignty over the land before it passed to the Anglo-Saxons.

Following Wace, Laȝamon recounts in the latter part of his narrative how, during the reign of the post-Arthurian British king, Carric, the Saxons in Britain banded together with a conqueror from Africa called Gurmund, seized the land and besieged Carric at Cirencester. But Carric proved a stubborn defender:

> Wel ofte Kariches men     comen ut of burhȝen
> and ræsden an Gurmunde     mid ræȝere strenðe,
> and sloȝen of his folke     feole þusende,
> and sende heom to helle,     heðene hundes alle.
> Karic wes swiðe goud cniht     and swiðe wel he heold his fiht,

---

[1] All citations are from the Cotton Caligula text of Laȝamon's *Brut* and all translations of this text are from *Laȝamon's 'Brut'*, ed. and trans. W. R. J. Barron and S. C. Weinberg (Harlow, 1995). References to Wace are from *Le Roman de Brut de Wace*, ed. I. Arnold, 2 vols. (Paris, 1938–1940), while references to Geoffrey of Monmouth are from *The 'Historia Regum Britannie' of Geoffrey of Monmouth*, I, or II (The Variant Version), ed. N. Wright (Cambridge, 1984 and 1988).

and faste he heold Chirchestre      mid strengðe þan mæste
þat ne mihte Gurmund      næuere mæren his ferde
ar he lette heom mid ginnen      biswiken wiðinnen.     $(14,570-7)^2$

The stratagem used by Gurmund to defeat Carric was to set fire to Cirencester by having sparrows return to their roosts in the city carrying lit pieces of tinder in nutshells attached to their feet. Laȝamon paints a graphic picture of a town ablaze, the wind fanning the flames, the inhabitants trapped and engulfed by fire (14,614–28). Laȝamon's contemporaries may have been unfamiliar with the story of Gurmund, but the graphic description of a town burning would have struck home. The town of Worcester, only some ten miles downstream from Areley-Kings, suffered at least four devastating fires between 1113 and 1202, memorable not only for the damage they caused, but also for the part they played in the campaign for the canonization of an Anglo-Saxon bishop. In 1113 a major fire broke out in Worcester, the flames spreading throughout the town and setting the roof of Worcester Cathedral alight. While the interior of the church was destroyed, amazingly, it seemed, the tomb of Wulfstan, the last Anglo-Saxon bishop of Worcester (1062–1095) survived unscathed. In 1147 fire once again engulfed Worcester and the cathedral was badly damaged. Bernard, bishop of St David's, in Worcester at the time, testified to the miraculous fact that, while the fire consumed all in its path, the tapestry spread over Wulfstan's tomb remained untouched by the flames. In 1189 yet another devastating fire set Worcester ablaze, and again in 1202, when the cathedral suffered damage once more.[3] It was after this fire, coinciding with the growing

---

[2] 'Carric's men repeatedly sallied out from the town and attacked Gurmund with furious might, and slew many thousands of his followers, despatching them, all heathen dogs, to hell. Carric was a very skilful warrior and conducted his defence very successfully, and stoutly defended Cirencester to the utmost of his power so that at no time was Gurmund able to defeat his forces until, by a trick, he caused them to be destroyed from within.'

    In the Variant Version of Geoffrey's *Historia* (§186–7), we hear that Gurmund, a pagan African king who has conquered Ireland, is recruited by the Saxons to drive the Britons under the post-Arthurian king, Carric, into Wales, and who then hands the country over to them. This is referred to by both Wace and Laȝamon early in their narratives (see pp. 27–8 of this paper and n. 18 below), but described in greater detail in its proper chronological context (lines 14,400–683) as part of the continuing narrative of conflict between the Saxons and the Britons for sovereignty of the land.

[3] For reference to the fire of 1189, see H. R. Luard, *Annales Prioratus de Wigornia AD 1–1377*, Annales Monastici, 4 vols., RS 36 (London, 1869), IV, p. 386. The fires of

interest in the cult of Wulfstan, that Mauger, the Norman bishop of Worcester, after consultation with the chapter, petitioned Pope Innocent III for Wulfstan's canonization. Pope Innocent had a commission of distinguished English clerics appointed to investigate the claims of sainthood. The commission's report, attesting to the miracles worked through Wulfstan's mediation, was conveyed to Rome in person by a delegation of Worcester monks. In April 1203 Wulfstan was canonized, and on 14 May a papal bull declared publicly the circumstances of Wulfstan's elevation, including testimony produced by the citizens of Worcester attesting to the many miracles performed at his tomb.[4]

Given the proximity of Areley-Kings to Worcester, local interest generated by the canonization of Wulfstan may have been the spur for Laȝamon's decision to record the Anglo-Saxon past for his contemporaries.[5] Furthermore he may very possibly have seen the now lost biography of Wulfstan, written in English sometime between 1095 and 1113 by Coleman, Wulfstan's chaplain for the last fifteen years of the bishop's life. Coleman, it has been argued, chose to write in English at a time when Latin was the commonly used and accepted linguistic medium for hagiographical biography, 'as a piece of conscious revivalism to emphasize the merits of Anglo-Saxon England',[6] and he could have provided Laȝamon with an important precedent for the use of English at a time when Latin and Anglo-Norman were the recognized languages of historical narrative. Regarding Laȝamon's ability to read Coleman's eleventh-century English, Laȝamon himself used what has been described as an 'archaic' form of English harking back to Old English models as his linguistic medium for narrating the early history of this island, and we know that in the early thirteenth century the 'Tremulous Scribe' was at work in Worcester Cathedral Library, annotating Old English texts.[7]

1133, 1147 and 1202 are discussed by E. Mason, *St Wulfstan of Worcester c. 1008–1095* (Oxford, 1990), pp. 272–3, 275–6 and 279.

[4] Mason, *St Wulfstan*, pp. 279–80.

[5] I discussed Laȝamon's interest in and knowledge of local topography and history as reflected in the *Brut* in '"By a noble church on the bank of the Severn": a Regional View of Laȝamon's *Brut*', *Leeds Studies in English* NS 26 (1995), pp. 49–62.

[6] A. Gransden, *Historical Writing in England*, 2 vols. (London, 1974 and 1982), I, p. 88.

[7] See C. Franzen, *The Tremulous Hand of Worcester: a Study of Old English in the Thirteenth Century* (Oxford, 1991), and W. Collier, '"Englishness" and the Worcester Tremulous Hand', *Leeds Studies in English* NS 26 (1995), pp. 35–47.

Laȝamon, like Coleman before him, made a deliberate choice to use English as his literary medium. What statement was Laȝamon making in the *Brut* about the Anglo-Saxon past, and what relevance, if any, did it have to Laȝamon's Anglo-Norman present?

Laȝamon's poetic history is, paradoxically, very largely a record, not of the earliest Anglo-Saxon kings, but of the earliest kings of the Britons, beginning with Brutus, Aeneas's great-grandson, and concluding with the reign of Cadwallader. It is only in the last two thousand lines or so of the poem (over sixteen thousand lines in all), that Laȝamon focuses the narrative more directly and in detail on the early Anglo-Saxon kings of Northumbria in the struggle between the Britons and the Anglo-Saxons for sovereignty over the island. The poem ends with the Britons dispossessed of their land and driven into Wales, and the Anglo-Saxon kings politically supreme:

> And Ænglisce kinges    walden þas londes,
> And Bruttes hit loseden,    þis lond and þas leoden,
> þat næuere seoðden mære    kinges neoren here.
> Þa ȝet ne com þæs ilke dæi,    beo heonneuorð alse hit mæi;
> iwurðe þet iwurðe,    iwurðe Godes wille.    (16,091–5)[8]

To see the shape of the past in Laȝamon's *Brut* as 'a recurrent pattern of land and people subject to continual conquest', and to describe it as a history 'not of the Britons but of the land of Britain', may be one way of accommodating the presence of both Britons and Anglo-Saxons in Laȝamon's narrative.[9] But while this view of the poem as a history of the land does not sit oddly with the presence in it of the Britons, the first settlers and rulers of this island, it is more difficult to account for his lengthy and largely sympathetic portrayal of their struggles against the treacherous Saxon would-be invaders, forerunners of the Anglo-Saxons who settled the island, the eventual successors of the Britons in ruling it, and who changed its name from Britain to England. But not only does Laȝamon express anti-Saxon sentiments in his poem; he deliberately

---

[8] 'And English kings gained sovereignty over these lands, and the Britons lost it, lost this land and the sovereignty of this nation so that never since that time have they been kings here. Such a day has not yet come, whatever may come to pass hereafter; come what may, let God's will be done.'

[9] M. Swanton, *English Literature before Chaucer* (Harlow, 1987), p. 176.

deepens the anti-Saxon perspective he found in Wace.[10] Laȝamon's antipathy towards the Saxons in the *Brut* has troubled critics of the poem. They have found it a matter of some perplexity that an English poet, writing in English when Latin and Anglo-Norman were the more usual languages of historical record, should sympathize with the Britons and hold up the Saxons to execration.[11]

One way of defending Laȝamon from the accusation that he vilified his Saxon ancestors is to claim that he made a deliberate distinction between the treacherous Saxons and the Angles, a term used almost exclusively towards the end of the poem for those who, 'untouched by Saxon guilt', were the true ancestors of the English, and gave their name to the land of England.[12] Under detailed examination, however, this hypothesis fails; Neil Wright points out that in the *Brut*, Hengest, the treacherous invading Saxon leader, describes his homeland as *Angles* (6,910–12), in direct contradiction to the equivalent passage in Wace (6,729–32), where Hengest states that he and his men come from *Saixone*. Wright argues, convincingly, that the distinction in usage between Saxons and Angles as titles for the ancestors of the English is not judgemental, but significant only in that Laȝamon uses the term *Angles* to identify the geographical origin of those Saxons who settled the land and to explain the etymology of the term 'England' (14,668–73).[13]

An alternative explanation for Laȝamon's hostile treatment of the Saxon ancestors of the English is offered by James Noble. He also sees a difference between Laȝamon's attitude towards the Saxon invaders who appear in the Arthurian section of the narrative and his attitude towards the post-Arthurian Saxons who settled the land, but argues that it is due to a 'distinction in the poet's mind between the would-be Saxon usurpers who were ultimately banished from Britain during Arthur's reign and *þa ilke þa weorn icorne* ['those chosen'] (14,677) – i.e. the Germanic

[10] See J. Noble, 'Laȝamon's "Ambivalence" Reconsidered', *The Text and Tradition of Laȝamon's 'Brut'*, ed. F. Le Saux (Cambridge, 1994), pp. 171–82. Noble cites several instances in the poem which 'attest to a systematic attempt on Laȝamon's part to vilify the Saxons to an even greater extent than Wace had succeeded in doing' (p. 172).

[11] See, e.g. *Arthurian Literature in the Middle Ages*, ed. R. S. Loomis (Oxford, 1959), p. 105, and D. Pearsall, *Old and Middle English Poetry* (London, 1977), p. 110.

[12] I. J. Kirby, 'Angles and Saxons in Laȝamon's Brut', *SN* 36 (1964), pp. 51–62.

[13] N. Wright, 'Angles and Saxons in Laȝamon's *Brut*: a Reassessment', *The Text and Tradition of Laȝamon's 'Brut'*, pp. 161–70.

immigrants who, some years later, are invited to assume stewardship of the island in the wake of Gurmund's invasion'.[14] Thus 'the apparent distinction in Laʒamon's mind between these two groups of Saxons who appear in his poem must be acknowledged as the source of the fact that the *Brut* qualifies as both a pro-English and an anti-Saxon statement'.[15] This second group, especially once converted to Christianity by St Augustine, 'gradually displace the Britons as heroes of Laʒamon's chronicle, the Britons demonstrating in each successive episode the degeneracy to which they have become prone without an Arthur to lead them'.[16]

It is certainly true to say that, as in Wace, the historical moment at which the name 'Britain' is replaced by 'England' occurs in Laʒamon's poem when Gurmund invades the country with his Saxon allies, devastates Britain, and the Saxons gain possession of the island.[17] But this moment of transference of dominion is anticipated much earlier in both poems, at the point in the narrative when the Britons, having

---

[14] Noble, 'Laʒamon's "Ambivalence" Reconsidered', pp. 171–82, at p. 181. Lines 14,668–75 are central to Noble's argument (I have cited both text and translation in this instance from Noble, p.180):

> Bisiden Allemaine is a lond       Angles ihaten.
> þer weoren iborne       þa ilke þe weorn icorne.
> þa Gurmund an hond       bitahte a þis kinelond
> alse he heom a forward hædde       ʒif he hit biwunne.
> Al his biheste       he heom bilaste.
> Of Englen heo comen       and þer-of heo nomen nomen.
> and letten heom cleopien ful iwis       þat folc þat wes Ænglis.
> & þis lond heo cleopeden Ængle-lond       for hit wes al on heore hond.

'Near to Alemaine is a land called Angle where were born those chosen to inherit this land should Gurmund succeed in winning it; he had promised it to them and he fulfilled his promise. From Angle-land they hailed and derived their name. They called themselves English, and, since it had been given into their possession, they called this land England.'

[15] *Ibid.*, p.181.

[16] *Ibid.* Noble concurs here with the view of F. Le Saux, *Laʒamon's Brut: the Poem and its Sources* (Cambridge, 1989), pp. 174–5. Wright holds a similar view, commenting that 'at the end of the narrative we find it is the English who serve as a model of unity and civilization' ('Angles and Saxons', pp. 169–70).

[17] Wace follows the First Variant Version of Geoffrey's *Historia* in placing the transference of political power from the Britons to the English at this chronological point in his narrative (13,635–58). The Vulgate Version defers the passage of dominion until late in the seventh century. See Wright, 'Angles and Saxons', pp. 162–4.

vanquished the giants, take possession of Albion. Having explained the change of the island's name from Albion to Britain, the latter name devised for it by its conqueror Brutus *æfter himseluan* 'in keeping with his own' (977), Laȝamon, following Wace, anticipates the later change from Britain to England:

> Gurmund draf out þe Brutuns;   and his folc wes ihaten Sexuns,
> of ane ende of Alemaine,   Angles wes ihaten.
> Of Angles comen Englisce men,   and Englelond heo hit clepeden.
> Þa Englisce ouercomen þe Brutuns   and brouhten heom þer neoðere
> þat neofer seoððen heo ne arisen   ne her ræden funden.   (989–93)[18]

The wording in Laȝamon at this point in the narrative does not refer to the granting of sovereignty to the Saxons by Gurmund. Instead it sets up a parallel between the occupation of Albion by the Trojan exiles under Brutus and that of Britain by the Anglo-Saxons under Gurmund, two transfers of power, each in turn bringing changes to the cultural identity of the land. These two conquests are paradigmatic of a history of settlement characterized by conquest and cultural change, a pattern specifically referred to by Laȝamon early on in the poem when the history of King Lud is narrated, whose successor, Cassibellaunus, was king of the Britons at the time of the Roman invasion under Julius Caesar:

> Swa is al þis lond iuaren   for uncuðe leoden
> þeo þis londe hæbbeð biwunnen   and eft beoð idriuen hennene;
> and eft hit biȝetten oðeræ   þe uncuðe weoren
> and falden þene ælden nomen   æfter heore wille
> of gode þe burȝen   and wenden heore nomen,
> swa þat nis her burh nan   in þissere Bruttene
> þat habbe hire nome æld   þe me arst hire onstalde.   (3,549–55)[19]

However lengthy and glorious the rule of the Britons is, it does not save

---

[18] 'Gurmund drove out the Britons, and his people were called Saxons, from a region of Germany which was called Angles. The English came from Angles, and they called the land England. The English overcame the Britons and brought them into subjection so that they never rose again nor prospered here.'

[19] 'So this whole country has suffered because of the foreigners who have conquered this land and then been driven out again; and then other foreigners have got possession of it and, in accordance with their wishes, have suppressed the old names of the major towns and changed their names, so that here in this island of Britain there is no town which retains the old name which was originally conferred upon it.'

them from domination by the Romans at one stage in their history and, ultimately, from displacement by the Anglo-Saxons. The fate of the Anglo-Saxon rulers, although beyond the narrative framework of the *Brut*, is parallel to that of the Britons; domination by the Danes at one stage in their history and, ultimately, displacement by the Normans. Those who are victorious at one historical moment become victims at another.

As to the more sympathetic treatment of the Anglo-Saxons compared with the Britons in the latter part of the poem, this is to simplify Laȝamon's narrative approach.[20] Ælfric, an early pagan Northumbrian king responsible for the massacre of British clerics, is referred to as *forcuðest alre kinge* 'the most wicked of kings' (14,878, repeated at 14,903). Yet not much further on in the narrative Ælfric and the British king Cadwan, previously at war, are reconciled, and Laȝamon now praises both kings for putting the interests of the country and people above their own territorial claims:

> Þer iwurðen sahte     þa kinges beie tweien,
> sæhte and some;   heo custen wel ilome.
> Þas kinges wel ilomen     mid luue heom icusten;
> eorl custe oðer     swulc hit weore his broðer,
> sweines þer ploȝeden   - blisse wes mid þeinen.
> Æluric wes king on londe     bi norðen þere Humbre;
> and Cadwan wes king sele     a suð half þere Humbre;
> blisse wes on hireden   mid balden þat kingen.     (14,991–8)[21]

It is not surprising, given Laȝamon's English ancestry – the proem gives his father's name as Leouenað (2) – and his priesthood, that the treatment of Oswald, Anglo-Saxon ruler of Northumbria, martyred in the *Brut* at the hands of Penda, the pagan Anglo-Saxon ruler of Mercia, is

---

[20] L. Johnson, 'Reading the Past in Laȝamon's *Brut*', *The Text and Tradition of Laȝamon's 'Brut'*, pp. 141–59, argues for a more complex attitude towards the Anglo-Saxons than simply a reversal of sympathies once they have been converted to Christianity. In what follows, my observations support her view.

[21] 'There reconciliation was effected between the two kings who kissed repeatedly; amity and concord were brought about. Again and again the kings kissed each other lovingly; noblemen embraced each other like brothers, warriors made merry there – the leaders were content. Ælfric was ruler of the land to the north of the Humber, and Cadwan was an excellent ruler south of the Humber; there was contentment among the followers of both those valiant kings.'

noticeably more sympathetic than that found in Wace. While Wace sees Oswald as noble and a man of courage (14,437), Laȝamon describes him twice as one of God's chosen elect (15,635 and 15,665). As Penda cuts him down, Laȝamon points out that *þis wes Seint Oswald þe a murðe wes aqvald* 'this was Saint Oswald who was murderously done to death' (15,688), the title *Seint*, as pointed out by Françoise Le Saux, not accorded Oswald in Wace, but repeated by Laȝamon at line 15,694.[22] Laȝamon portrays Oswald as a man spiritually inspired but naively trusting, whose trust is betrayed. Surprisingly however, Laȝamon paraphrases a prayer to the Cross which is in Wace, though he adds a pious element not in his source: Oswald has his men pray that should Penda prove treacherous God will avenge the wrong (15,671). This is, however, a somewhat odd sentiment in view of what happens subsequently to Penda: in a version which contradicts both history and Wace, Laȝamon has Oswald's successor, Oswy, killed in battle against Penda – the reverse of Wace – while Penda, badly wounded, flees and is heard of no more (15,834–47). This same Penda who, captured in battle by the British king Cadwalan, becomes his ally and a betrayer of fellow Anglo-Saxon kings, and is depicted consistently as a cruel and most treacherous king, is never specifically referred to in the poem as a pagan/heathen. And he is the same Penda who Laȝamon reminds us, in a comment not in Wace, *wes Mærwales fader, Mildburȝe alde-uader* 'was the father of Mærwal, the grandfather of Mildburge' (15,478). Mildburge is the female saint, descended from the Mercian royal family, who founded, in the late seventh century, the religious house of Much Wenlock in Shropshire, some twenty miles from Areley-Kings.[23]

The account of King Edwin of Northumbria, Oswald's predecessor, makes no mention of his Christianity although he was a devout Christian for the latter part of his seventeen-year reign, and his name in the Caligula manuscript of the poem has the contemporary Latin gloss *Sanctus Edwinus*. The focus, rather, is on his closeness to the British king Cadwalan in their youth and their later conflict over the sovereignty of the land. In speaking of the ravaging of the country by Edwin when he and the British king Cadwalan fall out (*his here wrohte on londe / harmes vniuoȝe* 'his army wrought great havoc in the land', 15,204), Laȝamon's

[22] Le Saux, *Laȝamon's 'Brut': the Poem and its Sources*, pp. 165–7.
[23] *Ibid.*, p. 165.

elaboration of Wace turns Edwin's abduction of a British woman into an abduction and rape, making Edwin's conduct in this instance seem more heinous.

In contrast, Cadwalan, a Christian king but at enmity with both Oswald and his predecessor, Edwin, is repeatedly described in such terms as *þan gode* 'the good' (15,301) and *þæ kene* 'the valiant' (15,438, 15,505 and 15,585). At Whitsuntide Cadwalan holds court in London (as did his predecessors Uther and Arthur), and the description of the assembly is reminiscent of that held by earlier kings of the Britons.[24] We are told that there was great rejoicing at this assembly among those who came to honour the valiant Cadwalan, for *þe king wes swiðe treowe – his treouðe wel he iheold* 'for the king was a man of great integrity – he held faithfully to his word' (15,746). Following the death in battle of Oswy, brother of the martyred King Oswald, Oswy's son, Osric, who had been lovingly reared in Cadwalan's household, successsfully petitions Cadwalan, his liege-lord, for his father's land. At this point in the narrative Laȝamon adds an approving note:

> God king wes Cadwaðlan, swa him wes icunden;
> he wes king hire seouen and feouwerti ȝere. (15,856–7)[25]

To describe Cadwalan as a good king does not entail praising a pagan since at this chronological point in the narrative the Britons, like the Anglo-Saxons, are Christian. Yet, as has been seen in the case of the Anglo-Saxon king Ælfric, a pagan king can be condemned at one moment for a dastardly act and recognized the next as acting in the best interests of the country. Equally, a Christian king is not immune to criticism. Cadwalan, described as a good king and ruler of the country, is also responsible, early in his reign, for bringing misery to the land when he and Edwin, childhood friends but subsequently enemies, go to war:

> Ædwine wes kempe; his men weoren kene.
> Cadwaðlan wes cniht god and he hafde muchel mod.
> Edwine wende ouer Humbre and Cadwaðlan to Lundene;
> þas kinges weoren wraðe – þa aræs þa weore.

---

[24] Cf. lines 15,736–46 with lines 9,229–41, 9,962–4, 11,085–9 and 12,130–5.

[25] 'Cadwalan was, in keeping with his nature, a good king; he was king here for forty-seven years.'

Heo riden and heo arnden,    heo herȝede and heo barnde;
heo sloȝen and heo nomen    al þat heo neh comen;
wa wes þan beondes    þa on londe wuneden.    (15,145–51)[26]

What is significant here is the lack of differentiation between Anglo-Saxons and Britons; the emphasis is rather on the harmful effects of regnal strife on the inhabitants of the country.[27]

It is understandable that Laȝamon, a parish priest, should highlight any moral shortcomings, and the heathen Saxon invaders of the Arthurian section of the narrative, seeking more often by foul than fair means to gain control of the land, are roundly condemned, even though they are ethnically at one with the Anglo-Saxons and thus the English. But Laȝamon's moral disdain is also clearly visible in the lengthy episode covering the treachery of Vortiger, British usurper of the British throne, responsible for inviting the Saxons, along with their chief, Hengest, to settle, and through marriage to Hengest's daughter, Rouwenne, plunging the country back into paganism.[28] Vortiger is described as *of vfele swiðe iwaer* 'well-practised in wrong-doing' (6,669 and 6,691), *swike ful deorne* 'a most subtle deceiver' (6,805), and, most frequently, *of elchen vuele . . . war* 'skilled in every evil practice' (6,899, 6,929, 6,956, 7,063, etc.). Laȝamon emphasizes, in over a thousand lines, Vortiger's treacherous deeds both before and after seizing the throne (6,487–8,101), and when Vortimer leads the Britons in an uprising against Vortiger, war between son and father is legitimized by the righteousness of the cause and the devout Christianity of Vortimer. In this instance warfare is seen as necessary to rid the country of a traitor and to restore the Christian faith.

As I have tried to show, any statement Laȝamon is making about the past cannot but be influenced by his background and outlook as a priest, and he often brings a moral/Christian dimension into his account of both

---

[26] 'Edwin was a noted warrior; his followers were bold men. Cadwalan was a brave warrior and he had great courage. Edwin crossed the Humber, and Cadwalan returned to London; both kings were enraged – war followed. They rode and galloped, they harried and burned; they slaughtered and seized all they came upon; the farmers, for whom the land was their livelihood, suffered misery.'

[27] The importance of firm regnal control in fostering unity within a kingdom, irrespective of the ethnic origins of the inhabitants, is discussed by S. Reynolds, *Kingdoms and Communities in Western Europe, 900–1300* (Oxford, 1984), ch. 8.

[28] The spelling of the names used here (Vortiger and Rouwenne) conforms to that used by Laȝamon.

British and early Anglo-Saxon kings.[29] But one needs also to acknowledge another Laȝamon, the historian who records that Julius Caesar, the
first conqueror of the Britons and a pagan, was at the same time the man
who *makede þane kalender þe dihteð þane moneð and þe ȝer* 'made the calendar
which orders the months and the years', and *dihte feole domes þe ȝet stondeð
ine Rome* 'made many laws still in force in Rome' (3,599–600), facts not
stated in Wace. Although Caesar is a ruthless adversary, Laȝamon at the
same time admits that he is *wis and swiðe iwar* 'wise and very shrewd'
(3,619, 3,653, 3,848, etc.). While acknowledging Caesar's inevitable
damnation as a pagan, it is nevertheless a matter of some concern for
Laȝamon that such a man, the wisest man on earth in his time, *into helle
sculde gan* 'should ever go to hell' (3,601).

This observation concerning Caesar is symptomatic of a narrative
stance which runs through much of the *Brut* and which promotes a more
detached and less partisan view of the historical process as it affects the
different racial and cultural entities vying for dominion. Right from the
beginning of his poem Laȝamon seems to have conceived it as an account
of the different peoples who shaped the history of England. The choice of
an archaized form of English may have more to do with the need for an
appropriate literary medium 'to mediate the history of the past' than with

---

[29] The Christian dimension within which the past operates is marked in the prologue by
Laȝamon's description of the first inhabitants of the island as those who occupied the
land

> æfter þan flode    þe from Drihtene com,
> þe al her aquelde    quic þat he funde,
> buten Noe and Sem,    Iaphet and Cham,
> and heore four wiues    þe mid heom were on archen.    (10–13)

'after the Flood sent by God, which destroyed all living creatures here on earth, save
Noah and Shem, Japhet and Ham, and their four wives who were with them in the
ark'.

References to the Flood were widespread, since the period from the Creation to the
Flood and from the Flood to Abraham counted as two of the seven ages into which
biblical history was divisible, and history for medieval annalists and historians was a
continuum, going back ultimately to the Creation. In a twelfth-century manuscript of
the *Worcester Chronicle* (Oxford, Corpus Christi College 157), thought to have belonged
to John of Worcester and localized, therefore, at Worcester Cathedral Priory in the
early twelfth century, there is, among other introductory diagrammatic genealogies of
Anglo-Saxon kings and bishops, one which draws a direct line of descent from Adam,
the four sons of Noah, and Abraham (fol. 47).

a desire to focus specifically on the historical identity of the Anglo-Saxons through their language.[30]

La3amon accepts it as a fact of history that the Anglo-Saxons succeeded the British as conquerors of the land. But interest in the English past is expressed within a context of historical continuity between British and English, based on their dual and successive occupation of the land. La3amon uses linguistic detail to both differentiate between and link the two groups of inhabitants. He shows an awareness of the different languages spoken by the British and the English respectively, explaining, for example, that Uther's cognomen, *Pendragun an Brutisc* 'Pendragon in the British language', is *Draken-hefd an Englisc* 'Dragon's-head in English' (9,097). At the same time, however, there is linguistic overlap. While the name of Arthur's shield *wes on Bruttisc Pridwen ihaten* 'was Pridwen in the British tongue' (10,554), Arthur's helmet, which had belonged to his father, Uther, was called *Goswhit* (10,552) – the English term 'goose-white' – a name omitted in Wace. Likewise, the occasional references to Arthur as 'King of England' and the similarity of his cognomen 'Britain's darling' to that given to Alfred the Great, 'England's darling', in early Middle English,[31] indicates a mode of thought which elides the ethnic distinction between Britons and Anglo-Saxons, and constructs a common heritage for the English.

What the unfolding historical record also reveals, however, is that the transfer of political power can obliterate the identities of the conquered. Twice in the narrative La3amon comments on the changing names of the country's capital city, called *Troye þe Newe* and later *Trinouant* by Brutus, then changed to *Lundene* by *Englisce men* and, bringing the historical record up to date, *Londres* by the *Frensca* (1,016–31 and 3,529–48). La3amon's emphasis throughout the narrative on the origin of placenames may be one way of recording the past, while simultaneously testifying to the suppression of this past through linguistic change.[32]

---

[30] L. Johnson, 'Tracking La3amon's *Brut*', *Leeds Studies in English* NS 22 (1991), pp. 1–27, at p. 15.

[31] *Middle English Dictionary*, s.v. *dereling* 1(c).

[32] La3amon's *Brut* is not the only poem to comment on the way language operates to obfuscate the past. The Anglo-Norman *Le Roman de Waldef*, written c. 1200–1210, acknowledges the linguistic displacement of the English past as a result of the Norman conquest and the change in language, but is confident that this past can be recovered through translation:

Laȝamon's account of the changing populations brings the historical record up to date by including a reference, as we have seen, to the most recent conquerors of the country, the Normans. In the only two references within the text to these people, Laȝamon refers to them once as *Frensca* and once as *Normans*, seeming not to differentiate between the two terms. The reference to the *Frensca* describes them as gaining control of London through conquest (1,030–1) while the Normans are seen as coming with *heore nið-craften* 'their evil ways' and harming the country (3,547–8). Noble regards these two negative comments as signalling Laȝamon's antagonism towards the Normans, 'the monstrous Normans who had all-too-recently deprived the English of their rightful heritage'.[33] For Lesley Johnson, however, there needs to be more evidence if a case is to be made for an anti-Norman stance.[34] Both Noble and Johnson, however, agree that the way events are narrated in the *Brut* would have encouraged those who formed the original audience for the poem to recognize or seek 'connections between earlier and later historical epochs and to exercise their historical imaginations in using a narrative about the political formations of the past to meditate upon those of the present'.[35] A view of the past in which both Britons and Anglo-Saxons held and then lost

'When the Normans seized the land, the great histories that had been made by the English and recounted by them were left behind, on account of the peoples shifting and the languages changing. Since then much has been translated, and greatly enjoyed by many, such as the Brut, such as Tristan' (39–47).

The poem has been edited by A. J. Holden (Cologny-Genèvre, 1984), and the translation of lines 39–47 is from S. Crane, 'Social Aspects of Bilingualism in the Thirteenth Century', *Thirteenth Century England* 6, ed. M. Prestwich, R. H. Britnell and R. Frame (Woodbridge, 1997), pp. 103–15, at p. 105. In Crane's view 'it is unlikely that *Waldef* and the many *Bruts* and *Tristans* translate from English estoires, but such an assertion is itself a way of linking Anglo-Norman to English culture' (p. 105).

[33] Noble, 'Laȝamon's "Ambivalence" Reconsidered', p. 181. Le Saux, likewise, infers some animosity on Laȝamon's part towards the Normans (*Laȝamon's 'Brut': the Poem and its Sources*, pp. 80–3, p. 175 n. 6, p. 222 n. 131 and p. 230), while M. Shichtman describes Laȝamon as 'a priest to a vanquished people', writing for an audience 'that had to tolerate but never fully accepted the authority and enthusiasms of its French conquerors' ('Gawain in Wace and Laȝamon: a Case of Metahistorical Evolution', *Medieval Texts and Contemporary Readers*, ed. L. A. Finke and M. B. Shichtman (Ithaca and London, 1987), pp. 103–19, at p. 114).

[34] Johnson, 'Reading the Past in Laȝamon's *Brut*', pp. 157–8.

[35] *Ibid.*, p.158.

35

political power could significantly affect the attitude towards a Norman presence contextualized within a historical pattern of changing populations in England.

The difficulty of making categorical statements regarding the attitude taken by Laȝamon towards the Norman present becomes apparent once we return him to his own time and locality. Wendy Collier cites a number of localized Worcestershire texts from the two centuries after the Norman Conquest in which anti-Norman/anti-French sentiments are expressed.[36] Yet Laȝamon himself, though of English parentage on his father's side, was clearly fluent in French. Moreover, the church at Areley-Kings, where Laȝamon was parish priest, was a dependent chapel of Martley church which, together with its dependent chapels, was a possession of the Benedictine abbey of St Mary at Cormeilles in Normandy.[37] And in the movement for the canonization of Wulfstan Laȝamon would have seen an example of the Norman present encompassing the Anglo-Saxon past. It was, after all, Mauger, a Norman, who oversaw the arrangements for Wulfstan's canonization in 1203, although it has been viewed as an act less of devotion to the Anglo-Saxon saint than of greed for the income from pilgrimage to the shrine.[38]

Another instance of cross-cultural linkage reaches to the highest level of government. In 1207 King John, disputing the papal appointment of Stephen Langton as Archbishop of Canterbury, appealed to a particular legend circulating about St Wulfstan which John interpreted as demonstrating Wulfstan's belief in the right of the monarch alone to appoint the higher clergy of the realm.[39] Furthermore, King John, himself a visitor to and supporter of Worcester Cathedral, adopted Wulfstan as his patron saint and insisted on being buried alongside him in Worcester Cathedral.

---

[36] Collier, '"Englishness" and the Worcester Tremulous Hand', pp. 41–3. Collier includes Laȝamon in her list of those who 'had no good opinion of the Normans' (p. 42).

[37] See Weinberg, '"By a noble church on the bank of the Severn": a Regional View of Laȝamon's *Brut*', p. 52.

[38] *Lawman: 'Brut'*, trans. R. Allen (London, 1992), p. xix. It is of relevance that 'adopting English saints and heroes and finding continuities between Anglo-Saxon and post-Conquest history served the Norman and Plantagenet dynasties' ideological claim to a long heritage in England' (Crane, 'Social Aspects of Bilingualism', pp. 103–15, p. 104).

[39] Mason, *St Wulfstan of Worcester*, pp. 113–14 and 281–2.

In the event, an Angevin king ended up lying between two Anglo-Saxon bishops of Worcester, St Oswald and St Wulfstan.[40]

A recurrent theme in Laȝamon's account of events in the past is that of a country vulnerable to internal strife and external attack. Kings who rule firmly and peacefully are commended even though these same kings may be subjected to disapproving comments concerning other less favourable attributes. Contextualizing King John within this view of king and country leaves him falling far short of good kingship, and an early thirteenth-century audience might be less concerned with the cultural affinities of King John than with the dangers facing England caused by a king who had antagonized his barons to the point of rebellion and was, at his death, 'struggling not to lose his kingdom to an invading foreign prince'.[41]

Whatever connections may have been intended or made between the view of the Anglo-Saxons in the *Brut* and the contemporary world of Laȝamon, the conclusion of the poem has *Ænglisce* kings ruling the country, the Britons having lost sovereignty and with no knowing when they will regain it. Laȝamon ends the poem with the line *iwurðe þet iwurðe, iwurðe Godes wille* 'come what may, let God's will be done'. This appears to be a proverbial saying and is extant in two other relevant texts.[42] In the early Middle English *Proverbs of Alfred*, (proverbial material ascribed to King Alfred), the saying is quoted in the context of man's obligation in the weakness and poverty of old age to thank God for all his goodness, 'and wheresoever you go, say at the end, come what may, may God's will be done'. A similar sense of putting one's trust in God in adverse circumstances, this time political rather than personal, is implied when the saying is quoted at the end of the entry for the year 1066 in the 'D' version of the *Anglo-Saxon Chronicle*.[43] This annal concludes with William

---

[40] *Ibid.*, pp. 282–3.

[41] R. V. Turner, *King John* (Harlow, 1994), p. 1.

[42] See Le Saux, *Laȝamon's 'Brut': the Poem and its Sources*, pp. 219–22. The modern English translation of the proverbial saying in these two texts is my own.

[43] D. Whitelock argues that the 'D' version of the *Anglo-Saxon Chronicle* (Cotton Tiberius B iv) was either brought to Worcester for use in compiling the *Worcester Chronicle* or, alternatively, that there was available to the compiler a manuscript very like 'D', but not 'D' itself, as the *Worcester Chronicle* has none of the Scottish entries of 'D'. See *The Anglo-Saxon Chronicle: a Revised Translation*, ed. D. Whitelock with D. C. Douglas and S. I. Tucker (London, 1961), p. xvi.

returning to Normandy, leaving Bishop Odo and Earl William behind, and we are told that these two 'built castles far and wide throughout the land, oppressing the unhappy people, and things went ever from bad to worse'. At the end of the annal are the words *Wurðe god se ende þonne God wylle* 'may the end be good when God wills it'.[44] Le Saux argues against any connection between these three occurrences of the proverb other than 'the similarity of the situations described', the context in all three instances being one of helplessness.[45] In her view Laȝamon is expressing helplessness in the face of Norman domination. But the uncertain future facing, once again, a strife-torn England and its inhabitants might provide a more appropriate early thirteenth-century context for the closing line of Laȝamon's *Brut*.[46]

---

[44] The word *god* is interlined, possibly by a later hand. See *Two of the Saxon Chronicles*, ed. C. Plummer, 2 vols. (Oxford, 1892–1899), I, p. 200.

[45] Le Saux, *Laȝamon's 'Brut': the Poem and its Sources*, p. 222.

[46] I wish to thank Dr Lesley Johnson and Professor Donald Scragg for reading earlier drafts of this paper and for their helpful suggestions.

# Kings, constitution and crisis: 'Robert of Gloucester' and the Anglo-Saxon remedy

## SARAH MITCHELL

In his preface to the *De excidio Brittonum* Gildas, after expressing his anxieties at the ills which have befallen the country of *Brittannia* and its inhabitants since the arrival of the *saxones*, comments:

> Condolentis patriae incommoditatibus miseriisque eius ac remedii condelectantis edicturum putet.[1]

This statement could also stand, I would propose, as an appropriate foreword to the metrical chronicle attributed to 'Robert of Gloucester',[2] although Robert's concerns are, of course, not with the Romanized Britain of the fifth century, but with the Normanized England of the late thirteenth and early fourteenth centuries.[3] Robert is not the first post-

---

[1] 'I sympathise with my country's difficulties and troubles, and rejoice in remedies to relieve them.' *Gildas: the Ruin of Britain and Other Works*, ed. and trans. Michael Winterbottom (London, 1978), pp. 13 and 87.

[2] The name 'Robert of Gloucester' is a convenient term for referring to the chronicle; my use of it is not intended to limit authorship to a single, identifiable, person. Even if it is the work of more than one person, the unity of the first-recension text – its polemical and ideological coherence – allows its analysis as a single whole.

[3] The chronicle is extant in two recensions, both containing the same material (with few alterations) until 1135, after which they divide, the first, and longer, recension detailing events until 1271 at which point the most complete manuscript is damaged; the second recension provides a different, but equally lengthy, account of the reign of Stephen, after which the history of the country to the accession of Edward I in 1272 is briefly recounted. The chronicle is datable to the late thirteenth/early fourteenth century. The earliest surviving manuscript (London, British Library, Cotton Caligula A.xi), which is of the first recension, has been dated, on palaeographical grounds, to between 1300 and 1330. A. Hudson, *An Edition of the Chronicle Attributed to Robert of Gloucester with a Study of the Original Language of the Poem*, unpub. D.Phil. diss., Oxford University, 1964, p. 5, dates it *c.* 1300–1325. W. A. Wright, *The Metrical Chronicle of Robert of Gloucester*, RS

Conquest historian to write in the English vernacular. Laȝamon is a notable predecessor. But Robert is of exceptional importance in the context of post-Conquest retrospects upon the Anglo-Saxon period in that, whereas Laȝamon terminates his *Brut* with the death of the last British king, Cadwallader, Robert brings the account of English history up to his own day, and distinctively looks at the Anglo-Saxon past from out of the context of contemporary, late thirteenth-century England. This is, potentially, a significant political standpoint, and indeed, I hope to show that Robert plainly does promote certain aspects of Anglo-Saxon England as important in the shaping of his own society.

A brief review of what Robert's chronicle is (and, indeed, is not) may help to provide some context for the following discussion. It is, for example, preoccupied with kings and governance. History, to Robert, comprises the succession of monarchs and their acts (good and ill) of policy. It is not solely a history of the English Church and people. It is not, like the 'Alfredian' chronicles, pro-dynastic establishment propaganda; it challenges the establishment of the day. It is not, like the *Peterborough Chronicle*, a monastic history, rather parochially assessing 'national' figures in terms of their impact upon the fortunes of the abbey or regional church. It is a national history. It is not a British history. It is English in an assertive and specific sense. It is not fabulous. It is concerned with traditional Christian polities. It is not Latin; it is not French. It is not merely antiquarian, nor (primarily) entertaining. It is a contemporary (and maybe proleptic) polemic.

---

86 (London, 1887), I, p. xl, dates it 1320–1330. Internal evidence confirms a date of composition around the turn of the century: the battle of Evesham – which occurred in 1265 – is described, where, notably, the 'author' claims personal witness and also names himself as Robert. Within the text Louis IX is also referred to as a saint. Louis was canonized in 1297. Thus, these are two *termini post quos* for the chronicle's composition, one of which also conveniently ties in the name traditionally associated with the chronicle, 'Robert of Gloucester'. My focus in this paper will be upon the first recension text, as, in its exposition of events near-contemporary with its composition (*c.* 1300), the author shows himself to be working to a different agenda from that of the second recension author, and it is this highly political agenda that I am interested in. The amendments to the text by the second recension author, and the continuation, indicate that this author was less politically motivated than the first; little involvement is shown in the politics of his day, his concern seeming to be merely to convey necessary information to his audience, rather than using it for his own polemical purposes.

Robert's concern with England is made apparent from the opening line of the work, where he states:

> Engelond his a wel god londe . ich wene ech londe best.[4]

His source at this point (Henry of Huntingdon) makes reference to Britain;[5] Robert is therefore immediately demonstrating an independence of thought, as well as illustrating a potential pro-English nationalistic stance.

The land he promotes may be a *wel god londe* but Robert, in the contemporary account of events that he gives near the end of his chronicle, makes it evident that this country is not without its problems. Disturbances which occurred within the author's own time are narrated: the barons' rebellion and the battle of Evesham, for example, and a rhetorical (and not undramatic) interjection is made part way into the account of the reign of Henry III to alert the audience to the forthcoming miseries he is to recount:

> Þe meste wo þat here vel . bi king henries day.
> In this lond icholle biginne . to telle ȝuf ich may.[6]
>
> (10,986–7)

It is the remedy which Robert proposes for this greatest of woes that comprises the 'highly political' agenda to which I referred; and it is this that I would like to explore here. It is my thesis that Robert sees this remedy lying in the Anglo-Saxon past of the country, which he deliberately sets up for purposes of comparison with thirteenth-century England. Robert selects the Anglo-Saxon material at his disposal and treats it in a way which strengthens his polemic; this, I believe, centres upon the highly sensitive issue of the legitimacy of kingship, and such related specifics as the criteria for selecting a rightful king (and the consequences of this selection for the country), the necessity of a formal

---

[4] 'England is a very good land, I believe the best of any land.' All references to the chronicle text are taken from *The Metrical Chronicle of Robert of Gloucester*, ed. Wright.

[5] Henry of Huntingdon's *Historia Anglorum* opens with the line: *Brittannia igitur beatissima est insularum, foecunda frugibus et arboribus.* See *Henrici Archideaconi Huntendunensis: Historia Anglorum*, ed. T. Arnold, RS 74 (London, 1879), p. 5.

[6] 'I will begin to tell, if I may, the greatest misery that happened in this land in King Henry's day.'

coronation, and the laws and customs that the monarch ought, once appointed, to uphold. This, I would argue, is part of his attempt to define and promote concepts of a kind of 'cultural Englishness' within a late thirteenth-century context, which he offers as some sort of remedy for the ills of his own day.

This motive is, of course, consistent with his choice of the English language in which to write. Research (such as that of Ian Short)[7] suggests that English was, by the end of the twelfth century, the mother-tongue of Norman descendants, and Anglo-Norman the acquired, second, language. Robert's choice of language was still innovative at this time when most records, official documents and literature were composed and circulated in Latin and Anglo-Norman, but, by virtue of writing in English, Robert potentially gained access to a large audience. The gradual resurgence of English as a written medium, of which Robert was a part, echoes that other revival of the English (that is, Anglo-Saxon) tongue as a written medium in the ninth century under the auspices of Alfred, who advocated the translation of certain books into English to aid the revival of learning.[8] The situation in thirteenth/fourteenth-century England was, quite obviously, different from that of ninth-century Wessex; the native English (in so far as such a group can be defined) were no longer the masters of their land, and the choice of writing in English was dependent upon different criteria from those which Alfred discusses. Whereas Alfred promoted the use of the vernacular to counter the limitations of Latin as a cultural vehicle, Robert was perhaps promoting it to counter the cultural oppression of Latin and Anglo-Norman which were entrenched as the formal, instrumental languages of an over-class. Even though English would seem to have been the mother-tongue of Norman descendants by this time, Anglo-Norman may still have been seen to be the language of

---

[7] I. Short, 'Patrons and Polyglots: French Literature in Twelfth-Century England', *Anglo-Norman Studies* 14, ed. M. Chibnall (Woodbridge, 1991), pp. 229–49, at p. 246, asserts that 'the natural dynamic of diglossia and practical bilingualism would have meant that by the middle of the twelfth century at the very latest the "Anglo-Normans" . . . had not only a passive but also an active command of English'.

[8] Alfred, in the preface to his translation of Gregory the Great's *Cura pastoralis* comments after detailing the decline of Latin as a language of learning: *me ðyncð betre, gif iow swæ ðyncð, ðæt we . . . sumæ bec, ða ðe niedbeðearfosta sien eallum monnum to wiotonne, ðæt we ða on ðæt geðiode wenden ðe we ealle gecnawan mægen, Sweet's Anglo-Saxon Reader*, revised by D. Whitelock (Oxford, 1988), p. 6, lines 56–9.

an over-class; Robert himself speaks of a perceived linguistic division in
society which, even if merely theoretical by 1300, would still appear to
have been a point of emotive appeal.[9] These languages may then have
been perceived, by Robert, to be the embodiment of, and an instrument
of, a royal governance whose credentials were suspect, and whose
imperfections were responsible for bringing ills upon the country.
Robert's English may be, in short, an anti-colonialist gesture, a rallying
standard for renascent Englishness.

Robert's strategy in the chronicle is to remind people that his
contemporary England has an English past which predates recent
Norman-usurped history, and which is, into the bargain, a past en-
shrining values of good, and Godly, governance which has, unhappily for
the people, been corrupted. His preoccupations are still essentially
directed by the nature of the 'wo' that he describes having befallen the
country in the reign of Henry III, but his search for a remedy is
inextricably involved in his attempts to assert a claim for Englishness.
The woes about which he complains are clearly defined. They are
primarily provoked by the behaviour of the monarch, and can be seen to
fall into three main categories of concern: first, a desire for English
freedom and autonomy; second, English traditional law as a guarantor of
that freedom and autonomy; and third, the harmony of the spiritual and
worldly, within the life and governance of the nation. These are
articulated by three specific and practical issues which Robert discusses:
the influx of foreigners into the country, the failure of the king to uphold
the traditional laws of the land, and the king's refusal to accept
ecclesiastical advice.

Robert's anxieties about foreigners are directed against the people
whom he describes as the French, particularly because of the preferment

---

[9] When recounting the aftermath of the Norman Conquest, Robert writes: '& þe
normans ne couþe speke þo . bote hor owe speche./ & speke frenss as hii dude
atom . & hor children dude also teche./ So þat heiemen of þis lond . þat of hor blod
come./ Holdeþ alle þulke speche . þat hii of him nome./ Vor bote a man conne
frenss . me telþ of him lute./ Ac lowe men holdeþ to engliss . & to hor owe speche
ȝute.' (7,538–43). Giraldus Cambrensis also equates Anglo-Norman with Latin as a
prestige language when he discusses his nephew's inability to converse in that tongue.
See W. Rothwell, 'The Role of French in Thirteenth-Century England,' *Bulletin of the
John Rylands Library* 58 (1975–1976), pp. 445–66.

given to them over the English; the increase in their numbers is attributed by him solely to the royal family:

> Þoru hom & þoru þe quene was  .  so much frenss folc ibrouȝt.
> Þat of englisse men  .  me tolde as riȝt nouȝt.
> & þe king hom let hor wille  .  þat ech was as king.  (10,992–4)[10]

This does not stand as an isolated instance of irritation expressed in the chronicle at the treatment of the English by the king; similar outrage is expressed at the preference given to the Normans after the Conquest:

> & kniȝtes of biȝonde se  .  & oþer men al so.
> He ȝef londes in engelond  .  þat liȝtliche com þer to.
> Þat ȝute hor eirs holdeþ  .  alonde monion.
> & deseritede moni kundemen  .  þat he huld is fon.
> So þat þe mestedel of heyemen  .  þat in engelond beþ.
> Beþ icome of þe normans  .  as ȝe nou iseþ.
> & men of religion  .  of normandie al so.
> He feffede here mid londes  .  mid rentes al so.
> So þat vewe contreies  .  beþ in engelonde.
> Þat monekes nabbeþ of normandie  .  somwat in hor honde.
>                                                       (7,578–87)[11]

The 'he' referred to is, of course, William the Conqueror, and Robert here demonstrates that he understands that the root of his contemporary problems lies in William's succession. Part of the complaint about the influx of the Normans into the land in 1066 and after is expressed in the present tense, comment being passed, for example, upon the fact that the heirs of those Normans who came over with William are still (*ȝute* 'yet') in control of lands belonging to *kundemen* 'natives'. Whilst these people atone for their sins by raising monastic foundations and churches

---

[10] 'Through them, and through the queen, so many French people were brought into the country that Englishmen were considered as nothing, and the king let them do as they wished, so that each was as a king.'

[11] 'He gave lands in England to knights from beyond the sea, and to other men also, so that they gained it with no effort, and their heirs still own much of it; in so doing, he disinherited many native men whom he considered his enemies, so that, as you can now see, the greatest part of the high men in England are descended from the Normans. He also endowed the men of religion from Normandy with lands and with rents also, so that there are few counties in England that are not somewhat in control of monks from Normandy.'

(7,588–601), their outward appearance as penitent christians is indicated to be a façade in another interjection by the chronicle's 'author':

> So varþ monye of þis heyemen . in chirche me may yse.
> Knely to god as hii wolde . al quic to him fle.
> Ac be hii arise & abbeþ iturnd . fram þe weued hor wombe.
> Wolues dede hii nimeþ vorþ . þat er dude as lombe.    (7,606–9)[12]

Robert's concerns may seem to be dictated solely by clerical self-interest (cf. his comments upon the imposed Norman abbacy of most English monasteries), but, if so, this is balanced in the text by a concern for the lay person, and hence of the general disruption of English inheritance by the Conquest; the wolf-like deeds of the Norman descendants are directed, he elaborates, against *sely bonde men* not the religious orders (7,610–11). That a situation of oppression and displaced rights is still pertinent to his own society Robert implies by the appeals he makes to his audience (*as ʒe nou iseþ, me may yse*) suggesting either that he expected them to be sympathetic to his views in recognizing this, or was conditioning them to accept this outlook.

Audience expectation also, perhaps, underlies the manner in which Robert discusses another of his main concerns, the customs of the land and English law. He continually uses the key term the *gode olde law* in the text, never giving any further definition of it. This phrase could be merely a casual reference to a code of law belonging to a perceived past golden age (used in the manner of the modern phrase 'the good old days' for example) but it becomes clear that it is understood to refer to a recognized code of laws, which are found encapsulated in the Magna Carta. It is these laws, Robert makes clear, that Henry III refuses to uphold:

> Þe riʒts of holichurche . & of þe gode olde lawe.
> Þat he adde of is chartre ymad . he gan him wiþdrawe.
> (10,890–1)[13]

Robert's order of specification might be of importance here. The 'rights of

---

[12] 'Many of these high men may be seen in church, kneeling to God as if they wished to quickly go to him. But when they have risen and turned away from the altar, they perform wolves' deeds, those who had formerly acted as lambs.'

[13] 'He began to withdraw from the laws of Holy Church and from the good old law of which he had made his charter.'

Holy Church' are made to stand separately from 'the law', and are given priority in this formula. This may merely be suggestive of clerical self-interest, but, it also reflects the ordering of the Magna Carta, which advises in its first 'chapter' 'that the English Church shall be free and enjoy her rights in their integrity and her liberties untouched'.[14] The charter which Robert mentions here is in fact the second re-issue of the Magna Carta of 1218[15] (the first re-issue occurred immediately after the accession of Henry), and, despite the vagueness of the term *gode olde lawe*, Robert seems to have some understanding of this charter's contents. Upon the first re-issue he comments:

> Þe king made is chartre  .  & grantede it wel vawe.
> Þe gode lawes of forest  .  & oþere þat wule were.  (10,637–8)[16]

It is perhaps pertinent to note that the forest laws were for the first time issued as a separate charter at this date, together with the Magna Carta, and it is with such general details that Robert seems to have had at least a passing familiarity. Indeed, it is possible that he may have encountered copies of these law codes; these charters were reproduced in the cartularies of Gloucester Abbey, for example. In the absence of any analysis by Robert of the *gode olde lawe*, the Magna Carta or the forest laws, evidence for his detailed knowledge of these legal documents is lacking. It may, then, be suggested that his interest in 'the law' is an aspect of his general concern with good governance; that is, his interest in the Magna Carta and its ancillary laws is theoretical rather than specific. Robert's interest in right laws and *costume* 'custom' can be traced back in the chronicle, and it can be seen to be a tradition that he perceives emanating from the Anglo-Saxon period, particularly from the reign of Alfred; the symbolic nature of his preoccupation may therefore be apparent.

The third of Robert's concerns about sovereignty is that the wise, normally ecclesiastical, advice which he perceives as essential to good rule is ignored by the king. This advice is often proffered by a saintly character in the chronicle, and in the time of Henry III comes from St Edmund of Abingdon, Archbishop of Canterbury:

---

[14] A. E. Dick Howard, *Magna Carta: Text and Commentary* (Charlottesville, 1964), p. 34.

[15] K. Feiling, *A History of England* (London, 1975), p.168.

[16] 'The king made his charter and granted it very gladly, the good laws of the forest, and other laws that existed formerly.'

> Þo sprong þer gret contek . bituene henri vr king.
> & þe erchebissop seint edmund . & noȝt vor lute þing.
> Vor þe king þo he adde iwiued . & an eir adde al so.
> He drou to oþer conseil . þan he was iwoned to do. (10,886–9)[17]

This description of Henry's defiance of the archbishop is closely followed by Robert's statement that he is now going to speak of the woes that fell in King Henry's day. It is this defiance Robert perceives as contributing to those woes.

Robert's remedy, like that of the monks of Canterbury in the eleventh-century *Anglo-Saxon Chronicle* fulminating against Eustace and the other arrogant foreigners favoured at Edward the Confessor's court,[18] is to expel the foreigners. This is supplemented by some less harsh criteria: that the king should uphold the traditional laws of the land and respect ecclesiastical advice. However, in order to fully understand the answer which Robert proposes for his country's contemporary problems, we need to return to an earlier part of the chronicle, particularly to that relating to the Anglo-Saxon period, as it is from here that his concepts of good and rightful kingship emanate.

Alfred is a central figure in Robert's discussion of kingship; from his reign, in Robert's account, stem all legitimate monarchs of the country. As the country which Robert promotes is England, it is natural that he should seek the seeds of hereditary kingship among the monarchs of the English royal house, rather than the French or British. His Anglo-Saxon kings are presented, however, in vignettes; even Alfred's life is given little space. Robert's method of emphasis is not to dedicate to this period more space than he attributes to the 'Matter of Britain', for example, but to demonstrate the conjoining of the regnal line with divine authorization. This occurs during the reign of Alfred's father, Æthelwulf, when Alfred, at the age of four, is taken on a visit to Rome. The account reads as follows:

> Þe pope leon him blessede . þo he þuder com.
> & þe kinges croune of þis lond . þat in þis lond ȝut is.

---

[17] 'Then a great strife arose there between Henry, our king, and the archbishop, St Edmund, and not over a small thing. Because the king, when he had married, and had an heir also, turned to other counsel, as he was inclined to do.'

[18] *Two of the Saxon Chronicles Parallel*, ed. C. Plummer and J. Earle, 2 vols. (Oxford, 1892 and 1899), MS E, annal 1048.

& elede him to be king   .   ar he were king iwis.
& he was king of engelond   .   of alle þat þer come.
Þat verst þus yeled was   .   of þe pope of rome.
& suþþe oþer after him   .   of þe erchebissop echon.
So þat biuore him   .   pur king nas þer non.      (5,327–33)[19]

As a consequence of this sacring ceremony, not only is Alfred anointed rightful king, but, as this ceremony is echoed between future kings and the archbishop (normally of Canterbury), they too are divinely appointed if they are of the blood of Alfred. The position of Alfred as the root from which all kings of England must derive is made clear in the interpretation of Edward the Confessor's death-bed prophecy. Edward's vision of a green tree which is cut in half, but eventually reunites, flowers and bears fruit was seen as a prophecy of the troubles which would afflict the land after his death, and their eventual cessation. In his *Gesta Regum Anglorum*, William of Malmesbury considers the first half of the prophecy (the severing of the tree) to have been accomplished, but sees no end to the miseries which afflict his country.[20] In contrast, Robert, following the interpretation given by Ailred of Rievaulx in his *Historia Regum Anglorum*,[21] identifies the green tree as England and the royal house of that country, and explains the nature of the tree's roots:

Þe more bitokneþ þe riȝte kunde   .   þat ech of oþere come.
Fram king alfred þe kunde more   .   þat verst was yeled at rome.

(7,242–3)[22]

There is a history of misinterpretation and manipulation of the portrayal of Alfred's first visit to Rome, beginning (apparently) soon after the event

---

[19] 'The pope Leo blessed him when he came there, and the king's crown of this land which is still in this land, and anointed him to be king before he was king. And he was king of England, of all who came there, he who was thus first anointed by the pope of Rome, and since others after him, by the archbishop each one, so that before him there was not a perfect king.'

[20] *William of Malmesbury: Gesta Regum Anglorum/The History of the English Kings I*, ed. R. A. B. Mynors with R. M. Thomson and M. Winterbottom (Oxford, 1998), pp. 414–16.

[21] Ailred of Rievaulx, 'Historia Regum Anglorum', PL 195 (Turnholt, 1855), pp. 711–38.

[22] 'The root betokens the correct race, that descends each from the other, from King Alfred the native root, who was first anointed at Rome.'

itself,[23] and Robert is not unusual therefore in using this episode for his own purposes. It had also been incorporated into the work of earlier chroniclers,[24] but its interpretation that as a consequence of this ceremony Alfred was the first 'perfect' king of the country is adopted from Ailred's *Genealogia* and adapted by Robert to further his own ends. By choosing to include this incident of Alfred's life, and in interpreting it in such a manner, Robert is diminishing the standing of those monarchs who preceded Alfred, fixing his contemporary monarchy in a clearly English past, and recognizing the necessity for the coronation of all future kings by the archbishop in order to claim legitimacy, and therefore ensure peace.

Robert's ideas here are ones which are consistent with coronation procedures in the thirteenth century. The English coronation *ordo* stemmed directly from Anglo-Saxon models; the 'Anselm' *ordo* by which Henry III was crowned to office, for example, was a late eleventh/early twelfth-century revision of an earlier tenth-century 'Edgar' *ordo*,[25] one essential alteration being that the chrism used to anoint the new ruler was replaced with a less holy oil, thus emphasizing that kingship was distinct from the priesthood. Nevertheless, the anointing ceremony was intended to elevate the standing of the king above the layman, and was a live issue in the thirteenth century, as a letter from Robert Grosseteste to Henry III discussing sacerdotal and kingly powers makes clear.[26] The coronation

---

[23] This anointing ceremony is mentioned in both the *Anglo-Saxon Chronicle* and Asser's *Life of Alfred*; although the dating of the latter text, and its dependency upon the former, has been the subject of some academic discussion, this does not detract from the importance of Robert's inclusion of material ultimately derived from these sources. By so doing he reflects a similar ideological allegiance to the house of Wessex, particularly to its claim to be the founding dynasty of the English monarchy. Cf. Plummer and Earle, *Two of the Saxon Chronicles*, 853 E, *Asser's Life of King Alfred*, ed. W. H. Stevenson (Oxford, 1904), p. 7, and *Alfred the Great*, trans. S. Keynes and M. Lapidge (Harmondsworth, 1983), p. 232.

[24] See *Symeonis Monachi Opera Omnia*, ed. T. Arnold, 2 vols., RS 75 (London, 1882–1885), II, p. 72; *Chronica: Magistri Rogeri de Houedene*, ed. W. Stubbs, 4 vols., RS 51 (London, 1868–1871), I, p. 36; *Willelmi Malmesbiriensis Monachi de Gestis Regum Anglorum*, ed. N. E. S. A. Hamilton, 2 vols., RS 52 (London, 1887–1889), I, p. 109.

[25] P. E. Schramm, *A History of the English Coronation* (Oxford, 1937), p. 37.

[26] This is letter CXXIV in *Roberti Grosseteste Episcopi Quandam Lincolniensis Epistolae*, ed. H. R. Luard, RS 25 (London, 1861).

49

procedure itself aided the idea of a historical continuity emanating from the Anglo-Saxon era. William the Conqueror had himself crowned in the same manner as his predecessor, Edward the Confessor, in order to legalize his right to the throne, and the words were retained in the *ordo* that he held office *hereditario iure*.[27] The three-fold Anglo-Saxon *promissio* of the king to his subjects was also retained in the coronation oath. The duties imposed upon the thirteenth-century monarch at his accession derived from that earlier period were firstly, to preserve the peace and protect the clergy and the people, secondly, to maintain good laws and abolish bad ones, and thirdly, to ensure the equitable administration of justice to all men.[28] It is the failure to maintain this list of promises which forms the basis of the concerns found in 'Robert of Gloucester's' chronicle. When it is realized that, from the time of John's repeat coronation oath in 1213, the monarch swore to uphold the laws of his predecessors, especially those of Edward the Confessor,[29] these further parallels demonstrate that Robert had at least a general and theoretical understanding of the laws which bound the king to his subjects, and was conscious of digressions therefrom. Robert also emphasizes that which is implicit in the coronation procedure: the monarch is the king of England, and is part of a long line of kings stretching back, with some discontinuity, to the Anglo-Saxon era (in his interpretation, to the days of Alfred). Thus, in his account, not only is Alfred blessed by the Pope, but also *þe kinges croune of þis lond* which, furthermore, *in þis lond ȝut is*. It is uncertain whether Robert refers to a literal or abstract crown, but what is of importance is that he considers it to be still in his country, and to be an English crown, not French, Norman or British. By acceding to, or wearing, this crown, the monarch thus lays claim to the authority invested in Alfred, and ought, accordingly, to uphold the laws emanating from that period.

The force of Robert's argument can only be fully understood when it is considered in the context of succession disputes which occur after Æthelred the Unready's death. By the application of Robert's criteria, Cnut, Harthacnut and Harold I are dismissed as illegitimate kings who disrupt the royal line from its rightful course, as, indeed, are Harold Godwinsson, William the Conqueror and William Rufus. Throughout

---

[27] Schramm, *A History of the English Coronation*, pp. 27–8.
[28] *Ibid.*, p. 196.   [29] *Ibid.*, p. 200.

the succession dispute between Harold and William, Robert holds up Edgar the atheling, the grandson of Edmund Ironside, as the *ri3t eir . . . of engelond . & kunde to be kinge* (7,745), as he is a direct descendant of the Anglo-Saxon royal line. To clarify this for his audience, Robert interprets the title *atheling*:

> Wo so were next king bi kunde  .  me clupede him aþeling.
> Þeruore me clupede him so  .  vor bi kunde he was next king.
>
> (7,276–7)[30]

The inverted repetition in line 7,277 of that which is described in the line above serves to make Robert's support of this member of the royal line as emphatic as possible. This is a matter of some importance for Robert as he considers that the succession of a wrongful king will bring miseries to the country. He does not explain his reasoning for thinking this, but since he maintains that a king obtains the throne legitimately only if he is anointed by the archbishop and if he is of the blood of Alfred because Alfred was anointed by the Pope (God's viceregent on earth), then it can be concluded that Robert perceives that the accession of a monarch who does not have such heavenly approval causes a breach in the proper order of the universe, resulting in troubles descending upon the kingdom. The accession of an illegitimate monarch is, for example, the reason for the defeat of the English people at the battle of Hastings:

> Þus lo þe englisse folc  .  vor no3t to grounde come.
> Vor a fals king þat nadde no ri3t  .  to þe kinedom.  (7,494–5)[31]

In his support of the rights of Edgar the atheling, Robert presents William as another illegitimate ruler who, though he *in more ri3te was* (7496) than Harold, he *in pur ri3te nas* (7,497). Robert is consistent in isolating each wrongful king, and in emphasizing the fact that a legitimate king has been correctly anointed. He intimates further that all people are bound by the laws governing coronation which have been implemented since Alfred's accession to the throne. Dunstan, for example, is loath to crown Æthelred the Unready because of the murder of his elder half-brother, Edward the Martyr. Osbern's life of the saint reports

---

[30] 'Whoever was next king by right of birth, he was called atheling; therefore he was called this because by right of birth he was the next king.'

[31] 'Thus the English people were defeated for nothing, for a false king who had no right to the kingdom.'

that there was such a reluctance to crown this king,[32] but Robert's exposition of the event applies his own criteria to the scene and explores this point of tension. Dunstan is Archbishop of Canterbury and therefore cannot deviate from his duty as outlined at the time of Alfred's anointing; he must crown Æthelred as he is the legitimate heir (by hereditary right if not morally):

> þis godeman seint dunston.
> Hatede muche to crouny him  .  ȝif he it miȝte vorgon.
> Ac þo it moste nede do  .  þoru pur londes lawe.      (5,902–4)[33]

The archbishop too, Robert makes plain, is constrained by the country's laws, and cannot, by omitting to crown him to office, avert the disaster that he prophesies is to befall the land because of the sins of Æthelred's mother.

Robert often makes a point of stating that the correct procedure has been followed with other, legitimate, kings; so, John's coronation is narrated:

> He let him crouni king  .  an holi þorsday iwis.
> At westmunstre in þe abbey  .  as þe riȝte crouninge is.
> Of þe erchebissop of kantebury.      (10,100–2)[34]

Robert's concern to establish that the coronation had been undertaken in the appropriate manner might be associated with the fact that the coronation was only considered to have its due effect if all of the forms had been observed and nothing omitted.[35] By the criteria here detailed, and indeed by those which were generally acknowledged at the time,[36] Henry III can be seen to be a legitimate king. He is of the blood of

---

[32] See Osbern's *Life of Saint Dunstan* in *Memorials of Saint Dunstan; Archbishop of Canterbury,* ed. W. Stubbs, RS 63 (London, 1874).

[33] 'This good man, St Dunstan, greatly disliked having to crown him, if he could have avoided it, but he had to do it because of the perfect law of the land.'

[34] 'He caused himself to be crowned king on Holy Thursday at Westminster in the abbey by the archbishop of Canterbury, as is the manner of the correct coronation.'

[35] Schramm, *A History of the English Coronation,* p. 10.

[36] *Ibid.,* pp. 39–40. Schramm notes how in 1140 forgeries from Westminster Abbey confirmed the right for the coronation to take place there; the right of the Archbishop of Canterbury (or one of his suffragans, but not the Archbishop of York) to crown the sovereign was also established at this time.

Alfred, as direct descent was assured after the marriage of Henry I to Matilda of Scotland (a descendant of the sister of Edgar the atheling and hence of Edmund Ironside), and he is crowned (the second time) at Westminster by the Archbishop of Canterbury.[37] Yet Robert makes it apparent that his kingship is not perfect, indicating that the duties of the king to his people bound up in the king's coronation *promissio* need to be upheld in order to ensure the peaceful reign of an ideal king.

I return here to Robert's complaint about Henry III that he does not follow the *gode olde lawe*. As has been seen, the expectation that the monarch should maintain such laws was an element of the *ordo* and ultimately had its roots in the Anglo-Saxon period. For Robert, the *gode olde lawe* is that encapsulated in the re-issues of the Magna Carta in the reign of Henry III, and, like the coronation ritual and hereditary right, it can be traced back in the chronicle to the pre-Conquest period, in this case, via the reign of John:

> . . . þe barons . nolde it þolie noȝt.
> Ne þe luþer lawes þat he huld . ac bede him wiþdrawe.
> Is luþer wille & granti hom . þe gode olde lawe.
> Þat was bi seint edwardes day . & suþþe adoun ibroȝt.
> Þoru him & þoru oþere . þat were of luþer þouȝt. (10,493–7)[38]

The Magna Carta itself does indeed make reference to the 'ancient and just customs' of the land,[39] and the *ordo* makes mention of the old laws which are to be preserved,[40] and it is these which Robert locates more firmly in the reign of the last rightful Anglo-Saxon king (Edward) as, indeed, does the coronation *ordo*. It is such phraseology ('ancient and just

---

[37] Robert describes both of the coronations of Henry III; the first at Gloucester which was given authority by the pope's legate, and the second at Westminster after the defeat of Louis IX (lines 10,560–73 and 10,655–7).

[38] 'The barons would not endure it or the evil laws that he upheld, but asked him to withdraw his evil will and grant them the good old law that existed in St Edward's day, and that was afterwards brought down by him and by others who were of evil thought.'

[39] Dick Howard, *Magna Carta*, p. 44.

[40] In the revised 1308 coronation *ordo* prepared for Edward II's accession, the wording was altered so that the king swore to uphold the laws of Edward I, not Edward the Confessor, and to maintain just, rather than old, laws. See Schramm, *A History of the English Coronation*, p. 206.

customs', 'old laws') which Robert converts into a colloquial phrase and adopts into his word-hoard (*gode olde law*); his recurrent use of it appears to be deliberate, enabling his audience to trace key concepts forward to their own time, and encouraging them to appreciate their heritage.

Robert, however, makes no claims for Edward the Confessor as a law-maker; he merely states that the laws reinforced in the Magna Carta were those which were around in the reign of this king. It is to Alfred again that we must look to find a law-making king whose dedication to his country Robert admires; twice he mentions the strong laws that Alfred passed, marking what he perceives to be their originality at the time:

> Þey me segge þat lawes beþ   .   in worre tyme vorlore.
> Nas it noȝt so bi is daye   .   vor þei he in worre were.
> Lawes he made riȝtuolore   .   & strengore þan er were.
>
> $$(5,389-91)^{41}$$

In Robert's admiration for Alfred's dedication to law-making at a time of national crisis, it may be possible to perceive a wish that such was the case in his own *worre tyme* of the barons' revolt. What he does indicate, however, is that the very laws which Alfred initiated, and which were passed, via the reign of Edgar, to Edward the Confessor's day, are now overturned.

Supplementing Robert's interest in the monarchs of the kingdom is a comparable and compatible preoccupation with the saints, and especially with their role of supporting and advising the sovereign. Of the fifty saints mentioned by Robert in the chronicle, almost half are of Anglo-Saxon birth or affiliation, while only six issue from the post-Conquest era. The Anglo-Saxon age is therefore presented as an era of saints, many of whom play an active role in the political situation of their time. Alfred receives the help of a saint when he retreats into the marshes of Athelney before the Danish advance. A vision of Saint Cuthbert assures him of his victory:

> Icham he sede Cuthbert   .   to þe icham ywent.
> To bring þe gode tydinges   .   fram god ich am ysent.
> Vor þat folc of þis lond   .   to sunnen hor wille al ȝeve.
> & ȝut nolleþ hiderto   .   hor sunnen bileue.

---

[41] 'It is said that laws are destroyed in wartime. It wasn't so in his day, even though he was at war, he made laws juster and more forceful than had existed before.'

Þoru me & oþer halwen . þat in þis lond were ybore.
Þat for ʒou biddeþ god . wan we beþ him biuore.
Vre lord mid is eyen of milce . on þe lokeþ þeruore. (5,342–9)[42]

The vision of Saint Cuthbert is a popular one in Alfredian legend,[43] but the insistence that the native saints of the country have actively invoked the help of God for Alfred, seems to be peculiar to Robert.

This prophetic utterance echoes those defensive and defiant moves which were being made by the monasteries across the country in the early post-Conquest period, but also at the time of the Viking invasions.[44] In these times of crisis, the relics of locally-honoured saints were raised up as protectors of the lands and privileges of religious communities, whose wrath would fall upon the oppressors of monastic houses, for example St Cuthbert at Durham. It is interesting, therefore, that Robert would appear – by virtue of his inclusion of this episode – to still uphold that long-standing faith in the protection of the land by its saints. As Robert perceives the country of his time to be a direct descendant of that of Alfred, then he may be suggesting that it too is protected by the same heavenly community, that it is the country of England (not a Normanized version of the same) which is being served. This group of saints does not operate in isolation from the monarch, however (it is often, indeed, a part of the regnal line); it would seem that they are mutually supportive forces. If a king is a descendant of Alfred, in Robert's view, then saintly support is often forthcoming in moments of need. In the event of such support being ignored, misery is inevitably brought to the country's population, as in the case of Eadwig, Æthelred the Unready and, indeed, Henry III.

Such is the situation in Robert's own time, and his remedy for these miseries is implicit in his presentation of historical events. The Anglo-Saxon period is constantly looked to as the source for the foundations of thirteenth-century society – from hereditary succession of the monarch to

---

[42] 'I am, he said, Cuthbert, I have come to you to bring good tidings; I am sent from God because the people of this land gave their will entirely to sins and still refuse, up to now, to leave their sins. Because of me, and other saints who were born in this land, who pray for you to God when we are before him, Our Lord looks on you with his eyes of mercy.'

[43] See *Alfred the Great*, trans. Keynes and Lapidge, pp. 211–12, and A. P. Smyth, *King Alfred the Great* (Oxford, 1995), p. 342.

[44] See D. Rollason, *Saints and Relics in Anglo-Saxon England* (Oxford, 1989), p. 11.

the laws of the land and the English language itself. Robert's anxieties about the influx of the French into the country is therefore based, I would suggest, upon a fear of the consequent disruption of the kingdom (and of associated English law and custom) which, as has been seen, he roots firmly in the age – and godliness – of the Anglo-Saxons.[45]

---

[45] I would like to express my thanks to Mr S. A. J. Bradley, Department of English and Related Literature, University of York, for his invaluable advice and comments on the draft of this paper.

# The *South English Legendary*: Anglo-Saxon saints and national identity

## JILL FREDERICK

While William's victory at Hastings in 1066 created a significant reconfiguration of Anglo-Saxon religious tradition, that tradition was by no means totally broken with.[1] Undoubtedly, William cut a punitive swathe through both English landscape and institutions over a period of months and years, placing Normans in positions of power throughout the country; the desolation that he and his army left behind is well-documented.[2] Nevertheless, the Normans had a huge investment in legitimizing William's claim to the Anglo-Saxon throne; if William wished to rule as Edward's rightful heir, he needed the co-operation of both ecclesiastical and secular leaders in England. William replaced key positions selectively, and perhaps more benignly than tradition has held: Stenton tells us that William 'made a serious attempt to govern England

---

[1] See, for instance, S. Ridyard's book, *The Royal Saints of Anglo-Saxon England: a Study of West Saxon and East Anglian Cults* (Cambridge, 1988), and her article, '*Condigna Veneratio*: Post-Conquest Attitudes to the Saints of the Anglo-Saxons', *Anglo-Norman Studies* 9 (1986), pp. 179–208, as well as A. Gransden, 'Traditionalism and Continuity during the Last Century of Anglo-Saxon Monasticism', *Journal of Ecclesiastical History* 40 (1989), pp. 159–207.

[2] A thorough account appears in F. W. Stenton, *Anglo-Saxon England*, 3rd edn. (Oxford, 1971); David Knowles's fundamental work, *The Monastic Order in England: a History of its Development from the Times of St Dunstan to the Fourth Lateran Council 940–1216*, 2nd edn. (Cambridge, 1963), describes the religious antagonism between Norman and Anglo-Saxon churchmen. Other sources for evidence of mutual religious scepticism are R. W. Southern, *St Anselm and his Biographer: a Study of Monastic Life and Thought 1059–c. 1130* (Cambridge, 1963), p. 249; *The Letters of Lanfranc, Archbishop of Canterbury*, ed. and trans. V. H. Clover and M. T. Gibson (Oxford, 1979), 1.19–29; *The Life of St Anselm, Archbishop of Canterbury, by Eadmer*, ed. and trans. R. W. Southern (London, 1962), p. 51, and M. T. Gibson, *Lanfranc of Bec* (Oxford, 1978), p. 171.

through men who had held high office in King Edward's day'.[3] In particular, the new Norman rulers of England skilfully retained the native religious tradition and put it to work towards their own purposes.[4] William maintained a relatively conciliatory attitude toward the English ecclesiastical hierarchy, at least in the first few years following the Conquest; Gibson writes that '[William's] principle is clear. The only bishops who were deposed were those involved in the recent revolts; otherwise William was content to wait for the death of an incumbent and then replace him with his own candidate'.[5] She asserts that, at least at first, the Anglo-Saxon establishment accepted William,[6] seeing, according to Stenton, little to be gained by overt disobedience.[7]

One of the English tradition's most enduring manifestations occurs in the post-Conquest survival of Anglo-Saxon saints. While Susan Ridyard concedes that tracing the precise means by which Anglo-Saxon saints endured is extremely difficult, she argues convincingly that their cults 'survived and even prospered in the decades following 1066'.[8] One written record bearing vernacular witness to the survival of these saints into the Middle English period, beyond the evidence provided by church calendars, is the so-called *South English Legendary*, a collection of saints' lives and temporale materials.[9] The *South English Legendary* (henceforth *SEL*) was obviously very popular from the number of manuscripts of it still extant from the fourteenth and fifteenth centuries,[10] so it is not

---

[3] Stenton, *Anglo-Saxon England*, p. 623.

[4] M. Chibnall, *Anglo-Norman England 1066–1166* (Oxford, 1986), p. 276; Ridyard, *The Royal Saints*, p. 7.

[5] Gibson, *Lanfranc of Bec*, p. 114.    [6] *Ibid.*, p. 113.

[7] Stenton, *Anglo-Saxon England*, p. 624.

[8] Ridyard, *The Royal Saints*, p. 251.

[9] Two editions of the *South English Legendary* have been published, both in the Early English Text Series. The first is that of C. Horstmann, *The Early South-English Legendary*, EETS OS 87 (London, 1887), which provides an edition of Oxford, Bodleian Library, Laud Misc. 108. The most recent, and the one on which the argument of this essay is based, is *The South English Legendary*, ed. C. D'Evelyn and A. J. Mill, vols. 1 and 2, EETS OS 235–6 (London, 1956), vol. 3, EETS OS 244 (London, 1959).

[10] According to M. Gorlach, *The Textual Tradition of the South English Legendary* (Leeds, 1974), pp. viii–x, there are twenty-five major manuscripts, nineteen fragments and eighteen miscellanies containing single *SEL* items, although the precise numbers are open to some small disagreement. See also A. Samson, 'The South English Legendary: Constructing a Context', *Thirteenth Century England I: Proceedings of the Newcastle Upon Tyne Conference 1985*, ed. P. R. Coss and S. D. Lloyd (London, 1986), p. 185, and

surprising that the transmission history is extremely complex, particularly as individual manuscripts are widely scattered in date and provenance.[11] To complicate matters further, the contents of the manuscripts vary considerably.[12] Nevertheless, it is true to say that most manuscripts contain a substantial proportion of Anglo-Saxon saints, and the D'Evelyn and Mill edition contains seventy-five saints' lives, of which thirteen are Anglo-Saxons.[13] The majority of the remaining lives in this compilation are of Latin saints, that is, any non-English or non-British saints,[14] and the distinction between the two categories, English and Latin, has both thematic and structural importance, as this study will demonstrate.

Following the appearance of Manfred Gorlach's comprehensive study of the textual tradition of the *SEL*,[15] scholars have begun to move beyond linguistic and textual analysis into critical interpretation of the collection, concentrating especially on the historical and political dimensions of the *SEL*.[16] One theme on which these articles have implicitly or explicitly commented is the *SEL*'s attention to matters English; in particular, Klaus Jankofsky argues that the *SEL*'s compiler manipulates his overall materials in a way designed to make them especially appealing to an English audience.[17] Jankofsky's contributions to any critical assessment of the

B. Boyd, 'A New Approach to the *South English Legendary*', *Philological Quarterly* 47 (1968), p. 494, for some variant figures. In addition, a nearly complete manuscript of the *SEL* was found and auctioned after Gorlach's survey: see O. S. Pickering and M. Gorlach, 'A Newly Discovered Manuscript of the *South English Legendary*', *Anglia* 100 (1982), pp. 109–23.

[11] Gorlach, *The Textual Tradition*, p. 1.

[12] 'In no two manuscripts is the list of saints' lives exactly duplicated in number and order': D'Evelyn and Mill, *The South English Legendary*, III, p. 3.

[13] While the D'Evelyn and Mill compilation contains no female Anglo-Saxon saints, other *SEL* manuscripts do include women, for instance Ætheldreda, Eadburga, and Mildthryth; see P. Acker, 'Saint Mildred in the *South English Legendary*', *The South English Legendary: A Critical Assessment*, ed. K. Jankofsky (Tubingen, 1992), p. 140.

[14] K. Jankofsky makes this distinction in 'National Characteristics in the Portrayal of English Saints in the *South English Legendary*', *Images of Sainthood in Medieval Europe*, ed. R. Blumenfeld-Kosinski and T. Szell (Ithaca, 1991), p. 83.

[15] Gorlach, *The Textual Tradition*.

[16] See T. Heffernan, 'Dangerous Sympathies: Political Commentary in the *South English Legendary*', *The South English Legendary: a Critical Assessment*, ed. Jankofsky, p. 3, and Jankofsky, 'National Characteristics in the Portrayal of English Saints', p. 89.

[17] K. Jankofsky, 'Entertainment, Edification, and Popular Education in the *South English Legendary*', *Journal of Popular Culture* 11 (1977), p. 707.

*SEL* are indispensable, but his observations provide a minimal interpretive framework.[18] Renee Hamelinck's approach suggests a more pointed structure for the *SEL*, identifying a political theme that unifies the selection of English saints' lives into a kind of narrative that, as a group, recounts the history of the English church from the time of St Augustine up to the time of the *SEL*'s composition.[19] In particular the legends outline the church's decline from its Anglo-Saxon prosperity to its weakened position under the Norman kings.[20]

Hagiography's didactic, even propagandistic, qualities have been often acknowledged, but Hamelinck's argument ignores a number of difficulties, including the arrangement of saints' lives chronologically by feast days in all manuscripts except Oxford, Bodleian Library, Laud Misc. 108. At the very least, the difficulty of dating and placing the many *SEL* manuscripts, and more specifically the manuscripts collated by D'Evelyn and Mill into one edited text, makes Hamelinck's argument problematic.[21] While acknowledging her insight into the political nature of the *SEL*, the present study proposes that the *SEL* contains a more emphatically political motif in a much less orderly arrangement. With their consistent and careful attention to details of English life and land,[22] especially in contrast to the dearth of similar details in the lives of the Latin and British saints, the Anglo-Saxon lives redefine and reclaim the saints as particularly English, as a means of establishing not just moral but political rectitude. By offering clear examples of loyal – indeed,

---

[18] See, for instance, his 'Personalized Didacticism: the Interplay of Narrator and Subject Matter in the *South English Legendary*', *Texas A & I University Studies* 10 (1977), p. 77.

[19] R. Hamelinck, 'St Kenelm and the Legends of the English Saints in the *South English Legendary*', *Companion to Early Middle English Literature*, ed. N. H. G. E. Veldhoen and H. Aertsen (Amsterdam, 1988), pp. 21–30.

[20] *Ibid.*, p. 21.

[21] Laud 108 is 'not typical of the collection at all' (Gorlach, *The Textual Tradition*, p. 3), while the 1956 edition by D'Evelyn and Mill, though helpful in many regards, does not offer a clear statement of the editorial principles guiding the combination of 'four somehow related manuscripts for a semi-critical text' (Gorlach, *The Textual Tradition*, p. 3). It is easy, as Gorlach points out, for the unwary reader to assume that the four manuscripts of D'Evelyn's composite edition are more closely related than, in fact, they are (*ibid.*, p. 219, n. 8). Nonetheless, the 1956 edition has its own virtues – 'a well-arranged and readable text,' in Gorlach's words (p. 3) – and can provide a reasonable field for inquiry.

[22] Jankofsky, 'National Characteristics in the Portrayal of English Saints', p. 85.

patriotically self-sacrificial – behaviour and constant reminders of English daily life, the *SEL* raises the symbolic value of the Anglo-Saxon saints well beyond the purely devotional.

The earliest threats to the English as a people came from the Vikings, and a number of the Anglo-Saxon saints' lives in the *SEL* (for instance, St Oswald, bishop, St Alphege, and St Edmund) chronicle the encounters between English and Danes. The structure of the life of St Oswald, tenth-century bishop of Worcester, underscores the saint's Englishness by withholding the events of his life until after the speaker outlines a battle between King Athelstan and some *heðene men* 'heathen men'.[23] Using this strategy, he first reminds us of Oswald's connection to the valiant king; the opening statement of the life confirms Oswald's connection to the throne:

> Of heie men he was icome . . .
> Sire Ode was is fader broðer  .  ðe kinges conseiler
> þat hext Iustice was of ðat lond . . .  (71.2–4)[24]

Ode, the king's highest counsellor and Oswald's uncle, emboldens the king on what appears to be the brink of defeat, asking

> . . . sire king wat is ðe
> War is ðin herte nou bicome  (72.18–19)[25]

and urging him, *take to ði scauberk  .  & ði swerd out drawe* 'seize your scabbard and draw your sword' (72.20). King Athelstan turns again to his foes and overcomes them. Only at this point in the story does the speaker return his attention to Oswald, absent from the narrative since the opening line. Creating such an explicit link between Oswald and Athelstan's victory over the Danes underscores for the audience the saint's political dimension and by extension, Oswald's Englishness. This implicit example of nationalism clarifies a phrase used earlier in the *SEL*, describing Wulfstan, bishop of Worcester, as *ðe kundest Englisse man* 'the truest Englishman' (11.96). In this victory over the Danes we see how a *kund* Englishman ought to behave.

---

[23] D'Evelyn and Mill, *The South English Legendary*, p. 71, l. 8. All further references to this edition will be made parenthetically within the text.

[24] 'He came from noble men . . . Sir Ode was his father's brother, the king's counsellor, who was the highest justice in that land.'

[25] 'Sir King, what are you doing? What has now become of your courage?'

A similar structural pattern occurs in the life of St Alphege, where the speaker seems more concerned with establishing Alphege's sacred credentials than with the events of the saint's life. Once he has situated Alphege's holiness, the speaker focuses on the important figures of Dunstan and Æthelwold, and their responses to Alphege rather than Alphege himself. With Alphege securely contextualized, however, the speaker turns the audience's attention to a danger besetting England. In the seventh year of Alphege's archbishopric,

> Þe luðer prince of Denmarch . gret poer wið him nom
> And wende hom her into Engelond . as hi dude er ilome
> For Deneis and men of Engelond . selde beoð ysome
> Þo ðis luðer prince & is men . to Englonde come
> Hy barnde & robbede al to gronde . & heiemen nome.
>
> (150.50–4)[26]

As the speaker has previously given Oswald a political dimension by linking him to King Athelstan, here he emphasizes that aspect of Alphege by contrast with Æthelred, especially the king's lack of fighting spirit (*So simple he was & so milde* [150.56], *þe king . . . was so milde* [150.61], *Of bataile he nolde noðing do    bote huld him euere stille* [150.65]) 'he did not wish to take part in warfare, instead he held himself back from battle'), and consequently *hadde ðe Denys    into Engelond hore wille* 'the Danes had their will throughout England' (150.66). By contrast, as the Danes assault Canterbury, Alphege willingly offers himself as a hostage. Additionally, after describing Alphege's martyrdom, the speaker editorializes:

> And in ðis manere ymartred [he] was . in oure Louerdes name
> For ðe loue of Engelond . ðat me broʒte so to ssame.   (154.185–6)[27]

This self-conscious link between the saint's religious and political martyrdom, martyred for the love of his *country*, suggesting the need for a regeneration of a national spirit, is unique to the *SEL*'s Anglo-Saxon lives. Alphege's life, then, offers not only another example of religious devotion,

---

[26] 'The evil prince of Denmark brought a great force with him and made his way to England, as he had frequently done before. For the Danes and the men of England were seldom at peace. Then this evil prince and his men came to England, robbed and burned everything, and captured high-born men.'

[27] 'And in this way he was martyred in our lord's name for the love of England, which men brought to such shame.'

but an act of religious martyrdom specifically linked to the political fate of England.

The life of St Edmund the king offers another example of anti-Danish sentiment and the link between religious and political power. Though here the enemies are designated merely as *Tuei princes of anoðer lond . ðat were of liðer ðoʒt* 'two princes of another land, who were of evil intent' (512.7), their names, Hubba and Hyngar, would have alerted an audience to their nationality. The two princes *Faste here red togadere nome . to bringe Engelonde to noʒt* 'together quickly devised their plan to bring England to destruction' (512.8) and, beginning in Northumberland, *ðer hi sloʒe to grounde/Robbede also & brende to noʒt . & destruyde al ðat hi founde* 'there they murdered, as well as robbed and burned everything, and destroyed all that they found' (512.11–12). While the description of Edmund's martyrdom is atypical because its graphic detail is more akin to the Latin lives than those of the English, the aftermath of Edmund's martyrdom demonstrates another method by which the *SEL* exhibits its concern with matters English: attention to the use of English as a language.

Hyngar hews off Edmund's head, leaving the body to lie in the field, his men bearing off the head and hiding it in *a durne stede . . ./Among ðicke ðornes* 'a secret place . . . among thorn bushes' (513.61–2). Although the body is easily found, *for hit nas ihud noʒt* 'because it was not well covered' (514.72), the saint's head remains hidden until, wondrously,

> . . . ðat heued bigan to grede
> As hit among ðe ðornes lai  .  & ðuse wordes sede
> Al an Englisch  .  her. her. her. as ðeʒ hit were alyue.
>
> (514.77–9)[28]

Of itself, this detail might be merely a linguistic anomaly, and it is not unique to this version of the life; Ælfric's life of St Edmund, written around 990, contains the same information.[29] However, it has a parallel in the life of St Kenelm, whose wicked sister has him killed after, at the age of seven, he succeeds his father Kenulf to the Mercian throne. Kenelm's traitorous guardian, Askeberd, leads the boy deep into the wood

---

[28] 'That head began to call out as it lay among the thorn bushes, and said these words all in English, "Here, here, here," as though it were alive.'

[29] For some discussion of this passage in Ælfric, see Jankofsky, 'National Characteristics in the Portrayal of English Saints', p. 87, n. 12.

of Clent (Worcestershire) and decapitates him beneath a tree, burying the body there. Just as Askeberd strikes off Kenelm's head, a white dove flies up into the heavens. At the new queen's command, no one may speak Kenelm's name, and his body lies forgotten in the valley of Coubach. Meanwhile, some years later, as the Pope is preaching at St Peter's in Rome, a white dove flies down from heaven, leaving a note on the altar. In letters of gold, and in English, the note reads,

> In Clent Coubach Kenelm kinges bern
> Lið vnder a ðorn heued bireued. (288.267–8)[30]

As with Edmund's *her. her. her.*, this English message leads to the discovery of the saint's body and its proper enshrinement at Winchcombe Abbey. These two instances unmistakably suggest that it is the *English* language that contains salubrious traits. Here the use of English leads to not only a proper understanding of moral behaviour, but to a wholesome effect on a political situation as well: in Kenelm's case, his wicked sister dies a justly unpleasant death, leaving a more appropriate ruler on the throne of Mercia.

Perhaps the most overt example of political statement, and political statement closer to the lives of the *SEL*'s contemporary audience, appears in the life of Wulfstan, eleventh-century bishop of Worcester.[31] Here, anti-Norman sentiments resound without equivocation as the speaker rehearses the state of England at Edward the Confessor's death: when

> . . . seint Edward ðe holy king . wende out of ðis liue
> To gret ruðe to al Engelonde . so weilaway ðe stonde
> For strange men ðer come suððe . & broȝte Engelond to gronde
> Vor Harald was suððe kyng . wið traison alas
> Þe croune he bar of Engelond . wuch wile so it was
> Ac Willam Bastard ðat was ðo . duk of Normandie
> Þoȝte to wynne Engelond . ðoru strengðe & felonye. (10.58–64)[32]

---

[30] 'In Clent Coubach Kenelm, the king's child, lies under a thorn bush, without his head.'

[31] Jankofsky, 'National Characteristics in the Portrayal of English Saints', p. 85. See also his article, '*Legenda Aurea* Materials in the *South English Legendary*: Translation, Transformation, and Acculturation', *Legenda Aurea: Sept siècles de diffusion*, ed. B. Dunn-Lardeau (Montreal, 1986), p. 322.

[32] 'St Edward, the holy king, left this life, to the great sorrow of all England. So in woe they stood, for foreign men came there afterwards and overpowered England. For Harold was king afterwards; through treason, alas, he bore the crown of England for a

Three key ideas emerge in this passage: (1) treason and betrayal mark William's victory, rather than superior strength or military strategy; (2) the result of this victory has grievous results for England; and (3) William himself understood the impropriety of his claim. The speaker reinforces these ideas in later passages as well:

No strengðe nadde ðe stronge men .  ðat icome were so niwe
Aȝen ðe baronie of Engelond .  ðe wile hi wolde be[o] triwe
Ac alas ðe tricherie .  ðat ðo was and ȝute is
Þat broȝte ðo Engelonde .  alto grounde ywis
Vor Englisse barons bycome somme .  vntriwe and fals also
To bitraie hom sulf and hore kyng .  ðat so much triste ham to
           (10.75–80)[33]

Willam Bastard was aboue .  Harald byneðe was
For hy ðat Harald triste to .  faillede him wel vaste  (11.84–5)[34]

Þis Willam Bastard ðat was kyng .  suððe him vnderstod
Þat he mid vnriȝt hadde yssad .  so many mannes blod
And ðere as ðe bataille was .  an abbey he let rere
Þat me clupeð Abbey of ðe Bataille .  ðat noble stont ȝut ðere.
           (11.87–90)[35]

In addition, these passages create a sense of the past in the present: treachery, as well as Battle Abbey, still exists in the speaker's England.

This version of Wulfstan's life certainly *re*-interprets the past in terms of the present, as the speaker recreates Wulfstan as an English patriot, almost a rebel priest, standing up to the immorality of the Norman usurper. He says:

time. But William the Bastard, who was then duke of Normandy, thought to win England through force and deceit.'
[33] 'No strength at all had the foreign men who were newly come against the barony of England. For a while they were faithful, but alas for the treachery that was then and still is, which utterly destroyed England, in truth. For some of the English barons became untrue, and false also, to betray themselves and their king, who had trusted them so much.'
[34] 'William the Bastard was above, Harold was beneath, because those whom Harold had trusted failed him completely.'
[35] 'This William the Bastard who was king, afterwards he understood that he had wrongly shed so many men's blood, and where the battle had been, he had an abbey built, which men call Battle Abbey, that nobly stands there still.'

As sone so [William] was kyng ymad   .   & all Engelond bysette
As he wolde mid strange men   .   ac noman ne miȝte hym lette
Þis holy sein Wolston   .   wel ofte him wiðsede
þat he wið vnriȝt hadde ido   .   a such vuel dede
And spak aȝen hym baldeliche   .   & ne sparede for no drede
For he was ðe kundeste Englisse man   .   ðat was of eny manhede.

(ll.91–6)[36]

But this passage contradicts the historical evidence. In his introduction to
William of Malmesbury's *Vita Wulfstani*, R. R. Darlington tells us that
'Wulfstan was among the first to submit to the conqueror after the Battle
of Hastings. He was looked upon more favourably by William I, and
before the year 1067 was out received from him two hides of land at
Cookley'.[37] Stenton lists Wulfstan among the participants at William's
'conclusive meeting with the English leaders . . . where he received an
oath of fealty' from many of the Anglo-Saxon leaders.[38] Indeed, Wulfstan
was one of a number of Anglo-Saxon prelates to maintain his see after a
council held in Windsor in 1069.[39] Consequently, the episode narrated
between 10.97 and 14.174, wherein both William and Lanfranc threaten
to remove Wulfstan from his bishopric, and the miracle that ensues (the
embedding of Wulfstan's crozier in the marble of St Edward's tomb in
Westminster) as a result of their threats, is not very likely to have
occurred. Darlington has demonstrated that removing Wulfstan was
never under consideration.[40]

But these examples of invasion and usurpation provide simply the
most explicit reminders of Englishness; other, more subtle, means of
reminding the audience of its heritage exist throughout the *SEL*. Perhaps

---

[36] 'As soon as William was made king, and he had filled all England as he wished with
foreign men, though no man could prevent him, this holy saint Wulfstan very often
told him that he had acted wrongly, done such evil deeds, and spoke against him
boldly, and never spared, out of fear, because he was the truest Englishman that came
from any stock.'

[37] *The Vita Wulfstani of William of Malmesbury*, ed. R. R. Darlington, Camden Society 3rd
series 40 (London, 1928), p. xxvii.

[38] Stenton, *Anglo-Saxon England*, p. 397.

[39] J. Godfrey, *The Church in Anglo-Saxon England* (Cambridge, 1962), p. 414. Godfrey
points out that because the changeover from Anglo-Saxon to Norman administration
was gradual, 'in 1073, at least a dozen English abbots still ruled their houses,'
including Wulfstan (p. 434).

[40] Darlington, *The Vita Wulfstani*, pp. xxxi–xxxiii.

most prominently, the lives of the Anglo-Saxon saints contain frequent, often extensive references to specific English settings, as well as to English geography in general, unlike the settings of the Latin lives which remain abstract. Even the lives of British saints such as Patrick and Bridget, which are quite a bit longer than many of the Anglo-Saxon lives, offer few details about where the events occur; the saints' nationality seems extraneous. Although all the Anglo-Saxon lives contain some geographical reference, the most elaborate and extensive occurs in the opening lines of the life of St Kenelm, which gives a detailed description of the Anglo-Saxon kingdoms, some sixty-five lines long (9–74):

> Vif kinges ðere were ðulke tyme  .  in Engelond ido
> For Engelonde was god and long  .  & somdel brod ðerto
> Aboute eiʒte hondred mile  .  Engelond long is
> Fram ðe souð into ðe norð  .  and to hondred brod iwis
> Fram ðe est into ðe west . . .  (280.9–13)[41]

This description, unlike the one found in the opening pages of Bede's *Historia Ecclesiastica*, is purely politically centred. The speaker offers topographical detail, for example, the names and situations of rivers, in order to lay out boundaries, linking towns and shires into kingdoms. Hamelinck points out that this long catalogue 'is meant to remind the audience of the history of the country – a history they could be proud of';[42] but it also recollects the country's present-day power as well. Throughout the Anglo-Saxon lives, the speaker links the past and present not only with judicious use of tag phrases such as 'and yet still is'[43] and verb tense, but with references to markers of important events, abbeys built and still standing, towns that were and remain important centres of English life.

Other links between the past and present exist as well, small reminders of important dates, genealogical (personal, political and religious) and historical information. The Anglo-Saxon lives are filled with what might appear to be extraneous material, digressions from the holy acts of saints. Certainly the Latin lives do not contain this kind of detail; they are far

---

[41] 'Five kings there were at that time, as it happens, in England, for England was good and long and partly broad as well. England is nearly eight hundred miles long from the south to the north, and two hundred broad, in truth, from the east to the west.'

[42] Hamelinck, *St Kenelm*, p. 27.

[43] Jankofsky, 'National Characteristics in the Portrayal of English Saints', p. 86.

more concerned, in contrast, with the events of a saint's life, particularly the painful itemizing of the process of martyrdom. The small instances of geographical, historical and genealogical information – often inextricable from each other – serve to create continually and reinforce the sense of national unity that emerges in the collection. Some of the more important and striking examples appear in the lives of St Edmund, St Swithun and St Aldhelm. St Edmund's life begins:

> Of ðat on ende of Engelond . kyng he was her bi este
> For of Souðfolc he was kyng . & of ðe contray wide
> For ðer were ðo in Engelond . kynges in eche side. (512.2–4)[44]

Swithun's background is laid out in the first lines of his life as well:

> Sein Swiððin ðe confessour . was her of Engelonde
> Biside Winchestre he was ibore . as ich vnderstonde
> Bi ðe kinges day Ekberd . ðis godeman was ibore
> Þat þo was king of Englelond . & somdel ek biuore
> Þe eiʒteðe king he was ðat com . after Kenewolf ðe kinge
> Þat sein Berin dude to Cristendom . in Engelond ferst bringe
> Ac seint Austin hadde biuore . to Cristendom ibroʒt
> Aðelbriʒt ðe gode kyng . ac al ðe lond noʒt
> Ac suððe it was ðat sein Birin . here bi weste wende
> And turnde ðe king Kynewolf . as oure Louerd him grace sende
> So ðat Ekberd ðat was king . ðo sein Swiððin was ibore
> Þe eiʒteðe was after Kynewolf . ðat so longe was biuore.
>
> (274.1–12)[45]

St Aldhelm's genealogy establishes his political credentials in the first four lines of his life:

[44] 'From that one end of England, he was king close to the east, for he was king of Suffolk, and of the country roundabout, for there was then in England kings on every side.'

[45] 'St Swithun the confessor was a man of England. He was born close to Winchester, as I understand. This good man was born in the day of King Egbert, who was king of England then and for a little while before that; he was the eighth king who came after Cynewulf, the king who St Birinus first brought to Christianity in England. But St Augustine had before brought to Christianity Æthelberht the good king, but not everywhere in the land. But afterwards it was that St Birinus came here from the west and converted the king Cynewulf, as our Lord sent him grace. So that Egbert who was king when St Swithun was born was the eighth after Cynewulf, that was so long before.'

> Seint Aldelm ðe confessour   .   was man of noble line
> Ibore he was in Engelonde   .   ðe kinges broðer sone Yne
> For Kenten was [is broðer]   .   ðat seint Aldames fader was
> And suððe was kyng after Ine   .   as God ȝaf ðat cas.   (211.1–4)[46]

Meanwhile the background material in the life of St Oswald emphasizes his religious genealogy, his link with St Dunstan and St Æthelwold:

> Seint Donston and seint Oswold   .   wardeins were ðerto
> And ðe bissop of Winchestre   .   seint Aðelwold ðat was ðo
> Þis ðre[o] bissops wende aboute   .   ðoru al Engelonde
> Ech luðer person he caste out   .   hom ne miȝte non atstonde.
> (75.123–6)[47]

The life which may participate most fully in this network of Englishness, however, is the life of St Edward the Martyr (d. 978).[48] Here the seeds of potential destruction have not entered from another country, but, as in the life of St Kenelm, are a product of betrayal from within the kingdom. Like Kenelm, Edward is killed, stabbed to death, not by heathen enemies of the English people but at the behest of a member of his own family as a way of acquiring the throne. After the young king's death, his traitorous assassin casts the body into a *durne stude* 'secret place' and *burede him wel uaste* 'buried him very deeply' (112.89–90). Still, St Dunstan, and others in the kingdom, suspect the worst, and even though Edward's half-brother Atheldred (i.e. Æthelred) is crowned king, men ride over the countryside to search for the murdered king's body. Eventually, as some good men from the town of Wareham seek the body,

> . . . ðo seie hy gret liȝt
> Aboute a place cler inou   .   as a piler stod upriȝt.   (114.133–4)[49]

They find and remove the body to give it a proper burial:

> Þere hy burede ðis holy body   .   wið gret honur & prute

---

[46] 'St Aldhelm the confessor was a man of noble lineage; he was born in England, son of King Ine's brother, for Kenten was his brother, who was St Aldhelm's father, and who then was king after Ine, as God ordained.'

[47] 'St Dunstan and St Oswald were wardens as well, and the bishop of Winchester, who was St Æthelwold then, these three bishops travelled about through all of England. Each evil person they cast out; none could withstand them.'

[48] D'Evelyn and Mill mistakenly took this life to be that of Edward the Elder (d. 924).

[49] 'Then they saw a great light around the place, as clear as if a pillar stood upright.'

> A chapel ðer is arered   .   as ðis holy body lay
> In ðe toun of Waram   .   ðat stont ȝute to ðis day      (114.142−4)[50]

although ultimately,

> þis men ladde ðis holy body   .   wið gret honur & prute
> To ðe abbeie of Ssefteburi   .   ðer as it lið ȝute.      (116.203−4)[51]

The details of this saint's life and death place it in the tradition of Englishness found in the *SEL*: marked by allusions to specific place names (the towns of Wareham and Corfe, for instance), it encourages its audience to make connections between the period of Edward's life with that of its own. For instance, describing the site of the king's final hunt, *a vair wode in Dorsete* 'a pretty wood in Dorset', the narrator explains:

> Þat fair wode was ðulke tyme   .   ac nou he is al adoune
> Bote ðornes & ðunne boskes   .   ðat stondeð biside ðe toune.
>                                                       (111.43−4)[52]

In the town of Corfe itself, he tells the audience, *A strong castel ðer is nou . ac ðo nas ðar non ðere* 'there is now a strong castle, but then there was none' (111.49). Even the murder weapon itself provides a material link between the two eras:

> A long knif it was & smal inou   .   as me may ȝute ose[o]
> For in ðe churche of Cauersham   .   it hað ȝare ibe[o].      (112.79−80)[53]

And again the various genealogies − personal, historical and especially religious − are present and inextricable from one another. Edward is identified as the son of Edgar and the half-brother of Æthelred (110.3 and 8). His connection with St Dunstan is established within the first twenty-five lines, and in turn, Dunstan's hearty approval of Edward (110.22−3). Their link is emphasized by Dunstan's intuitive understanding of the treachery behind Edward's death, and his unwillingness to crown Æthelred (113.103−5). After Edward's death, the emphasis falls on the

---

[50] 'There they buried his holy body with great honour and ceremony; a chapel was built where this holy body lay in the town of Wareham, which stands yet to this day.'

[51] 'These men took this holy body with great honour and ceremony to the abbey of Shaftesbury, where it lies yet.'

[52] 'At that time it was a pretty wood, but now it is completely covered in thorn bushes and thin undergrowth that stands beside the town.'

[53] 'It was a long knife and very narrow, as men may yet see, because it has been to hand in the church at Caversham.'

haven offered to the martyred king's body by holy men and women of the church (115.165–70), one of whom is Edward's own sister, Edith.

Perhaps most interestingly, although unsurprisingly, the narrator of the saint's life has rewritten the historical Edward to accommodate a political and religious agenda, in much the same manner as Wulfstan's life has been rearranged. Edward is presented in his life as

> . . . meok & milde inou   .   & fair of fleiss & felle
> Deboner to speke wið   .   and wið pouere men mest
> Chast and wis of conseil   .   and prute he louede lest
> Wilde men ne louede he noȝt   .   ðat recheles were of ðoȝte
> Ac wisemen he drou to him . . .                    (110.16–20)[54]

Stenton offers another picture, however: Edward 'had offended many important persons by his intolerable violence of speech and behaviour', and despite his canonization, many people had a long memory for his angry outbursts.[55] And while the narrator tells his audience that

> God pais ðer was in Engelond   .   & loue & ioye inou
> Richesse and al oðer god . . .                    (111.25–6)[56]

Stenton observes, 'Little can be gathered about the character of Edward's reign beyond a vague impression of disorder'.[57] Perhaps it was the brutality and treachery of Edward's murder that moved him into the rank of saints, and overrode the natural loyalty of the common people to Edward's successor,[58] but this saint's life presents another example of the intermingling of religious and political that moves the *SEL* beyond the boundaries of a simple legendary.

Not all the Anglo-Saxon saints' lives contain this sort of material, local or otherwise; the life of St Oswald king and martyr – perhaps the briefest in the *SEL* – contains only two short episodes in which the narrator merely elliptically describes the *bataille nome/Atte toune of Marsfeld*

---

[54] 'Very meek and mild, and attractive in every respect, courteous to speak with, and with powerful men most virtuous and wise of counsel; and he loved ceremony least, and wild men, who were reckless of thought, loved not at all. But he drew wise men to himself.'

[55] Stenton, *Anglo-Saxon England*, p. 372.

[56] 'There was good peace in England, and much joy and love, wealth, and every other good.'

[57] Stenton, *Anglo-Saxon England*, p. 372.

[58] *Ibid.*, p. 374.

(358.32–3) – perhaps Oswestry, in Shropshire.[59] St Alban would not be recognizable as English but for the first and last lines of his life:

Seint Albon ðe holyman  .  [was] her of Engelonde . . .
Seint Albon ymartred was  .  here in Engelonde
Biside a toun ðat Wincestre  .  me clupede ich understonde
Þere is nou a chirche arered  .  and a gret abbeie also . . .

(238.1; 241.93–5)[60]

However, even here the speaker takes care to merge past and present with a reference to Winchester. The life of Cuthbert contains little concrete information about England; the opening line tells us he *was ibore  .  here in Engelonde* 'was born here in England' (118.1), while in the rest of the narrative geographical or temporal referents are almost absent, perhaps because of his northern affiliations.

Even though the representation of Anglo-Saxon saints in the D'Evelyn/ Mill version of the *SEL* is not comprehensive, nor do all those included participate thoroughly in the pattern this study argues for, the consistent, in fact constant, presence of this motif of national feeling seems abundantly clear. Nonetheless, its implications are cloudier. For instance, the issue of audience continues to be an important one: to whom was this political encouragement offered? In what spirit was it offered? Hamelinck provides a partial answer in closing her discussion of the life of St Kenelm: 'Perhaps more strongly than in any other of the legends it expresses the longing for the old Anglo-Saxon times when God's grace so openly rested upon England and its inhabitants'.[61] But this explanation seems too simple: the *SEL* is not an exercise in nostalgia, despite its interest in the Anglo-Saxon past.[62] Consciously or not, it reflects the historical trends and tendencies that began to manifest themselves in the thirteenth and fourteenth centuries, the need to consolidate the bound-aries of England as well as the growing sense of English nationalism that

---

[59] *Ibid.*, p. 82.

[60] 'St Alban, the holy man, was from England . . . St Alban was martyred here in England near a town that, I understand, men call Winchester, where there is now a church built, and a great abbey as well.'

[61] Hamelinck, *St Kenelm*, p. 30.

[62] See, for instance, J. Campbell, 'Some Twelfth-Century Views of the Anglo-Saxon Past', *Essays in Anglo-Saxon History* (London, 1986), pp. 209–28, and most recently, T. Turville-Petre, *England the Nation: Language, Literature, and National Identity 1290–1340* (Oxford, 1996).

appears to have been developing concurrently with the re-emergence of the English language as the dominant tongue. That this pattern of a developing sense of Englishness appears in so many distinctly regional manuscripts, across the span of more than a century, seems unmistakable evidence that this concern for identity was indeed a *national* one.[63]

[63] I am grateful to a number of people for their assistance with this essay: Professor Gernot Wieland for first suggesting the topic; Professor Klaus Jankofsky for reading the paper in an earlier form and offering the benefit of his considerable expertise in the subject; Professor Robert Babcock for offering guidance on several points of inquiry; Professor Phillip Pulsiano for bibliographical assistance; and Ms Diane Schmidt, of Moorhead State University's Inter-Library Loan Office, for helping me gather the necessary source materials. Any inaccuracies and difficulties are the result of my own intransigence.

# King Ælle and the conversion of the English: the development of a legend from Bede to Chaucer

### JOHN FRANKIS

Chaucer's Man of Law's Tale has not generally been discussed as a work embodying a view of Anglo-Saxon England and this aspect of the tale is admittedly not conspicuous. Nevertheless the tale is partly set in Anglo-Saxon England and has a central figure, Alla, who is an identifiable historical character, the sixth-century Anglo-Saxon king Ælle. Gower has a version of the same story in *Confessio Amantis* II. 586–1612, and in this version the references to Anglo-Saxon England are slightly more detailed than in Chaucer, though still apparently peripheral. To focus on the Anglo-Saxon element in the tale as told by Gower and Chaucer because of its intrinsic interest need not imply that previous criticism of these works has been at fault in not giving prominence to this element: neither Gower nor Chaucer seems to make very much of the English setting, and in each case the tale is obviously and primarily a moral romance concerning a suffering heroine, whose exemplary function seems little affected by whatever historical and geographical elements the setting may have. Gower explicitly presents his version of the Constance-story as a moral tale against envy and detraction (*CA* II. 383–586) but Chaucer's attitude to his version is not made explicit in this way (the remarks on poverty in the Man of Law's Prologue give little in the way of clues to the interpretation of the tale). Chaucer's motive in having the tale narrated by the Man of Law is not obvious, and the placing of this apparently self-contained tale in the whole sequence of *The Canterbury Tales* is a problem that has been frequently but inconclusively discussed: references to discussion of these matters are given in *The Riverside Chaucer* and they need not be pursued here, though it may be that a consideration of the

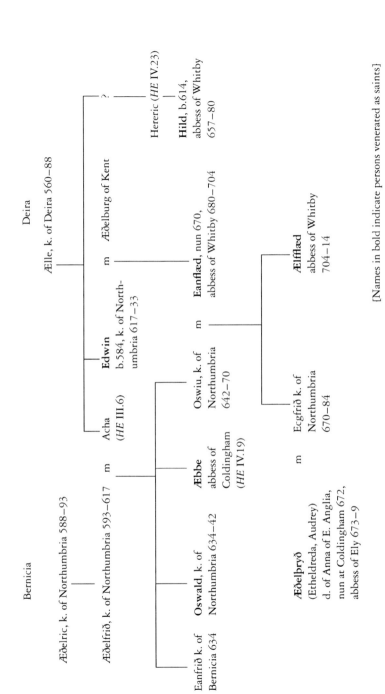

Bernicia

Deira

Æðelric, k. of Northumbria 588–93

Ælle, k. of Deira 560–88

Æðelfrið, k. of Northumbria 593–617  m  Acha (*HE* III.6)

Æðelburg of Kent

?

Hereric (*HE* IV.23)

**Hild**, b.614, abbess of Whitby 657–80

**Edwin** b.584, k. of North-umbria 617–33  m  Æðelburg of Kent

**Eanflæd**, nun 670, abbess of Whitby 680–704

Oswiu, k. of Northumbria 642–70

**Ælfflæd** abbess of Whitby 704–14

Ecgfrið k. of Northumbria 670–84  m  **Æbbe** abbess of Coldingham (*HE* IV.19)

Eanfrið k. of Bernicia 634

**Oswald**, k. of Northumbria 634–42

**Æðelþryð** (Etheldreda, Audrey) d. of Anna of E. Anglia, nun at Coldingham 672, abbess of Ely 673–9

[Names in bold indicate persons venerated as saints]

Northumbrian Royal Saints

75

Anglo-Saxon aspects of the tale will ultimately clarify the achievement of both Gower and Chaucer.

The Constance-story as told by Gower and Chaucer does not on the face of it tell us very much about fourteenth-century views of Anglo-Saxon England, but this subject is very much to the fore in the story as it appears in the source used by both poets, the Anglo-Norman chronicle by the early fourteenth-century Dominican friar Nicholas Trevet. There the story appears as part of a wider account of Anglo-Saxon and European history, and is seen more clearly as a tale, almost a myth, of the bringing of Christianity to pagan Anglo-Saxons. The story has often been discussed as a member of a large category of tales of accused queens and persecuted women, an exemplary tale of fortitude and patience, but what distinguishes the story as told by Trevet, Gower and Chaucer from even such a close analogue as the Middle English romance of *Emaré*, not to mention the many remoter tales of falsely accused heroines, is its historical element, including its comments on Anglo-Saxon England.[1] Some of the 'accused queen' analogues have quasi-historical settings, but none that I know of has the specific relevance to a particular event in history that distinguishes Trevet's tale. There is no known source for Trevet's combination of this traditional exemplary tale and the particular historical setting, although imaginative, but largely groundless, conjectures concerning hypothetical precursors have not been lacking.[2] Until convincing evidence for such a source appears, however, it is better to assume that the historical setting for the story in this Anglo-Norman chronicle was substantially devised by Trevet; it throws considerable light on his view of Anglo-Saxon England and was probably devised for a historiographical purpose. Trevet's claim to a source in 'ancient Saxon chronicles' may therefore be seen as a fiction of a familiar kind, like Geoffrey of Monmouth's alleged book in the British language (*Historia Regum Brittaniæ*) and other claims to mysterious and untraceable sources that

---

[1] On analogous tales see M. Schlauch, *Chaucer's Constance and Accused Queens* (New York, 1936), and other studies listed in J. Burke Severs, *Manual of Writings in Middle English*, I. *Romances* (New Haven, 1967), pp. 120–32, 136–8 and 278–91; there is a later survey in *Le Bone Florence of Rome*, ed. C. F. Heffernan (Manchester, 1976), pp. 3–17. For Chaucer and Gower I refer to *The Riverside Chaucer*, ed. L. D. Benson (Oxford, 1988), and to *The Complete Works of John Gower*, ed. G. C. Macaulay, 4 vols. (Oxford, 1899–1902); the *Riverside Chaucer* refers (pp. 856–8) to numerous relevant studies.

[2] For example A. B. Gough, *The Constance-Saga*, Palaestra 23 (Berlin, 1902), pp. 1–22.

several medieval authors deploy in order to impart to fictitious narratives an aura of venerable antiquity and authority. There is, as said, no known source in any English chronicle for the whole tale of Constance as told by Trevet, but it is undeniably a story that uses material from English chronicles, and Trevet was a notable historian. He was chiefly famous in his day for writings on theological and philosophical subjects that are not of concern here, but he was also a historian with a remarkably wide knowledge of what passed for history at the time, a man of great learning whose reading covered a wide range of historical texts.[3]

In view of the romantic and fantastic nature of the Constance-story it is perhaps surprising how much historical material actually underlies it in Trevet's version. The remarks with which he introduces the story are interesting: he begins by referring to what we today think of as orthodox history, telling how *Thiberie Constantin emperour* chose as his successor a soldier from Cappadocia named *Moris*, and gave him his daughter *Constaunce* in marriage. This is historically correct: Tiberius Constantinus, emperor of Byzantium 578–82, having no son, gave his daughter Constantina (*sic*) as wife to Mauricius, who succeeded him as emperor and ruled from 582 to 602. After a relatively long and effective rule Mauricius was ousted in a revolt led by Phocas, one of his generals, and killed

[3] There is still no adequate edition of Trevet's *Chroniques*; most useful is A. Rutherford, *The Anglo-Norman Chronicle of Nicholas Trivet* (Ph.D. thesis, University of London, 1932), a work that urgently needs replacing, though for its time and purpose it is learned and thorough; any statements about Trevet's *Chronicle* must be to some extent provisional until a new edition appears. There is a good edition of Trevet's Constance-story by Margaret Schlauch, 'The Man of Law's Tale', *Sources and Analogues of Chaucer's Canterbury Tales*, ed. W. F. Bryan and G. Dempster (New York, 1941), pp. 162–81. On Trevet as a historian see R. J. Dean, 'Nicholas Trevet, Historian', *Medieval Learning and Literature: Essays presented to R. W. Hunt*, ed. J. J. G. Alexander and M. T. Gibson (Oxford, 1976), pp. 328–52; and R. J. Dean, 'The Manuscripts of Nicholas Trevet's Anglo-Norman *Cronicles*', *Medievalia et Humanistica* 14 (1962), pp. 95–105. On Trevet's writings in general see B. Smalley, *English Friars and Antiquity in the Early Fourteenth Century* (Oxford, 1960), pp. 58–65 and other references in the index. My references to Trevet are as far as possible to Schlauch, otherwise to Rutherford. On Geoffrey's 'ancient book', see *The Historia Regum Britanniæ of Geoffrey of Monmouth*, ed. N. Wright (Cambridge, 1984), p. 1; some of the best known claims to untraceable and probably fictitious sources are listed in P. J. Frankis, 'Laʒamon's English Sources', *J. R. R. Tolkien, Scholar and Storyteller*, ed. M. Salu and R. T. Farrell (Cornell, 1979), pp. 64–75, at pp. 74–5, and such claims are considered in the wider context of medieval forgeries in M. T. Clancy, *From Memory to Written Record* (London, 1979), pp. 250–7.

together with his sons; Constantina and her daughters were later executed for their part in a conspiracy against Phocas.[4] It is particularly important for the present study that Mauricius was emperor when Gregory the Great was elected pope in 590, for Mauricius was officially responsible, according to the custom of the time, for confirming Gregory's election. Gregory's letters to Augustine of Canterbury in England (included by Bede in *Historia Ecclesiastica* I. 23–32) are dated according to the regnal year of Mauricius, who as emperor was the secular authority ultimately responsible for the mission to England. The basic historical facts about Mauricius and Gregory were familiar in England both from Bede and from the *Anglo-Saxon Chronicle*; the latter notes the accession of Mauricius (583E, added later in A) and the election of Gregory (592E, added later in A), both presumably as a prelude to the recording of Augustine's mission (596E, added later in 595A). The fact that these entries appear, not as part of the original chronicle as represented by the Parker manuscript (A), but as entries in the relatively late Laud manuscript (E) or as later additions in A, suggests that ascribing a significant role in the conversion of England to Mauricius was a late development. The additions in the Parker manuscript, probably of the twelfth century, seem to be clearly motivated at this point: the interpolator evidently felt that the original record of late sixth-century events was insufficiently informative concerning the conversion of the English, so he inserted a series of references under the years 560, 565, 583, 592 and 595, giving the main events of the process as he understood it, and it is noteworthy that this group of interpolations begins after the record of the accession of Ælle in 560, and Mauricius and Gregory both have a conspicuous place in it.[5] The dual responsibility of Mauricius and Gregory for the mission to England also appears in the widespread story of how the emperor overcame Gregory's reluctance to accept election as pope. This story has various forms: in some the emperor simply overrules Gregory's objections to holding papal office, but in others an imperial official, presumably anticipating the emperor's wish to confirm Gregory's election, intercepts

---

[4] For the historical facts see M. Whitby, *The Emperor Maurice and his Historian* (Oxford, 1988); on the death of Constantina see *Chronicon Paschale 284–628 AD*, trans. M. and M. Whitby (Liverpool, 1989), pp. 144–6.

[5] See *Two of the Saxon Chronicles Parallel*, ed. C. Plummer, 2 vols. (Oxford, 1892–1899), I. pp. 18–21; for the addition to MS A, see *The Parker Chronicle and Laws, a Facsimile*, ed. R. Flower and H. Smith, EETS 208 (1941), fol. 6b.

and destroys Gregory's letter asking to be excused so that it never reaches the emperor.[6] It is this latter version that is narrated by Ælfric in his homily on St Gregory, and the significance of the story is shown by its being placed between the episode of Gregory and the English slaves and the account of Augustine's mission, implying that Christianity came to England because Mauricius ensured that Gregory became pope. Ælfric incidentally refers to Mauricius as Gregory's *gefædera*: this term is explained by the story (quoted, for example, in the *History of the Franks* by Gregory of Tours) that Gregory, while papal nuncio in Constantinople, stood as godfather to a son of Mauricius, demonstrating the closeness of the association of the emperor and the future pope.[7]

The basic facts of Roman-Byzantine history concerning Tiberius Constantinus and Mauricius, familiar in medieval England in a variety of sources, are set out by Trevet as being just one version of history, *come dient les vns cronikes* ('as some chronicles say'). He then goes on to say that a different version of history is given in ancient Saxon chronicles, *come dient les aunciene cronikes de Sessouns*, and this is essentially the story that we are familiar with in Chaucer's Man of Law's Tale. In this story, leaving aside the traditional motif of the persecuted heroine, Constaunce, the daughter of the Roman emperor, arriving alone in Northumbria after many adventures, converts various people among the pagan Saxons, including their king Alle, whom she marries; she bears him a son who is baptized Moris (the French form of Mauricius), who eventually, after all the adventures are over, becomes emperor of Rome when Constaunce's father dies. These alternative versions of history differ in that orthodox history makes Mauricius the son-in-law of the emperor, but 'the chronicles of the Saxons' make Moris his grandson, who allegedly came to the throne as a lad of seventeen. In this latter version (historically

---

[6] The former version appears in Giraldus Cambrensis, *Speculum Ecclesiae* iv. 34–8: *Opera*, ed. J. S. Brewer, RS 21, IV (1873), pp. 342–7; the latter in Paulus Diaconus, *Vita Sancti Gregorii*: PL 75, col. 81.

[7] *Ælfric's Catholic Homilies, Second Series*, ed. M. Godden, EETS SS 5 (1979), p. 75: homily ix, ll. 93–108. Gregory of Tours, *Historia Francorum* X. 1 (PL 71, col. 527), also has the story of the tearing up of Gregory's letter. See further M. R. Godden, 'The Sources of Ælfric's Homily on St Gregory', *Anglia* 86 (1986), pp. 79–88, and his 'Experiments in Genre: the Saints' Lives in Ælfric's *Catholic Homilies*', *Holy Men and Holy Women: Old English Prose Saints' Lives and their Contexts*', ed. P. E. Szarmach (Albany, N.Y., 1996), pp. 261–87, at pp. 275–6.

impossible in view of the short reign of Tiberius) events have been reshaped so that Anglo-Saxon history is made to impinge on Roman history, in much the same way as Geoffrey of Monmouth had earlier reshaped events to make British history impinge on Roman history in his story of how the British Helena's son became the emperor Constantine. The parallel between these stories is more specific in the light of the universally held belief (curiously not mentioned by Geoffrey) that it was Constantine who established Christianity in the Roman empire; Trevet actually exploits this implicit parallel, for in his story the Roman son of an English king is ultimately responsible for making England Christian, just as earlier the Roman son of a British princess had made Rome Christian; in each tale the religious impulse comes from a saintly woman. There is even a link between the two stories in the name of a central character in each: the Roman leader that Helena marries is Constantius, while the Roman princess that Ælle marries is Constantia (forms of her name are discussed below).

There are good reasons for choosing Ælle to fill the role of a link between England and Rome. We may think of him today as a rather shadowy figure about whom very little is known for certain, but in Anglo-Saxon and post-Conquest English tradition he was one of the best known of all Anglo-Saxon kings: this was largely due to Bede's famous and often repeated story of Gregory's encounter with the English slave-boys in Rome.[8] We should think of Gregory's word-play on the names of the nation, realm and king of the English boys not as a series of rather unfeeling jokes in dubious taste, but as showing the recognition of a series of divine signs. Bede's story gives the earliest recorded mention of the name of Ælle, king of Deira, and its importance here is that from

---

[8] *Historia Regum Britanniæ*, ed. Wright, pp. 51–5; Bede, *HE* II. i (see *Bede's Ecclesiastical History of the English People*, ed. B. Colgrave and R. A. B. Mynors (Oxford, 1969), pp. 132–4 (henceforth abbreviated *HE*)). Another version of the story appears in *The Earliest Life of St Gregory the Great*, ed. B. Colgrave (Cambridge, 1968), pp. 90–1 (ch. 9); the story is frequently repeated by subsequent chroniclers throughout the Middle Ages and beyond. The sixth-century Ælle seems, perhaps surprisingly, never to have become confused with the ninth-century Northumbrian king of the same name who also achieved legendary status: see Frankis, 'Views of Anglo-Saxon England in post-Conquest vernacular writing', *Orality and Literacy in Early Middle English*, ed. H. Pilch (Tübingen, 1996) and n. 13 below. On Gregory's word-play see also N. Howe, *Migration and Mythmaking in Anglo-Saxon England* (New Haven, Conn., 1989), pp. 119–20.

Bede onwards the name of Ælle was indissolubly linked with the conversion of the English. Bede's bare mention of the name may be supplemented with information elsewhere in his *Historia Ecclesiastica* and also in the *Anglo-Saxon Chronicle*: from these sources it may be deduced that the historical Ælle, a pagan, ruled Deira from 560 to 588; on his death Deira came under the rule of Bernicia, making a united North-umbria, and Ælle's four-year-old son Edwin was forced into exile. In 617, Edwin, supported by Rædwald of East Anglia, won a victory in which his Bernician rival Æðelfrið was killed, and Edwin became king of a united Northumbria. Through the influence of his Christian (Kentish) wife, as well as various other factors set out by Bede (*HE* II. 9–14), Edwin was converted to Christianity and baptized in 627. It thus came about that Christianity was brought to Northumbria by the son of that same Ælle whose name inspired Gregory's hope of a mission to England and his cry of 'Alleluia!' Edwin's defeated rival, Æðelfrið, of the royal line of Bernicia, was incidentally Edwin's brother-in-law, for he had married Ælle's daughter Acha (*HE* III. 6); one effect of this is that the Bernician offspring of Æðelfrið (including Oswald and his brothers) and the Deiran relatives of Edwin could all claim descent from Ælle, so that Ælle, like Penda of Mercia half a century later, could be seen as the progenitor, although pagan, of a royal family containing numerous holy men and women venerated as saints. Ælfric's 'Life of St Oswald', for example, emphasizes the relationship between Edwin and Oswald (both venerated as saints) and passes over the fact that Edwin killed Oswald's father and drove Oswald and his brothers into exile, and in the post-Conquest period this relationship is likewise emphasized by Laȝamon: *he wes ihaten Oswald . . . he wes of Edwines cunne.*[9] In fact, Ælle's reputation as a founding-father of Anglo-Saxon Christian civilization by no means diminished after the Anglo-Saxon period, and the post-Conquest develop-ment of his fame is nowhere better shown than in William of Malmesbury's statement (following a reference to the story of Gregory

[9] *Ælfric's Lives of Saints*, ed. W. W. Skeat, EETS 94 and 114 (1890 and 1900), II. pp. 124–43: 'St Oswald', lines 7 and 110; *Laȝamon: Brut*, ed. G. L. Brook and R. F. Leslie, EETS 277 (1978), lines 15,618–20. M. Miller, 'The dates of Deira', *ASE* 8 (1979), p. 38, argues that Bede presents the Deiran royal family so as to make Edwin its central figure. See also D. Rollason, 'Hagiography and Politics in Early Northumbria', *Holy Men and Holy Women*, ed. Szarmach, pp. 95–114.

and the English slaves) that this king was the main cause of Christianity among the English: *Alla . . . maxima occasio Christianitatis genti Anglorum fuerit.*[10] Reference to Ælle, usually in connection with the story of Gregory and the slaves, becomes a commonplace in post-Conquest chronicles,[11] and many also refer to Mauricius and Gregory in connection with Augustine's mission to England, including the Middle English chronicles of 'Robert of Gloucester' and Robert Manning. The latter in particular states that he is going to tell a story of the emperor Maurice (15,107–9), but what follows is an account of the mission of Gregory and Augustine without any further reference to Maurice.[12] There is however apparently no writer before Trevet who links the names of Mauricius and Ælle in one unified narrative, though they were in fact contemporaries, with Ælle apparently somewhat older than Mauricius, though perhaps hardly enough to have been his father.

A fundamental impulse for the fictitious association of Maurice and Ælle that we find in Trevet must lie in the body of legends that had grown up round both these figures. Ælle as a motivator of Gregory's mission to England and as the progenitor of a royal family of saints has already been mentioned, and it need only be added how important the theme of a holy dynasty was, both in history as seen by Anglo-Saxon writers (notably Bede and the compilers of the *Anglo-Saxon Chronicle*) and as an essential part of the post-Conquest view of Anglo-Saxon England. The importance of the concept of a royal family of saints has been

---

[10] William of Malmesbury, *De Gestis Regum*, ed. W. Stubbs, RS 9 (1887), I. p. 45 (Lib.I. p. 45). The context contrasts the Christian fame of Ælle (deriving specifically from the story of Gregory) with the undeniable fact of his paganism, but sees the conversion of his son Edwin as the logical progression of God's plan *(sane ad filium eius manavit electio)*.

[11] See, e.g., Matthew Paris, *Chronica Majora*, ed. H. R. Luard, RS 57 (1872), I. p. 245: *Elle rex Deirorum de quo in vita beati Gregorii papae fit mentio* 'Ælle, the king of Deira, of whom mention is made in the Life of Pope Gregory'; likewise *The Chronicle Attributed to John of Wallingford*, ed. R. Vaughan, Camden Society, 3rd series, 90 (1958), pp. 3–4; and *Liber Eliensis*, ed. E. O. Blake, Camden Society, 3rd series, 92 (1962), p. 20. Gaimar, *L'estoire des engleis*, ed. A. Bell, Anglo-Norman Text Society 14–16 (1960), does not have the story of the slaves, but in 1,035–44 he links the names of Ælle and Edwin with the spread of Christianity in England.

[12] *The Metrical Chronicle of Robert of Gloucester*, ed. W. Aldis Wright, RS 86 (London, 1887), I. p. 334 (lines 4729–31), and *The Chronicle of Robert Manning of Brunne*, ed. F. J. Furnivall, RS 87, vol. II (London, 1887), p. 524 (15,099–120).

demonstrated by D. W. Rollason and I have shown elsewhere that the Mercian family of saints descended from Penda figures prominently in a range of post-Conquest writings, notably the *South English Legendary* and several saints' lives in Anglo-Norman.[13] There is ample evidence in the cult of Anglo-Saxon saints that the family descended from Ælle constituted such a dynasty of royal saints (see genealogical chart), and the continued veneration of many of these saints in the post-Conquest period at a number of centres (especially York and Durham, but also Coldingham, Whitby and Ely) guaranteed that the names of many of them were still widely known in the fourteenth century, particularly to a historian as widely read as Trevet, and a popular saint was always liable to attract or inspire exciting stories. It is thus hardly surprising that someone, Trevet or some unknown precursor, should have felt that Ælle, commemorated in the Gregory-legend and also the progenitor of so many saints, deserved a legend commensurate with those of his descendants, especially if it could be made to combine the views that Augustine's mission to England was on one hand ultimately due to Ælle, and on the other ultimately the responsibility of Mauricius.

The evidence for a Mauricius-legend is perhaps less familiar. Among the late Roman emperors he appears as a reasonably just and effective ruler, and his empress, Constantina, clearly had a reputation for piety on the evidence of Pope Gregory's letters to her. At some point after his death there grew up a legend of Mauricius as a martyr, as so often happened with Christian rulers who died a violent death. Mauricius was apparently never venerated as a saint, but the legend developed that, out of his piety, he prayed to God that he might be allowed to pay the penalty for his sins in this world instead of in the after-life. He was thereupon commanded in a vision to yield to the usurper Phocas, who had him killed together with his sons. This Mauricius-legend developed in the Byzantine world in the seventh century and it was clearly known in England by *c.* 1200, when it was recorded by Giraldus Cambrensis; it was repeated some half-century later by Matthew Paris, and in the fourteenth century Trevet tells the same story.[14] Particularly noteworthy here is the

---

[13] D. W. Rollason, *The Mildrith Legend* (Leicester, 1983); J. Frankis, 'Views of Anglo-Saxon England in post-Conquest vernacular writing', pp. 227–47, at pp. 237–8.

[14] For Gregory's letters to Constantina see *Gregorii I Papae Registrum Epistolarum*, ed. Paulus Ewald and Ludovicus M. Hartmann, Monumenta Germaniae Historica, Epistolae in Quarto (Berlin, 1957), I. pp. 324–9 (Lib. iv, ep. 38–9). On the origins of

fact that in these later versions the name of Tiberius's daughter had changed: originally *Constantina* (after her father Tiberius Constantinus, and presumably implying a connection with the emperor Constantine the Great), by the time of Giraldus she has become *Constantia* (the form of the name underlying Trevet, Gower and Chaucer), a name charged with allegorical potential, so that she becomes an exemplum of constancy. The narrative in the *Chronica Majora* of Matthew Paris is of possible relevance to Trevet's version, since the account of Mauricius is interlinked with that of Ælle. Matthew does not assert any connection between them; indeed his compilation is in the form of brief entries, mainly on a yearly basis, covering many aspects of history; but in his narrative the pattern of history displays them as contemporaries. He first mentions the rule of Ælle (I. 245), then the accession of Mauricius (I. 250); the death of Ælle and the eventual accession of Edwin follow, together with Augustine's mission (I. 254–5), and there follows the legend of the death of Mauricius and Constantia (I. 260–1). These episodes are interspersed with other material, so that they do not constitute a unified narrative combining Ælle and Mauricius, but Matthew (or some other chronicler) may well have given Trevet the basic impulse for such a narrative.

Some understanding of Trevet's motives in devising the Constance-story may be obtained from examining the way in which the story is placed in the whole sweep of history presented in his chronicle. A striking feature of the Constance-story is that it is quite unique in Trevet's chronicle as a whole. The chronicle, in spite of numerous inaccuracies of detail, is a masterpiece of constructive organisation, displaying a version of history from all sources known to the author: biblical (from the creation to Christ), classical (the Roman world) and medieval (post-Roman history down to the author's own time). In this last section, although there is an obvious focus on English history, the narrative encompasses the whole of western Europe. Not surprisingly in such an enormous range of material, the treatment of any one episode is inevitably summary, and there are few incidents that receive more than a single page of narrative, and only one that gets more than a few pages. The

the Mauricius-legend see Whitby, *The Emperor Maurice*, pp. 105–7, 124 and 325; for the later development in England see Giraldus Cambrensis, *Opera*, I (1861), pp. 184–5 ('De Invectionibus', Lib. vi, cap. 25); *idem*, *Opera*, VIII (1891), p. 121 ('De Principis Instructione', Dist. i, cap. 20); and Matthew Paris, *Chronica Majora*, I. p. 260.

Constance-story is this single exception to the pervasive brevity of narrative: occupying over twenty pages in Rutherford's edition, it demonstrates an entirely different narrative method marked by a wealth of expansive detail, including characterization and dialogue; it thus stands out as the most conspicuous story in the whole of history as recorded by Trevet, for no other event is narrated at such length and with such dramatic force. Moreover, it represents events of a different kind and on a different level: if the rest of the chronicle is history, then this episode is something other than history, though it is not simply romance disconnected from history. We might rather see it as a historical fiction devised to give new insights into history. The attention that Trevet, like many other post-Conquest chroniclers, gives to the Anglo-Saxon period derives from a recognition that this was the period when Christianity became established among the English, and the prominence that Trevet gives to the Constance-story reflects its nature as a conversion-legend. The placing of the story in the historical narrative also makes this clear. Trevet follows Bede, the *Anglo-Saxon Chronicle* and several later chroniclers in his general outline of the Anglo-Saxon settlement and the development of the separate kingdoms, and his account of the early Northumbrian kings naturally includes *Alla* and *Edwyn le fytz Alla* (Rutherford edition, p. 191), leading in turn to the story of Gregory and the English slaves with its reference to Ælle as king of Deira (p. 199). There follows an apparent digression into contemporary Spanish history, relating the triumph of Catholic orthodoxy over the Arian heresy among the Visigothic rulers of Spain (p. 199). This in turn is followed (pp. 200–22) by the familiar Constance-story, with its opening reference to *Alle auant nomé, que estoit le secund rei de Northombre*, 'the aforementioned Ælle, who was the second king of Northumbria', reminding us that the story concerns an Anglo-Saxon king already identified as having a well attested place in history and legend. Later in the story, when Alle departs for Rome and eventual reunion with his wife and son Moris, he appoints as regent another, presumably older, son, Edwin, whose mother is not named: *baila la garde de soun reaume a Edwyn son fitz, qu'esteoyt le tierz roy apres luy*, 'he entrusted the rule of his kingdom to his son Edwin, who was the third king after him' (Schlauch edition, p. 178); in this detail Trevet adds to the historical authenticity of his fiction. The story reaches its happy ending and Trevet glances at the successful reign of Moris (Rutherford edition, p. 222) and illustrates this with an encomium of

St Gregory, commenting on his liturgical reforms and referring to the well-known story of his deliverance of the soul of the emperor Trajan, indicating Gregory's role in bringing salvation to the heathen (p. 223). The focus broadens with references to Mahomet and St Brendan as contemporaries, and only then turns to Augustine's mission (p. 224). The Constance-story is thus placed in between the story of Gregory and the slaves (p. 199) and the account of the papal mission to England (p. 224), so that it has the appearance of a legend demonstrating the working out of God's plan for the conversion of the English. One may compare Ælfric's homily on Gregory (n. 7 above), which similarly places a 'Mauricius-story' between the tale of Gregory and the slaves and the account of Augustine's mission. Trevet then dates this mission and the subsequent conversion of the English by reference to the reign of Moris, and there follows the legend of the death of Moris as a voluntary martyrdom (pp. 225–6). We then return to Anglo-Saxon history with an account of Edwin *le fitz Alla* (p. 230), and the narrative broadens into a survey of the royal families of English saints, beginning with the descendants of Penda, getting into something of a muddle with Oswald and the Northumbrian saints (Trevet actually fails to exploit to the full the sanctity of Ælle's descendants), and concluding with Anna of East Anglia and his four saintly daughters, the most famous of whom, Æðelðryð (Audrey) of Ely, married a Northumbrian king descended from Ælle.

Set in this historical context the Constance-story is not only an alternative version of history that happily combines the roles of Ælle and Mauritius as progenitors of Christianity in England, but it is also a version that can be reconciled with orthodox history if we see it as susceptible to some degree of allegorical interpretation: the faith of Rome triumphs in England because of the acceptance of the principle of constancy in the face of suffering, with the overcoming of trials through faith, while Rome in turn benefits from English faith. Alternatively, and more specifically, Constance represents the Church, cruelly persecuted by some, accepted with love and devotion by others, but surviving by the grace of God; coming from Rome, she is rejected by the Saracens but finds an illustrious place in English history, and her English offspring play an important role in the subsequent history of the Christian faith. Trevet's capacity for this kind of allegorized narrative is demonstrated by his treatment of the Orpheus myth in his commentary on Boethius, familiar to students of medieval literature as a source for Henryson's

*Orpheus and Eurydice*.[15] Incidentally, the Christian-Saracen opposition demonstrated in the Constance-story has its historical counterpart in Trevet's reference to St Brendan and Mahomet as contemporaries in the western and eastern extremities of his world.

Finally, one striking detail further illustrates Trevet's way of thinking and of shaping his material. As already mentioned, the story of Gregory and the slaves, a logical introduction to the theme of Ælle and conversion, is actually separated from the Constance-story by a digression into Spanish history with a story that is substantially accurate, even if told with predictable bias. Hermingild, eldest son of the Visigothic king Levigild, married a Catholic princess and was converted by his wife to orthodoxy; the Visigothic royalty were Arians at this time, and Hermingild was killed by his father for betraying the family faith (actually, according to modern historians, for joining a Byzantine conspiracy to break Visigothic power in Spain). When Hermingild's younger brother succeeded to the throne shortly afterwards, he abandoned the Arian heresy in favour of Catholic orthodoxy, as if inspired by the martyrdom of his elder brother. This story may look like an irrelevant digression from the English theme that precedes and follows it, but two things about it give it relevance at this point. The first thing to note about this edifying tale of a man who dies for his faith is that, like Ælle in the story that follows, Hermingild is converted to the true faith by his wife. The second point lies in the name of the martyr-prince, Hermingild. Names compounded on *-gild* are well attested throughout the Germanic world as masculine names and they are particularly common in this Visigothic royal dynasty. They seem not in fact to have been so common among Anglo-Saxons (the legendary Ingeld is an obvious example, and the *Anglo-Saxon Chronicle* 829F refers to an abbot Felogild who became Archbishop of Canterbury, but few others seem to be recorded), so we may be surprised that when Trevet needed a female name for the wife of the Saxon commander who received Constance on her arrival in Northumbria, the name he chose was

---

[15] The relevant portion of Trevet's text is printed in *The Poems of Robert Henryson*, ed. D. Fox (Oxford, 1981), pp. 384–92. For a more elaborate allegorization of an analogous 'accused queen' tale, 'Merelaus þe Emperour', see *Early English Versions of the Gesta Romanorum*, ed. S. J. H. Herrtage, EETS ES 33 (1879), pp. 311–22; here the accused queen represents the soul of man; this English version is from the fifteenth century, but the original Latin *Gesta Romanorum* was a thirteenth-century composition and its moral allegory represents a mode of thought current in Trevet's time.

Hermingild, which he had just used in a narrative from historical sources where it is unmistakably a man's name. The most likely explanation is that Trevet was already familiar with Hermingild, or something very like it, as a woman's name, and it is in fact a plausible post-Conquest variant of the Old English female name *Eormenhild*. The most famous holder of this name was widely venerated as another royal saint (Florence of Worcester, *s.a.* 675, refers to her as *Eormengilda*); she was the daughter of Erconberht, king of Kent, married the pagan Mercian king Wulfhere (son of Penda) and was reputedly responsible for converting him to Christianity; she reigned as queen during his lifetime and after his death she became a nun and followed her mother (a former queen of Kent) as abbess, first of Minster-in-Thanet and later of Ely (her daughter incidentally was St Werburg).[16] Eormenhild was thus a link between the royal saints of Kent and Mercia, but the particular significance of her role as regards Trevet's narrative is that she was a Christian who converted her pagan husband, which of course is what happens in the Constance-story. In Trevet's narrative the lady Hermingild wishes to embrace the faith of her Christian guest Constance, but feels unable to do so while her husband is a pagan; when a miracle is performed through Hermingild, however, her husband accepts her faith and they are baptized by a British bishop brought from Wales for the purpose, whereupon they break up the mahomets they had formerly worshipped and throw them in the privy (Schlauch edition, p. 169). Trevet's narrative thus gives us in succession Hermingild, a Visigothic prince converted by his wife; Hermingild, a Northumbrian noblewoman who converts her husband (just as the historical Kentish Eormenhild-Ermengild converted her Mercian husband); and of course Constance, the Roman princess who converted her husband King Ælle (Trevet, perhaps unfortunately, does not repeat Bede's story of Edwin's conversion by his Kentish wife). A pervasive theme of the Constance-story, the spiritual power of women, is thus pre-echoed in its immediate context; it is of course a familiar biblical theme and is recurrent in Anglo-Saxon hagiography, but this highlighting of the theme is particularly appropriate in a work addressed, as this chronicle was, to a nun of royal birth.

Summing up, one can say that for Trevet, as for many other post-Conquest chroniclers, the Anglo-Saxon age was important as the period

---

[16] See references given in D. H. Farmer, *Oxford Dictionary of Saints* (Oxford, 1978), p. 135, under *Ermengild*.

when the English became Christians, and the details of the process by
which this conversion began to take root were so important as to merit the
devising of a special legend, the Constance-story, which may be seen as a
religiously motivated transformation of Anglo-Saxon and Roman history.

Where Trevet (or some unknown precursor) took a widely attested
exemplary tale of a persecuted heroine and adapted it to a historical
setting in order to make a statement about the conversion of the English,
his successors, Gower and Chaucer, largely restored the tale to its original
status as a moral romance. The historical setting is no longer a prominent
part of the tale: both poets refer briefly to it, but neither makes very
much of it; Gower has a few more specifically English references than
Chaucer does, but both are more informative about the Roman element
than they are about the English setting. The attitude of each writer to the
English setting may be demonstrated from the respective references to
Edwin: Trevet had set out the historical facts clearly before the tale began
and these are repeated when Alle, departing for Rome, entrusts his realm
to *Edwyn son fitz, qu'esteoyt le tierz roy apres luy*, (Schlauch edition, p. 178);
Gower retains the reference to Edwin but does not say what his relationship to Alle was, perhaps implying the possibility that he was a nephew
or cousin or something more distant:

> He made Edwyn his lieutenant,
> Which heir to him was apparant.     (*CA* II. 1,319–20)

Gower's Alle thus still has an approximate position in relation to a known
Anglo-Saxon king, but Chaucer omits all reference to Edwin, thus
divorcing Alle from any specific place in Anglo-Saxon history. A similar
decline in the specifically Anglo-Saxon aspects of the tale appears in the
references to the English language. Trevet twice mentions this: first, when
Constance arrives in Northumberland, we are told that she can converse
with the people in English because she has been well educated: *ele lui
responda en Sessoneys . . . come cele qu'estoit aprise en diverses laungages*, 'she
answered him in Anglo-Saxon, as one who had been instructed in various
languages' (Schlauch edition, p. 168); and second, when Hermingild
heals the blind Briton, her alleged English words are quoted in the
Anglo-Norman narrative: *Hermigild . . . lui dist en sa laungge Sessone,
'Bisene man, in Iesu name in rode ysclawe, haue thi sight'*, 'Hermingild said to
him in her Anglo-Saxon language, "Blind man, in the name of Jesus who
died on the cross, receive your sight"' (Schlauch edition, p. 170). In

Gower's version there is no suggestion that the language of the English differs from Constance's native tongue: conversation is recorded as if it presented no problem and Hermingild's words to the blind man (based on Trevet's account and retaining the distinctive word *bysne*, 'blind') are simply presented as part of an English linguistic totality, narrative and dialogue alike, with nothing to distinguish the speech from its context. Chaucer, aware of the possible linguistic problem, obviates it by making his Northumbrians speak a form of Constance's own language, thus diminishing their Englishness:

> A maner Latyn corrupt was hir speche,
> But algates therby was she understonde.
> (Man of Law's Tale (=MLT) 519–20: see note in *Riverside Chaucer*)

Hermingild's words to the blind man are omitted by Chaucer, as indeed is the fact that the miraculous cure was actually performed: we are simply told, *Custance . . . had hire wirche / The wyl of Crist* (MLT 566–7), as if the ensuing miracle were so inevitable and predictable that it need not be recorded in full (there is nothing in surviving manuscripts to suggest that anyone other than Chaucer was responsible for this surprising omission). There is thus, as we pass from Trevet through Gower to Chaucer, a descending scale of specified Englishness in the setting of the tale (it does not matter in this respect whether Gower's version actually preceded Chaucer's, as now seems to be generally thought). This is also reflected in the geographical references: Gower retains (and actually augments) Trevet's references to Knaresborough (the only English town named in their versions of the tale), but Chaucer omits the name.[17] Unlike Trevet

---

[17] See Schlauch edition, p. 172 and *CA* II. 943, 1,001, 1,264 and 1,273, with Gower multiplying the number of references; why Trevet introduced Knaresborough, and why Gower repeated it so emphatically, is not at all clear: the messenger travelling between (apparently) Elda's residence on the Humber and Alle's army in Scotland would take a rather circuitous route in order to pass through Knaresborough, though Trevet refers to the town as being *entre Engleterre e Escoce* (Schlauch edition, p. 172). No doubt Trevet's (and presumably Gower's) knowledge of northern English geography was rather vague, but the particular significance of Knaresborough for them is unclear; it was famous as the residence of the hermit Robert of Knaresborough (d. 1218) and from the mid-thirteenth century there was a monastery there of the Trinitarian order (devoted to the ransoming of prisoners taken in the crusades): see *The Metrical Life of St Robert of Knaresborough*, ed. J. Bazire, EETS 228 (1953), pp. 17–22, and references there cited; the relevance of this to the Constance-story remains to be explained.

and Gower, Chaucer does not mention the Saxons or name the Roman emperor, so that all we can deduce of the date of his tale is that it takes place when Rome was Christian and England was not, but his version still has a vestigial English element (see MLT 508, 578, *Northumberlond*, and 1,130, *Engelond*), which distinguishes it from his other tale of a persecuted heroine, the Clerk's Tale; the latter, with its references to Petrarch, has a contemporary framework and a strongly Italian location that contrast with the antique setting and vestigial Englishness of MLT. In Trevet's *Chronicle* the Constance story is clearly closely involved with Anglo-Saxon history and reflects an implicit view of Anglo-Saxon England; in Gower's version the English setting is still present, but in Chaucer the English element is more elusive: the contrast between Roman and English in Chaucer's tale is in fact less prominent than the contrast between Christian and pagan. This appears in Chaucer's relatively detailed account of the retreat of British Christianity before pagan invaders, who, far from being identified as Anglo-Saxons, are in fact left unnamed:

> In al that lond no Cristen dorste route;
> Alle Cristen folk been fled fro that contree
> Thurgh payens, that conquereden al aboute
> The plages of the north, by land and see.
> To Walys fledde the Cristyanytee
> Of olde Britons dwellynge in this ile;
> Ther was hir refut for the meene while.

> But yet nere Cristene Britons so exiled
> That ther nere somme that in hir privetee
> Honoured Crist and hethen folk bigiled,
> And ny the castel swiche ther dwelten three.     (MLT 540–50)

This account is actually more specific than anything in Trevet's tale, where there is only brief reference to the situation: *les Bretounz auoient ia perdu la seingnurie del isle*, 'the Britons had by then lost control of the island' (Schlauch edition, p. 168) and *lez . . . Sessouns qe auoient dounque la seignurie de la terre estoient vnquore paens*, 'the Anglo-Saxons, who now had the rule of the land, were still pagans' (Schlauch edition, p. 169), though there is a cross-reference to an earlier part of the chronicle where the subject had been dealt with more fully. For Chaucer the survival of Christianity in Wales seems more important than the identity of the pagan invaders responsible for this situation. Gower on the other hand underplays the religious situation, noting only Constance's sorrow on finding that there was no Christianity in the land (*CA* II. 745–6). In Chaucer the English location still has some vestigial significance, but the poet does not expound, even implicitly, any clear view of Anglo-Saxon England; he plays down national references and gives greater prominence to the religious element, and the emphasis on universal religious aspects at the expense of particular national considerations may well have given Chaucer's version a wider appeal in his own day and for some time afterwards. If we are looking for a view of Anglo-Saxon England in fourteenth-century literature, then Trevet's work is clearly very rewarding, and the versions of the Constance-story in Gower and Chaucer may appear relevant largely in so far as they retain, however faintly, traces of Trevet's subtle and sophisticated learning. Obviously neither poet is to be blamed for focusing his attention elsewhere, and it would be absurd to pretend that Trevet's narrative artistry (though by no means negligible) is preferable to that of Gower or Chaucer: each writer has his own particular purpose and writes accordingly; but we may be pleased that the two poets incidentally helped keep alive some of the medieval traditions of the pre-Conquest past, even though it was not their prime concern.

# Saxons versus Danes: the anonymous Edmund Ironside

## LEAH SCRAGG

Defending his decision to write of the distant past rather than to reflect upon contemporary events, Sir Walter Ralegh commented in the Preface to his *History of the World* (1614):

> I know that it will be said by many, that I might have been more pleasing to the Reader, if I had written the Story of mine own times; having been permitted to draw water as near the Well-head as another. To this I answer, that whosoever in writing a modern History, shall follow truth too near the heels, it may happily strike out his teeth. There is no Mistress or Guide, that hath led her followers and servants into greater miseries . . . It is enough for me . . . to write of the eldest times: wherein also why may it not be said, that in speaking of the past, I point at the present, and tax the vices of those that are yet living, in their persons that are long since dead; and have it laid to my charge. But this I cannot help, though innocent.[1]

Ralegh's wisdom (born of bitter experience) in refraining from drawing his water too near the wellhead is amply vindicated by the private histories of those writing for the Elizabethan-Jacobean stage. An attack on the Catholic Church and the Spanish monarchy in Middleton's *A Game at Chess* (1624),[2] for example, led to the closure of the Globe theatre and a warrant for the dramatist's arrest, while the 'seditious' material of *The Isle of Dogs* (1597) resulted in the imprisonment of Jonson and two fellow actors. As Ralegh's Preface indicates, however, the notice of the

---

[1] Quoted from *Sir Walter Ralegh: Selected Writings*, ed. G. Hammond (Manchester, 1984), pp. 149–50.

[2] The years to which plays are assigned refer throughout to date of first performance and are drawn, unless otherwise stated, from *Annals of English Drama: 975–1700*, ed. A. Harbage, rev. S. Schoenbaum (London, 1964).

authorities could be evaded by turning one's attention to 'eldest times', and through them taxing the vices not of the dead but the living. Ralegh's awareness that his own history might be interpreted in this light bears witness to the readiness of his contemporaries both to read and deploy historical material as a species of coded comment upon the present – a process of trans-historical exchange at work in the drama from as early as the 1530s. In Bale's *King John* (1538), for example, the eponymous hero's attempted repudiation of the Pope and the consequent division of loyalties among his subjects has an obvious application to Henry VIII's breach with Rome, and the ensuing sixteenth-century tensions between spiritual and political obligations. The smoke screen afforded by the past was not always entirely efficacious, as both textual[3] and performance records[4] reveal, but it did provide Renaissance writers with a degree of freedom to explore contentious issues, and it is this freedom which accounts, in some measure at least, for the extraordinary popularity of the history play in the latter half of the sixteenth century.

Though for the twentieth-century playgoer the principal achievements of the Renaissance stage are its comedies and tragedies, for the Elizabethan (as opposed to the Jacobean) spectator the dominant form of the period was undoubtedly the history play. From the modern, post-Shakespearian perspective the form tends to be equated with the chronicle histories of the 1590s, notably Shakespeare's two major tetralogies dealing with the Wars of the Roses, but in fact the genre is far broader than the Shakespearian canon suggests, embracing biblical and classical subjects (e.g. Peele's *David and Bethsabe*, c. 1581–1594 and Lyly's *Campaspe*, 1583),[5] episodes from European history (e.g. Marlowe's *The Massacre at Paris*, 1593) and material from yet further afield (e.g. the anonymous *Tamar Cham*, c. 1587–1592). The scope of interest in British history was not restricted, moreover, to the period of upheaval stretching from the death of Richard II to the accession of Henry Tudor. A number

---

[3] For a full account of censorship during this period, see J. Clare, '*Art made tongue-tied by authority*': *Elizabethan and Jacobean Dramatic Censorship* (Manchester, 1990).

[4] See, for example, the summoning of Augustine Phillips before Chief Justice Popham in 1601 to justify a performance of Shakespeare's *Richard II* by the Lord Chamberlaine's Men on the eve of the Essex rebellion (cf. E. K. Chambers, *The Elizabethan Stage*, 4 vols. (Oxford, 1923, corrected 1951), II. pp. 204–5.

[5] For the date of *Campaspe*, see *Campaspe: Sappho and Phao*, ed. G. K. Hunter and D. Bevington, Revels Plays (Manchester, 1991), pp. 4–5.

of plays are concerned with Celtic and Romano Britain (e.g. the anonymous *King Leir, c.* 1588–1594 and Hughes's *The Misfortunes of Arthur,* 1588), while numerous dramas chart the exploits of notable monarchs (e.g. Peele's *Edward I,* 1590–1593), or military heroes such as the Black Prince (e.g. the anonymous *Edward III, c.* 1590–1595). The Anglo-Saxon period did not escape the notice of playwrights eager for new material to satisfy a burgeoning public taste. A cluster of plays on Anglo-Saxon subjects was commissioned (or acquired), for example, by the theatrical impressario, Philip Henslowe, towards the close of the sixteenth century for performance by the Admiral's Men, including items on Vortigern, Guthlac, Hardicanute, and Earl Godwine and his sons. Unfortunately, very few plays on the pre-Conquest period have survived to modern times. The anonymous *A Knack to Know A Knave* (1592) is technically set in the reign of Edgar but deals exclusively with sixteenth-century abuses, while Athelstan plays a minor role in Dekker's *Old Fortunatus* (1599), and a rather more major one in *The Welsh Ambassador,* a much later play by the same dramatist. Of the remaining items, Brewer's *The Lovesick King* (1607–1617) conflates folk tale and romance, Middleton's *Hengist, King of Kent or The Mayor of Queeenborough* (1620–1622) and the related *Birth of Merlin* (?1622) are discussed by another contributor to the present volume,[6] while the anonymous *Edmund Ironside,* the only surviving example of an Elizabethan history play set firmly in the Anglo-Saxon period, is the subject of this essay.

*Edmund Ironside,* otherwise entitled *War Hath Made All Friends,* has been the focus of considerable critical controversy. The date of composition, an issue crucial to other problems, remains uncertain. Though there is evidence that the piece looks back to a number of plays from the first decade of Shakespeare's career,[7] suggesting that it may belong among that

---

[6] See below, pp. 107–21. Shakespeare's *Macbeth* should perhaps be included among Jacobean plays on this period in that it includes references to Edward the Confessor, while troops from England contribute to Macbeth's overthrow. For the date of *Hengist* and *The Birth of Merlin,* see below, pp. 108–9 and note 4.

[7] For parallels with the Shakespearian corpus (adduced in support of Shakespeare's authorship), see *Shakespeare's Lost Play: Edmund Ironside,* ed. E. Sams (London, 1985), pp. 225ff. For a more sceptical analysis of the evidence, see *'Edmond Ironside' and Anthony Brewer's 'The Love-sick King',* ed. R. Martin, The Renaissance Imagination: Important Literary and Theatrical Texts from the Late Middle Ages through the Seventeenth Century (New York and London, 1991), pp. 363–9.

group of items on Anglo-Saxon subjects produced by Henslowe at the turn of the century, arguments have been advanced for dates as early as *c*. 1588 and as late as 1647, though the latter, at least, has no recent support.[8] Questions of authorship and literary/dramatic success have produced even less unanimity. The interest attaching to the play derives not from its Anglo-Saxon subject matter, but from its ambiguous association with the Shakespearian canon, the argument that the play dates from the 1580s enabling it to be claimed, by those convinced of Shakespeare's authorship, as one of the dramatist's earliest experiments in the use of chronicle material, anticipating rather than echoing the two great tetralogies. For those, like Eric Sams, committed to this position, the play inevitably is a considerable success, potentially 'impressive in stage performance', alive 'with vigorous and diverse characterisation', written in a style 'lit by flashes of real poetry', with 'highly sophisticated wordplay', and 'continuous dramatic irony'.[9] A very different view of the drama obtains, however, among those scholars unconvinced of an early date and less committed to Shakespeare's authorship. To the editor of the Malone Society edition, for example, the play is 'devoid of dramatic structure', while its author lacks any 'dramatic skill' and can 'scarcely be called a poet'.[10] Nevertheless, though a critical consensus upon date and literary merit has yet to be achieved,[11] on two points, at least, some agreement does exist. The Malone Society editor's proposition that the piece constitutes 'the most important extant dramatization of Anglo-

---

[8] For a survey of views on the date of the play, see Sams, *Shakespeare's Lost Play*, pp. 9ff. The earlier date is espoused by Sams himself, the later by J. O. Halliwell-Philipps, *A Dictionary of Plays* (London, 1860), p. 62. The ownership of the play is discussed in relation to its date by Martin, *'Edmond Ironside' and Anthony Brewer's 'The Love-sick King'*, pp. 370–5.

[9] Sams, *Shakespeare's Lost Play*, pp. 51 and 52.

[10] *Edmond Ironside or War Hath Made All Friends*, ed. E. Boswell, Malone Society (Oxford, 1927), pp. xi and xii.

[11] For an indication of the current range of attitudes to the question of authorship, see the debate triggered in the *TLS* by an article by E. Sams (13 August 1982, p. 879): R. Fleissner (3 September, 1982, p. 947), P. Xuereb (3 September, 1982, p. 947), M. Jackson (10 September, 1982, p. 973), R. Proudfoot (17 September, 1982, p. 1010), E. Sams (24 September, 1982, p. 1037), R. Proudfoot (8 October, 1982, p. 1102), R. Proudfoot (22 October, 1982, p. 1162), E. Sams (29 October 1982, p. 1193), P. Milward (19 November 1982, p. 1273), and G. Taylor (1 April 1983, p. 328).

Saxon history'[12] remains unchallenged, while one similarity to the Shakespearian canon is indisputable – the source upon which the dramatist draws in constructing his play.

*Edmund Ironside* is unique among Renaissance dramas on pre-Conquest subjects in that it is firmly set within the Anglo-Saxon period and is entirely devoid of fairy tale or fantastic elements.[13] Like the majority of Shakespeare's history plays, the principal source of the drama is Holinshed's *Chronicles*, first published in 1577 and enlarged in 1587, though the source material is augmented by a rudimentary ahistorical sub-plot designed to widen the social scope. The play centres upon the complex sequence of events following the death of Æthelred the Unready in 1016, and is broadly faithful to the complicated history of the period that Holinshed relates. The action opens soon after the death of Æthelred and the coronation of Edmund Ironside in London, with Canutus calling upon the nobility to uphold his earlier election to the throne. Having accepted the hospitality of the Earl of Southampton, and precipitately married his daughter, Canutus learns of the defeat of his army in the north, and decides to march against Edmund himself. Edmund repulses an attack upon London, pursuing and defeating his rival in a series of encounters, though he comes close to losing a crucial battle following a false report of his death. A fresh onslaught from the Danes leads to the departure of Emma's sons, Alfred and Edward, for the safety of Normandy, while Edmund suffers a defeat through the treachery of a duplicitous noble. The battle is not decisive, however, and the armies again come together, but a major confrontation is averted by a proposal to settle the matter by single combat. As in Holinshed, Canutus again proves no match for Edmund, but the latter nevertheless embraces his offer of friendship and agrees to divide the kingdom between them.

In structuring his play the dramatist conforms to his source not merely in the ordering of the episodes, but in the emphasis that he places upon the divided loyalties of both Danes and Saxons, and on the influential part played by the treacherous Edricus, duke of Mercia, in the historical process. For Holinshed, the sequence of events that he relates exhibits the

---

[12] Boswell, *Edmond Ironside*, p. xii.

[13] Brewer's *The Lovesick King* offers a useful contrast here in that it deals with the same period (though with scant regard for historical fact) but includes the fairy-tale rags-to-riches story of Thornton and his support of a non-historical King Alfred.

fall of a glorious England under Edmund, the role played by a disloyal subject in the destruction of the realm, and the rise of a major political figure, destined to stamp his imprint upon the national life. The period is thus dominated, for the historian, by three strong individuals – Edmund, Edric and Canute – and the dramatist follows the chronicle in constructing his play around their contrasting personalities. It is from the playwright's treatment of these three figures, and the peoples that the two leaders represent, that some insight may be gained into Elizabethan attitudes to the Anglo-Saxons, and the relevance of early eleventh-century English politics to late sixteenth-century concerns.

The anonymous playwright's Edmund is recognizably derived from the charismatic figure depicted in the source. From the outset he is presented as an accomplished military leader, for whom Canutus is no match either on the battle-field or in single combat. It is the rumour that the Saxon king has fallen that causes the near defeat of the English forces at Worcester (cf. 993ff.),[14] while in the hand-to-hand confrontation that takes place at the close of the play the Dane is forced to sue for a pause in which to catch his breath (1,978–85), and is finally obliged to concede defeat (1,998). Edmund is not simply presented, however, as an outstanding warrior. His first lines in the play express his concern for his soldiers' well-being, and it is his self-abnegating care for the commonwealth that defines his concept of kingship throughout. His magnanimity is evident in his readiness to allow Canutus to catch his breath during a combat upon which the fate of the kingdom depends, and it is his readiness to attribute a similarly honourable cast of mind to others that makes him vulnerable to the wiles of the traitor, Edricus. Though dedicated to his destruction, Edricus himself is forced to concede that he is 'gracious in the people's eyes' (1,836), while Leofric and Turkillus, whose sons are held hostage by Canutus as pledges of their loyalty, elect to sacrifice their own heirs rather than desert a king who

> for good regard of merit and desert
> for honour, fame and true nobility
> is rightly termed mirror of majesty. (248–50)

Edmund's virtues, however, are not presented as unique to himself, but

---

[14] All references to the play are to Sams, *Shakespeare's Lost Play*. Line numbering in this edition is consecutive thoughout, rather than by act and scene.

as characteristic of the people he leads. While the dramatist is alive to the confusion of loyalties complicating the history of this period (Canutus's army, for example, is made up of both Saxons and Danes, cf. 1,073–86), he makes a clear distinction between the national characters of the two peoples, defining the Saxons as 'Englishmen' (cf. 198), while the Danes look to a 'foreigner' (854) as their king. The contrast between the two races is established in the first scene of the play when Edricus, having urged Canutus to bridle the rebellious Saxons and yoke them like slaves, receives the following, somewhat non-naturalistic, rebuke from Uskataulf, one of the officers of the Danish prince:

> Accomptest thou, Edricus, the *Saxons* fools
> or rather, hardy, wise and valorous?
> . . .
> Witness the many combats they have fought,
> *Denmark* our country's loss by them and theirs
> with many other witnesses of worth.
> . . .
> Recall the former perils we have passed
> whose dear-bought times are freshly yet in mind
> the tyranny your [Canutus's] father *Sveynus* used
> in tithing people, killing 9 of 10.
> What did ensue? Why, loss of many holds
> bloodshed and war, rebellion, sword and fire
> for they are Englishmen, easy to rule
> with lenity, so they be used like men,
> patient of right, impatient of wrong,
> brooking no tyranny in any sort
> but hating and revenging it with death.          (178–202)

Similarly, after the defeat of his forces at Worcester, Canutus draws a distinction between the conduct of the Danes who fought in the battle and the courage of the Saxons both on the opposite side and among his own troops:

> CANUTUS: Now by these heavens above our wretched heads
> ye are but cowards, every one of you.
> Edmund is blessed. Oh had I but his men
> I would not doubt to conquer all the world
> in shorter time than *Alexander* did
> but all my Danes are *Braggadochios*

and I accursed to be the general
of such a flock of fearful runaways.

. . . . . .

USKA[TAULF]: My noble lord, our countrymen are safe.
In all these broils English 'gainst English fight.
The Danes or none or very few are slain.
CANUTUS: *Turns towards Uskataulf*
It was a sign ye fled and did not fight.
Is't not a dishonour unto you
to see a foreign nation fight for me
whenas my home-bred countrymen do run
leaving their king amongst his enemies?                    (1,065–86)

Whereas the treatment of Edmund and the Anglo-Saxons clearly constitutes a heightened reworking of Holinshed's concept of the glory of early eleventh-century England, the presentation of Canutus involves a more significant adaptation of the source. A number of the incidents that are selected for dramatization are notable for the adverse light that they shed on the Danish leader, while unhistorical material is added to augment the presentation of a headlong ruler, given to explosions of anger and susceptible to mischievous advice. In the scene that begins at 383, for example, he resolves to marry Southampton's daughter within minutes of meeting her, commenting on the 'small ado' with which he has dealt with such a 'weighty matter' (453–4). In the following scene, he orders the mutilation of two young hostages, following the defection of their fathers, a command carried out on stage in a protracted episode that lends a minor incident in Holinshed considerable dramatic weight. His ungoverned rage after his defeat at Worcester is prejudicial, as his own officers recognize, to the morale of his army as a whole (cf. 1,105–10), while his readiness to defeat Edmund by treachery meets with disapproval even among those most closely allied to his cause (cf. 1,551–9). The Danes whom he leads are inferior, as he is, to the Saxons in battle, while their bloodthirstiness, matching his ruthlessness, is constantly stressed:

MESS[ENGER]: Haste, haste, king Edmund to relieve thy land
Which is oppressed by multitudes of Danes.

. . .

They prey upon thy subjects cruelly
like hungry tigers upon silly kids

sparing not ancient men for reverence
nor women for [their] imbecility
nor guiltless babes for their unspotted life
nor holy men, their madness is so rife.          (1,332–53)

It would be wrong to suggest, however, that the dramatist's changes to his source material lead to a simple good and bad opposition between the two kings. Edmund's nobility is shown as exposing him to deception, while the flaws in Canutus' character make him a far shrewder politician, capable of using the corrupt Edricus for his own purposes, while fully understanding his duplicitous nature. Early in the play, for example, following the defeat of his forces by Edmund, Canutus calls for Edricus to advise him, responding to the gross flattery to which he is treated by consciously exhibiting the lengths to which a time-serving politician will go in order to pander to those in power:

> Come hither, Edricus. Oh, strange miracle
> see you not in the heavens prodigious signs?
> Look how the sun looks pale, the moon shines red,
> the stars appear in the perturbed heaven
> like little comets, and not twelve o'clock.
> What is the cause then that the stars are seen?
> EDRICUS: I see them well, my lord, yet know no cause
> unless it shows the fall of *Ironside*.
> CANUTUS: Surely it doth. Look now they are all gone.
> 'Tis night, 'tis dark, beware ye stumble not
> lend me your hand, but first go fetch a torch
>                                *Exit Edricus*
> to light me to my tent, make haste I pray.
> He's gone to fetch a torch to light the day!
>                                *Enter Edricus*
> EDRICUS: My lord, the misty vapours were so thick
> they almost quenched the torch.
> CANUTUS: True as all the rest. I say thy wit is thick.
> Gross flattery, all-soothing sycophant
> doth blind thy eyes and will not let thee see
> that others see thou art a flatterer.          (783–801)

The episode establishes the Dane's clarity of judgement, whereas Edmund elsewhere is deceived, allowing the audience to accept the probity of the alliance made in the final scene, when magnanimity and shrewdness are formally united.

It is in the treatment of Edricus, rather than Canutus, however, that the most significant discrepancies are evident between the play and its chronicle source, providing an index to the dramatist's intention. Like Holinshed's Edricke, the anonymous playwright's Edricus is responsible for a succession of acts of betrayal designed to promote the Danish cause, motivated not by loyalty to Canutus but a ruthless pursuit of self-interest. The dramatist's self-seeking Mercian, however, is a far more ambiguous creation than his chronicle antecedent. A lengthy soliloquy early in the play establishes (unhistorically) that he was raised by Ethelred the Unready from a lowly condition, while his mother later reveals that he is the bastard son of a soldier, conceived during a visit to a fair (cf. 498–500).[15] Though he himself is ignorant of this aspect of his ambivalent status, his conduct throughout the play conforms to Renaissance assumptions regarding the class of beings to which he belongs.[16] Dislocated from the social order by virtue of his unnatural birth, he recognizes no allegiance to either of the kings he purports to serve (cf. 307–31), behaves callously towards his mother and putative father (cf. 535–55), is vicious in his stance towards his countrymen (cf. 150–62) and dedicates himself solely to his own advancement (cf. 278–331). Delineated as a self-conscious villain, he is aligned, moreover, by the dramatist with the Vice of the medieval Morality play, both implicitly, through his intimate relationship with the audience (cf. 278ff.) and explicitly through the announcement that he can 'play an *Ambodexter's* part' (330) – a reference to the Vice of Thomas Preston's *Cambises* (1558–1569).

The unnatural status of the play's traitor and his role as a self-conscious advocate of evil serves to broaden the implications of his acts of betrayal from the political to the spiritual sphere, and this wider dimension of the action is also evident through the part played in the drama by the Archbishops of Canterbury and York. In the scene that opens at 812, for example, a violent confrontation takes place between the two clerics, bearing witness to a schism that extends beyond the battle for the throne.

[15] Randall Martin suggests that the source for his illegitimacy may be Richard Grafton's *A Chronicle at Large* (1569): see '*Edmond Ironside*' *and Anthony Brewer's 'The Love-sick King'*, pp. 15–16.

[16] For a full discussion of the presentation of the figure of the bastard on the Renaissance stage, see my unpublished M.A. dissertation, *The Bastard in Elizabethan and Jacobean Drama*, University of Liverpool, 1964.

Canterbury, who supports Canutus, also upholds the authority of the Pope, while York stands for Edmund and an England free from papal intervention, cf.:

> CANTER[BURY]: Why bends not the presumptuous knee of York
> when Canterbury speaks? Cannot the curse
> of God and me, the metropolitan
> under the *Pope* of all *Dominians*
> within this realm of England, cause thee fear
> proud irreligious prelate? Know my power
> stretcheth beyond thy compass even as much
> as Rome doth mine. Then quiver when I curse
> and like a child indeed prostrate thyself
> before my feet, that thy humility
> may move me to absolve thy former sins
> and set thee free from hell's damnation.
> YORK: Traitor to God and to thy lawful king
> where thou dost bless I curse, where curse I bless.
> As thou art bishop, my commission
> stretcheth as far as thine . . .
>                     No Canterbury, no,
> I humble me to God and not to thee.
> A traitor, a betrayer of his king
> a rebel, a profane priest, a Pharisee
> a parasite, an enemy to peace
> a foe to truth and to religion
> . . .
> You are a champion for the devil and Canutus
> I fly not from thy curses.            (814–59)

Clearly, Anglo-Saxon England under its native sovereign is conceived here, not simply as a glorious kingdom in military terms, but as a realm in touch with a Christianity uncorrupted by the power of Rome, a view consonant with that of sixteenth-century theologians who supported the translation of the Bible into English by Anglo-Saxon precedents. The fate of the church is thus bound up in the physical conflict and is part of a larger battle between good and evil in which Edricus functions as a corruptive agency on more than one level.

The spiritual dimension of the play's action, implicit in the confrontation between the two prelates, is further enforced by a range of references to biblical and homiletic material. Edmund's first two speeches, for example, while indicating the humane nature of his leadership through his concern for his soldiers' welfare, also define him as a type of St Martin:

> A worthy captain seeing a tall soldier
> march barefoot, halting, plucked off his own shoes
> and gave them to the soldier, saying, 'Fellow
> when I want shoes then give me these again.' (351–4)

Similarly the terms in which he welcomes the return of Leofric and Turkillus from their enforced alliance with Canutus echo the parable of the prodigal son and invite identification with the good shepherd:

> One sheep that was lost I more rejoice to find
> than twenty other which I never missed. (371–2)

In the scene following the defeat of his forces by treachery, the king is seen by his followers as a type of Christ, while the Danes become the Jews thirsting to kill him, and Edricus both the Devil and another Judas:

> EDMUND: Vild *Edricus*, all this proceeds from him
> I saved his life and he doth thirst for mine.
> Ungrateful wretch, hellish incarnate devil!
> For sure no man was ever so unkind
> unto his king and loving countrymen.
> Disloyal and unfaithful sycophant
> it grieves my vexed soul to think on thee.
> ALFRIC: Let it not grieve you, rather joy to think
> you are escaped from the hands of him
> that sought like Judas to betray his lord
> into the hands of bloodthirsty Danes.
> . . .
> EDRICUS: All hail unto my gracious sovereign!
> EDMUND: *Judas*, thy next part is to kiss my cheek
> And then commit me unto *Caiaphas*. (1,615–45)

The relationship that the dramatist sets up between his principal figures thus functions, through a web of correspondences, on both public and private levels, and has spiritual as well as political dimensions. Edmund Ironside is at once a worthy king betrayed by a disloyal subject, the defender of a kingdom in both political and spiritual jeopardy, a representative of mankind at risk from diabolic forces, and ultimately a type of Christ. The alliance forged through the king's magnanimity in the closing scene of the play consequently has far wider ramifications than the corresponding military/political accommodation effected in the source. Not only is the kingdom freed from the ravages of a destructive conflict, but Edmund's offer of friendship is seen by Canutus as bringing 'heavenly physic to [his] earth-sick soul' (2,016), implying a species of redemption, while the defeat of the malign forces embodied in Edricus offers the hope of *'everlasting* peace' (my italics, 2,053). Though the temporal uncertainty of the resolution is evident in the continuing resentment of Turkillus and Leofric (cf. 2,034–8) and the dissimulated hostility of Edricus (cf. 2,056ff.), in the moment that the leaders of the two forces formally embrace, the audience is afforded a glimpse of a 'joy unspeakable' (2,031), momentarily achieved within the human sphere.

Though the success of the dramatist's reworking of his source material is open to question, the reasons underlying his choice and handling of his subject matter are not difficult to deduce. The political situation in the early years of the eleventh century, as recorded by Holinshed, corresponds to that which attracted sixteenth-century playwrights to other periods of English history, with the realm riven between rival claimants to the throne (cf. Shakespeare's *Henry VI, Parts 2 and 3, c.* 1590–1592), the autonomy of the kingdom threatened by foreign intervention (cf. Shakespeare's *King John,* 1591–1598), and the subject torn between conflicting loyalties to lineal and *de facto* kings (cf. Shakespeare's *Richard II,* 1594–1595). The interest in the situations explored in these plays is clearly related to public anxieties during a period in which the succession to the throne was far from assured, the experience of civil war was fresh in the national memory, and foreign intervention remained a continuing threat. For the English spectator at the close of the sixteenth century, the possibility of Spanish troops on English soil, supporting a Catholic claimant to the throne and attracting the loyalties of one segment of the community, was a deeply disturbing contingency informing the circumstances of day-to-day life, enabling a ready equation to be made between events on the stage and contemporary concerns.[17] At the same time, the correlation established during this period between the reformed church and that of pre-Conquest England[18] permitted the appropriation of the

---

[17] For a discussion of the interaction between the play and contemporary Catholic propaganda, see R. Martin, *'Edmond Ironside' and Anthony Brewer's 'The Love-sick King',* p. 43.

[18] See Matthew Parker's *De Antiquitate Britannicae Ecclesiae* (1572).

Anglo-Saxon kingdom to the support of a theological position. The drama is clearly written from a Protestant standpoint, and is concerned to legitimate an England free from papal domination by reference to an Edenic past. The play's Anglo-Saxon subject matter thus allows the playwright to reflect upon contemporary issues, and to support a particular sectarian viewpoint, without exposing himself to censure, safeguarding both himself and the interests of the company for which he wrote by refraining from drawing his water too near the wellhead.

While consciously promoting a sixteenth-century project, however, the anonymous author of *Edmund Ironside* is also unconsciously forwarding the very different venture upon which the contributors to the present volume are engaged. In appropriating eleventh-century England to the cause of sixteenth-century political and theological nationalism, he simultaneously affords the twentieth-century reader an Elizabethan view of the Anglo-Saxons. For him, the Saxons are emphatically 'Englishmen' (933), confirming his sense of cultural continuity, and the lineal successor to the throne of England is a courageous, high-minded, and truly Christian king. The Queen whose husband Ironside succeeds 'hath not her peer upon the earth / for wisdom, suffering and for patience' (1,512–13), while the king's followers, a 'generation like the chosen Jews' (145), are not only hardy in battle, 'stubborn, unwieldy fierce and wild to tame' (146), but 'easy to rule' (198) in times of peace, if treated with 'love and lenity' (205). Whereas for the writer to whom the play has been so contentiously attributed the significance of nomenclature is a matter of dispute, for the author of *Edmund Ironside* it is deeply significant, affording a key to national character. In the view of this sixteenth-century dramatist, at least, the Saxons' names

> discover what their natures are,[19]
> more hard than stones, and yet not stones indeed.
> In fight, more than stones detesting flight
> in peace, as soft as wax, wise provident.                    (180–3)

---

[19] The sense here depends upon the derivation of 'Saxon' from Latin *saxa* 'stone'.

# New times and old stories: Middleton's *Hengist*

## JULIA BRIGGS

In rereading and reworking history, each generation picks up what it needs or recognizes or understands, and leaves out what it finds uninteresting or obscure. History is a process of partial appropriation, focusing on points of similarity or difference. When Thomas Middleton dramatized the first invasion of Britain by the Saxons in his play *Hengist, King of Kent*, he acknowledged this at the outset, explaining that he was reworking a traditional legend as a tale for his own times. The monk Raynulph (Higden), acting as prologue, reminded the audience that

> Fashions that are now Calld new
> Haue bene worne by more than you,
> Elder times haue vsd ye same
> Though these new ones get ye name,
> So in story whats now told
> That takes not part with days of old?
> Then to proue times mutuall glorye
> Ioyne new times loue, to old times storye.    (Chor. i. 11–18)[1]

The story he proceeded to tell was one that interested contemporary historians whose several versions reflected their developing sense of nationhood and of the need for myths to support that concept.[2] While the details might vary, the main outline had been established by Geoffrey of Monmouth in his *Historia regum Britanniæ*.[3] It was the tale of

---

[1] All quotations from the play and references to it are to R. C. Bald's edition (New York and London, 1938), though Bald's superscript letters are not reproduced here.

[2] See R. Helgerson, *Forms of Nationhood: the Elizabethan Writing of England* (Chicago and London, 1993).

[3] *Geoffrey of Monmouth: the History of the Kings of Britain*, trans. L. Thorpe (Harmondsworth, 1966). Numbers of books and sections are given in the text.

Vortiger(n), the proud tyrant who persuaded Constans (Constantius, in Middleton's play), eldest son of Constantine, to leave his monastery and become king. Constans was subsequently killed by his own bodyguard, and his younger brothers, Aurelius Ambrosius and Uther Pendragon, fled to Brittany (*Historia*, vi. 6–8). Vortiger, who had engineered his murder, was then elected king himself. He was then troubled with border wars until Hengist and Horsa came to his aid with warriors from Saxony in long ships. Vortiger rewarded Hengist with as much land as could be contained within a thong cut from a bull's hide, and Hengist built Thong Castle on his land. Vortiger meanwhile had fallen in love with Hengist's daughter, Renwein (variously, Rowena, Ronix, or, in Middleton's version, Roxena), and married her, giving Hengist Kent as his fiefdom (vi. 9–12). Vortiger's son Vortimer became king and led the British against the Saxons, but was poisoned by his Saxon stepmother (vi. 13–14). After his death, Hengist made a truce with Vortiger at Mount Ambrius (more usually, Salisbury) which he then broke, massacring the British lords and taking Vortiger prisoner (vi. 15–16). After ceding substantial areas of eastern Britain to the Saxons, Vortiger retreated to a Welsh stronghold where he was killed and his castle burnt to the ground by Aurelius Ambrosius, who in the meantime had slain Hengist in battle (viii. 1–6). After the death of Aurelius, Uther Pendragon inherited the throne and was eventually succeeded by his more famous son, Arthur.

The events that followed the defeat of Hengist and the death of Vortiger, as related by Geoffrey of Monmouth, form the subject of William Rowley's play *The Birth of Merlin*, which was probably written to cash in on the success of *Hengist*, since it acts as a sort of sequel or spin-off from it.[4] More than twenty years earlier, Philip Henslowe's company had performed a Vortiger (or 'Valteger') play in repertory from December 1596 to April 1597, and this had been followed by a 'uterpendragon' play, in repertory from April to June of 1597.[5] Both plays are now lost, but as sequels their relationship may have paralleled that of *Hengist* and *The Birth of Merlin*, in which Uther Pendragon ('the Prince') is the hero. Rowley's

[4] *The Birth of Merlin* is reprinted in *The Shakespeare Apocrypha*, ed. C. F. Tucker Brooke (1908; Oxford, 1971) since its 1662 title page attributes it to William Shakespeare and William Rowley. F. G. Fleay proposed 1622 as a probable date of composition for it, which would allow it to be read as a sequel to Middleton's *Hengist*.

[5] R. T. Foakes and R. T. Rickert, *Henslowe's Diary*, (Cambridge, 1968), pp. 55–6 and 58–9.

play capitalizes on Middleton's most dramatic effects: it deploys a 'Blazing Star' at the beginning of Act IV, scene v (fireworks would have been used to represent the burning of Vortiger's castle at the end of Middleton's play), and like *Hengist*, it includes a love triangle involving a treacherous young Saxon woman, Artesia.[6] As in Middleton's sub-plot, there is a great deal of clowning involved: Merlin is born as a small boy with a long beard, resembling nothing so much as a hairy 'Hartichoke' (III. iv. 53). His mother, Jone Goe-too't, has been deceived by the Devil disguised as a gallant (the play's sub-title is 'The Child Hath Found His Father'). Her brother is the clown, and Rowley, who was an actor as well as a playwright, might have written this part for himself. Rowley was collaborating with Middleton on *The Changeling* at about the same time, or soon afterwards.

Middleton's *Hengist* has traditionally been dated between 1615 and 1622, but Roger Holdsworth has narrowed this down to 1620–1622.[7] It is the first surviving play in which Old English is actually spoken on stage, and its subject matter reflects that renewal of interest in the history and language of pre-Norman Britain which is also demonstrated by the popularity of chorographic and historical writings – works such as William Harrison's *Description of England* (1587), William Camden's *Britannia* (1586), Richard Verstegan's *A Restitution of Decayed Intelligence in Antiquities* (1605), John Speed's *History of Great Britaine* (1611), Samuel Daniel's *Historie of England* (1613), and Michael Drayton's chorographical poem *Poly-Olbion* (1613), itself inspired by Camden's *Britannia*. The study of Anglo-Saxon had recently been revived by scholars such as Laurence Nowell, John Leland and William Lambarde, whose *Perambulation of Kent* is an important work of chorography.[8] The

---

[6] The use of fireworks in the final scene of *Hengist* is discussed by R. C. Bald in his edition (pp. 124–5), by A. Lancashire in 'The Emblematic Castle in Shakespeare and Middleton', *Mirror up to Shakespeare: Essays in Honour of G. R. Hibbard*, ed. J. C. Gray (Toronto, 1984), pp. 235–8; and by L. Thomson, '"On ye walls": the Staging of *Hengist, King of Kent*, V. ii', *Medieval and Renaissance Drama in England* 3 (1986), pp. 165–76. 'A Blazing Star' is called for in the stage directions at the opening of the last scene of Middleton's *The Revenger's Tragedy*.

[7] Holdsworth, 'The Date of *Hengist, King of Kent*', *N&Q* 38 (1991), pp. 516–19.

[8] Helgerson, *Forms of Nationhood*, esp. ch. 3, 'The Land Speaks'; on the sixteenth-century revival of Anglo-Saxon, see *Anglo-Saxon Scholarship: the First Three Centuries*, ed. C. T. Berkhout and M. McC. Gatch (Boston, Mass., 1982), esp. R. E. Buckalew on 'Nowell, Lambarde and Lelande: the Significance of Laurence Nowell's Transcript of Ælfric's Grammar and Glossary', pp. 19–50.

history of England tended to be related in terms of its several different conquests: the frontispiece to *Poly-Olbion* portrays Hengist (though not quite dressed in 'fashions that are . . . new'), with the three other conquerors of Britain, Brut the Trojan (first celebrated by Geoffrey of Monmouth), Julius Caesar and Duke William of Normandy. For his *Restitution*, Richard Verstegan engraved his own illustration of 'The Arryval of the First Anceters [sic] of Englishmen out of Germanie into Britaine', 'therewithall to shew the manner of the apparel which they wore, the weapons which they vsed, and the banner or ensigne first by them there spred in the feild' (pp. 116–17).[9]

Thomas Middleton was appointed City Chronologer in 1620, and there may be a link between the play's historical content and his new post, since nowhere else did he attempt to dramatize British history for the public stage,[10] though there is disappointingly little evidence to suggest that he took any serious antiquarian interest in his material. The study of Old English was considered particularly important by those jurists such as John Selden and Sir Edward Coke, who hoped to establish English law upon traditional precedent, rather than to adopt a version of the codified Roman law widely used on the Continent; and also by theologians like Matthew Parker, Elizabeth's first Archbishop of Canterbury, who was eager to find evidence of the British Church's early independence of Rome (and thus its anticipation of the Reformation).[11] A self-consciously learned dramatist, Ben Jonson, maintained close links with his old schoolmaster, the historian William Camden, and dedicated the first folio of his *Works* to him, but if Middleton had comparably close connections with any of the scholars of Anglo-Saxon England, there is no evidence for it in this play. Indeed there is little evidence that Middleton's investigation of his historical material took him much beyond Shakespeare's favourite source, Raphael Holinshed's *Historie of England* and *Historie of Scotland*, probably supplemented with Fabyan's *Chronicle*.[12]

The Old English words in the play are spoken by Hengist as a signal to

[9] See T. D. Kendrick, *British Antiquity* (London, 1950), p. 118.

[10] Bald, ed., *Hengist*, p. 135.

[11] See Helgerson, *Forms of Nationhood*, chs. 2 ('Writing the Law') and 6 ('Apocalyptics and Apologetics'), and T. H. Leinbaugh, 'Ælfric's *Sermo de Sacrificio in Die Pascae*: Anglican Polemic in the Sixteenth and Seventeenth Centuries', in *Anglo-Saxon Scholarship*, ed. Berkhout and Gatch, pp. 51–68.

[12] Bald, ed. *Hengist*, pp. xxxviii–xxxix.

his Saxons when they meet the British forces 'Vppon ye plaine nere salsbury' (Chor. iv. 10). The Saxons have concealed long knives or 'seaxes' about them, and at the watchword *'Nemp yor sexes'* (IV. iii. 35, 52) will draw them and attack the assembled British lords. The phrase was spoken in Saxon so that the British lords should not understand it and so be put on their guard, but it had come to be particularly linked with the Saxons through the derivation of their name from their 'seaxes', the distinctive knives or short swords they carried.[13] This legendary 'Night of the Long Knives' was first recorded by 'Nennius' in his *Historia Brittonum*, where Hengist commands *'Eu, nimet saxas!'* (46). The phrase, variously spelled, turns up in the several medieval accounts of these events derived from Geoffrey of Monmouth's *Historia*, where Hengist bids *'Nimet oure saxes!'* (vi. 15). Geoffrey adapted and expanded the story from Nennius, linking it with Merlin, whom he credits with having brought the Giant's Ring (elsewhere, the hanging stones, or Stonehenge) from Ireland by magic, to commemorate the spot where the British were massacred (viii. 10–12).[14]

Middleton passed up an opportunity to include further phrases from Old English when he avoided showing on stage another traditional episode in this story, that of Hengist's daughter's pledge to Vortiger. In Middleton's play, the incident is reported by a gentleman:

---

[13] Richard Verstegan, *A Restitution* (London, 1605), pp. 21–2; John Speed, *The History of Great Britaine* (London, 1611), p. 285; Michael Drayton, *Poly-Olbion*, The Fourth Song, 386–8:

> And of those crooked Skaines they us'd in warre to beare,
> Which in their thundring tongue, the *Germans*, *Handseax* name,
> They Saxons first were call'd:

*The Works of Michael Drayton*, ed. J. W. Hebel, 5 vols. (Oxford, 1961), IV, p. 79. These characteristic knives, now known as scramasaxes, were single-bladed and sometimes curved or angled along the non-cutting edge, as can be seen from illustrations in *London and the Saxons* by R. E. M. Wheeler, London Museum Catalogues 6 (London, 1935), plates xiv, xv. Leah Scragg has pointed out to me that the anonymous play of *Edmund Ironside* includes an alternative etymology for the Saxons, deriving their name from the Latin *saxa* 'a stone':

> 'Their names discover what their natures are,
> more hard than stones, and yet not stones indeed.'     (I.i.181–2)

[14] Nennius, *British History and Welsh Annals*, ed. and trans. J. Morris (London and Chichester, 1980), section 46, pp. 32 and 73.

> She takes a Cup of gold and midst ye armye
> Teaching her knee a Current Cheerefulness
> Wch well became her, dranck a liberall health
> To ye Kinges ioyes and yours, . . .                    (II. iii. 202–5)

Nennius relates that Hengist's daughter acted as cup-bearer at a banquet given by her father for Vortigern (37). Geoffrey of Monmouth names the daughter Renwein, and describes how she greets Vortigern with the words, '*Laverd King, was hail!*', to which, he was told, the proper answer was '*drinc hail*', thus establishing in Britain the ancient custom of passing the wassail bowl (vi. 12). Middleton does not record the ritual exchange of the pledge itself, instead observing that Roxena carried a cup of gold, a detail mentioned by Geoffrey but here intended to remind his audience of the emblematic figure of the Scarlet Woman of the Apocalypse 'having a gold cup in her hand full of abominations and filthiness of her fornication'. Margot Heinemann has pointed out a later identification of Roxena with the Scarlet Woman, in the final scene of the play.[15]

Today, the stories of Vortiger, of the Salisbury plain massacre and Renwein's pledge, set between the reigns of Constantine and Uther's magical shape-changing to beget Arthur, are thought of as legends, deriving from Geoffrey's imaginative, accumulative but wholly unreliable *Historia* rather than from the less fanciful accounts of the Saxon invasion supplied by Gildas, Bede and the earliest entries in the *Anglo-Saxon Chronicle*.[16] From an early stage, a few historians had questioned Geoffrey's account of the founding of Britain. Polydore Vergil, in particular, had alerted Renaissance historians to its inconsistencies, but contemporary historiography had, in any case, begun to distinguish more carefully between different types of source material. In his detailed notes to Drayton's *Poly-Olbion*, the jurist John Selden queried whether the Saxons had been invited to England by Vortiger, as Geoffrey of Monmouth had claimed, since 'the stories of *Gildas* and *Nennius* have no

---

15 Revelation 17:4. See M. Heinemann, *Puritanism and Theatre: Thomas Middleton and Opposition Drama under the Early Stuarts* (Cambridge, 1980), p. 141.

16 Gildas, *The Ruin of Britain and Other Works*, trans. M. Winterbottom (London and Chichester, 1978), esp. sections 22–4, pp. 25–7; Bede, *A History of the English Church and People*, trans. L. Sherley-Price (Harmondsworth, 1955), I.15, p. 56; *Two of the Saxon Chronicles Parallel*, ed. C. Plummer, 2 vols. (Oxford, 1892–1899), entries for 449–473, pp. 12–15. T. D. Kendrick's *British Antiquity* traces the rise and fall in reputation of Geoffrey of Monmouth's *Historia*.

such thing'. Middleton followed Geoffrey in representing Hengist and his company 'as banished their country' by lot. In discussing the origins of the Picts, Selden warned Drayton against relying on Geoffrey of Monmouth: 'the Print in that and much other mistakes . . . the grosse differences of time make all suspicious; so that you may as well beleeve none of them as any one'. His advice is 'Rather adhere to learned *Camden*'.[17]

Hengist himself, however, had acquired a degree of historical credibility by having been named, with Horsa, in Bede's *Historia* as leaders of invading Germanic tribes, and the *Anglo-Saxon Chronicle* recorded a series of battles that he fought in Kent, at one of which Horsa is said to have been slain. William of Malmesbury, writing of *The Kings before the Norman Conquest*, referred to the battles mentioned by the Anglo-Saxon chronicler and recorded Hengist's daughter acting as cup-bearer to Vortiger, but made no mention of the massacre of the British lords on Salisbury plain. Holinshed was well aware that the various chronologies of Bede, the *Chronicle* and of Geoffrey's *Historia* did not correspond. He retold the story so as to include as many of these narratives as possible, while pointing out that there were substantial discrepancies between his sources: 'William of Malmesbury writing of this Vortimer, or Guortigerne, and of the warres which he had against the Saxons, varieth in manner altogither from Geoffrey of Monmouth, as by his words here following ye maie perceiue'.[18] Holinshed thus alerted Middleton to the doubtful status of the material he was dramatizing, and part of the playwright's purpose in presenting Raynulph Higden, a monkish chronicler, as the play's narrator, may have been to defuse criticism of its accuracy by deliberately emphasizing its legendary nature (Higden was the author of the *Polychronicon*, a fourteenth-century history that included topographical material, though Middleton seems only to have known it by reputation). His antiquity was not intended to confer authenticity so much as to introduce an element of the picturesque, following the theatrical precedent set by John Gower who acts as Chorus and interpreter of the dumb-shows in Shakespeare's *Pericles*, speaking in a stiff, archaic

[17] Hebel, *Works of Michael Drayton*, IV, pp. 91 and 161.
[18] William of Malmesbury, *The Kings before the Norman Conquest*, trans. J. Stephenson (repr. Lampeter, 1989), pp. 9–10 (sections 6–8); Raphael Holinshed, *The Historie of England* (London, 1587), ch. 4, p. 80.

four-stress metre, much as Higden does in Middleton's play. Although Middleton's interest in the history of the Anglo-Saxons was strictly limited, he recognized that the status of the material he was using was that of legend, rather than history: for him, its dramatic appeal lay in the repeated contests for kingship and rule in ancient Britain, and what the stories of such contests might be made to mean to audiences during the reign of James I. This gave him a freer hand, but not a wholly different purpose from that of the age's more scholarly historians.

The widespread Elizabethan interest in chorography, the history of places, is reflected throughout the play, manifesting itself particularly in the curious topographical specificity of its subtitle, 'The Mayor Of Quinborough', the title under which it was widely known and first printed by Henry Herringman in 1661. Queenborough is the main town on the Isle of Sheppey: it had been founded by Edward III with a mayor and two burgesses, when he built a garrison above it in 1386. The comic sub-plot lends specificity to the more general references to Kent. Late in the play, Symon, the mayor of Queenborough, plays upon the proverbial phrase 'in Kent and Christendom', when he insists that the 'the king of Christendom' is not more welcome to him than Hengist, king of Kent, adding, by way of explanation to the audience, in case they had missed the point, that the Saxons were, however, not yet Christians:

> For you must immagine now neighbors this is
> The time yt Kent stands out of Kirsondom
> For he thats King there now was never Kirsond;   (V. i. 44–46)

This kind of frame-breaking explanation was familiar from medieval Mystery plays. Middleton followed William Lambarde's *Perambulation of Kent* (1569) in locating Hengist's stronghold, Tong Castle (named by Vortiger at III. iii. 334), near Sittingbourne in Kent. Geoffrey of Monmouth had linked Hengist's settlement with Virgil's tale of the founding of the citadel of Carthage on as much ground as could be encompassed by a bull's hide,[19] naming his castle 'Thanceastre' (vi. 11). Tong Ceastre or Tong Castle had traditionally been located in Lindsey, but since the *Anglo-Saxon Chronicle* recorded Saxon invasions of Thanet and Kent, and the earliest battles had taken place there, Lambarde claimed Tong Castle in northern Kent as a more probable site for

---

[19] 'Taurino quantum possent circumdare tergo', *Aeneid*, I. 368.

Hengist's stronghold, on the basis of 'common opinion (conceived upon report, received of the elders by tradition)'. He even identified its site: 'the ditch and ruines of this olde Castle do yet appeere at Tong Mill where you may see the water drayned from the Castle ditch, to serve the corn Mill.'[20] The town of Queenborough is not far from Tong as a side-note to Fabyan's *Chronicles* also observes, though Fabyan also located Tong Castle in Lindsey.[21] Curiously, access to Queenborough, and the island as a whole, was via the King's town of Middleton, or Milton on the mainland (Sheppey was technically within the Hundred of Milton), and while no firm links have been established, Middleton's family may well have come from there, ultimately.

The sub-plot of Middleton's play concerns Symon the Tanner whose hide provided Hengist with his thong and who later, in a development that parallels and comments on the struggle for power in the main plot, competes for the mayoralty of Queenborough with Oliver the Puritan Weaver. The tanning industry is introduced early on by the presence of a fellmonger among a group of working men who petition the King in Act I, scene ii. Various explanations have been advanced for this oddly precise location of the sub-plot: 'Quinborow', as it was often spelled and pronounced, suggests a bawdy quibble on 'quim'. More interestingly, Heinemann has argued that the play's events allude to the disputed election of MPs at Queenborough, which began late in 1620 and rumbled on for some years, though it would certainly have been topical when the play was written.[22] From 1605, when Philip Herbert became Baron Herbert of Shurland (a large estate on Sheppey), the Herbert family had links with the island. In 1615, his elder brother William, third Earl of Pembroke, became patron of the King's Men, for whom the play was almost certainly written;[23] in the following year, Philip Herbert was appointed Constable of Queenborough Castle. His predecessor in this post had been Sir Edward Hoby, a former MP for Queenborough, who in the same year, 1616, had written an anti-Catholic pamphlet that took the form of a dialogue between the mayor, the minister and a learned rustic,

---

[20] William Lambarde, *Perambulation of Kent* (London, 1576), pp. 221–2; see also pp. 225–8.

[21] Bald, ed., *Hengist*, p. xxxviii.

[22] Heinemann, *Puritanism and Theatre*, pp. 144–8.

[23] Bald, ed., *Hengist*, p. xiv.

one Nick Groom,[24] and this may well have been known to Middleton. The pamphlet was probably provoked by the smuggling of Catholic propaganda into England via Sheppey, though it may also allude to an earlier dispute over tithes between the Minster church on Sheppey (formerly part of the Abbey) and that at Queenborough, in 1607, when citizens complained to the King at having to pay dues to the Minster when they employed their own curate. The initial success of Symon the Tanner in being elected mayor, and his subsequent humiliation at the hands of the players/cheaters parallels the initial success of Vortiger and his deception by the Saxons, by Roxena and Hersus, and by Hengist's pretended truce at Salisbury plain.

Topical references in the sub-plot may have functioned to alert the audience to the way that national history influences present and future destinies, connecting itself to the present time either through analogy, or through ancient blood ties: thus Shakespeare's *Macbeth* alluded to James I's ancestors and descendants through Banquo and the line of kings that sprang from his loins. *Lear*, like *Gorbaduc* in the previous century, had dramatized the threat of the divided kingdom and the disinherited child, while *Cymbeline* celebrated the triumphs of peace-making, where 'Pardon's the word for all'. Like Shakespeare, Middleton wrote chiefly for the King's Men, and, though his sympathies were often with Protestant disapproval of courtly extravagance, in 1618 he celebrated James's efforts to unify England and Scotland with an anti-duelling pamphlet, *The Peace-maker*. In *Hengist* the association of kings with peace-making is picked up by St Germanus, the missionary priest who, accompanied by Bishop Lupus, counsels the monk Constantius in the play's early scenes, advising him that it is his duty to leave the monastery because

> Who's borne a Prince is borne for generall peace
> Not his owne onely, heaven will looke for him
> In others buisnes, and require him their;          (I. i. 101–3)

Constantius replies that heaven has provided his brothers to preserve the country's peace, but in the end he is forced to forgo his hopes of private peace in favour of the claims of public service. The word 'peace' is repeated four times in the course of a twenty-five line discussion (I. i.

---

[24] J. Briggs, 'Middleton's Forgotten Tragedy *Hengist, King of Kent*', *RES* NS 41 (1990), pp. 493–5.

101–26). Constantius's sense of oppression in royal office recalls that of James who similarly suffered from

> . . . noyse and paines
> Clamors of suitors, iniuryes and redresses,
> Millions of riseing actions with the sun,
> Like laws still ending and yet neuer Dun. (I. i. 141–4)

One major change Middleton made in adapting this material to the King's sensibilities took the form of an omission, rather than an addition: in all the various versions of the story, the Picts had played a key role. According to Geoffrey of Monmouth, it was Constans's bodyguard of Picts who murdered him (vi. 7–8) and it was Pictish anger at Vortigern's slaughter of the bodyguard in revenge that prompted their retaliation (vi. 9), so that Vortigern's need for military support against them guaranteed Hengist and his mercenaries a warm welcome. Middleton knew from his sources that Vortiger, whether he had summoned the Saxons or not, had gratefully accepted their help in fighting off the Picts; he had drawn on Holinshed's detailed account of the British wars against the Picts in his *Historie of Scotland*, where Middleton also found the particular form of Roxena's name that he adopted. But the perfidy of the Scots, particularly of those close to the King, was hardly an auspicious topic for the King's Men to perform. Middleton's careful silence about their role may be contrasted with that of another contemporary treatment of the subject – that of Thomas Carleton's Latin tragedy *Fatum Vortigerni*, performed at the Catholic seminary in Douai in 1619. Here two of the King's guards are slain by Vortigern for their part in Constans's death, but the third escapes to become the leader of the Picts, only to be defeated and slain by Hengist in Act II.[25] This play, too, is likely to have included contemporary political allusions, probably to the treachery of the Scots, though the marriage of Vortigern to Ronix (Carleton's variant form for Roxena) seems to refer to the marriage of Henry VIII and Anne Boleyn, disastrous from a Catholic point of view.

Vortiger did not merely fail to unite the kingdom, he actually broke it

---

[25] *Fatum Vortigerni* is London, British Library, Lansdowne 723. It is usefully summarized by G. R. Churchill and W. Keller in 'Die lateinische Universitats-Dramen in der Zeit der Königen Elisabeth', *Shakespeare Jahrbuch* 34 (1898), pp. 258–64. The identity of the author was pointed out by W. H. McCabe in a letter in the *TLS*, 15 August 1935: see Bald, ed., *Hengist*, pp. xxiii.

up, surrendering whole regions of it to the Saxons. After the Salisbury plain massacre, Hengist forced Vortiger to declare him King of Kent, a title whose oddity resonates in the title of the play:

> Never was King of Kent yet
> But who was generall King                   (IV. iii. 105–6)

objects Vortiger. 'I'le be ye first then, / Euerything has begining' replies Hengist, adding that he also wants Norfolk and Suffolk thrown in for good measure. Although the invaders were finally defeated, with Hersus slain and Hengist captured, the Saxon conquest of England which brought with it the overthrow of 'the Religion, Lawes, Language, and all'[26] was only temporarily deferred.

For all its chroniclers, religious difference was considered a crucial aspect of the Saxon invasion. In Middleton's version, Vortiger initially refuses to grant land to Hengist and his Saxons on the grounds that they are 'misbeleevers' (II. iii. 9):

> But for y'are strangers in religion Cheifly,
> Wch is ye greatest alienation Can bee,
> And breeds most factions in ye bloods of men
> I must not grant you that.                   (II. iii. 34–7)

In the wake of the Reformation, difference of religion was recognized as a potential threat, and the Protestant Church compared itself to the early Church in respect of foreign persecution. Bede (and Gildas) had explained the Saxon invasion as a punishment ordained by God for the people's weakness, an interpretation that would have struck a familiar note in the early seventeenth century.[27] For those Protestants who had been driven into exile by Mary Tudor and her Spanish consort, men like John Foxe and John Ponet, there was a further analogy to be drawn: Vortiger's marriage to Hengist's daughter was for Foxe 'an example to all ages and all countries what it is first to let in foreign nations into their dominions but especially what it is for princes to join marriage with infidels'. Ponet in *A Shorte Treatise of politike power* enlarges upon Ronix's role in placing her own countrymen 'nyghest the kyng, . . . in all offices and holdes, and

---

[26] Samuel Daniel, *The Collection of the History of England* (London, 1634), p. 9.
[27] Bede, *History of the English Church*, i.15, pp. 56–7; Gildas, *The Ruin of Britain*, esp. sections 21, 22, pp. 24–6.

at leyngth the lande was ouerrunne and possessed of Straungers'.[28] The dangers of foreign marriages, so vividly present to the Marian exiles, became a renewed threat as James the Peace-Maker attempted to establish dynastic marriages for his children with both Protestant and Catholic royalty in Europe. With his daughter married to a Protestant prince, he attempted to marry his son Charles to the Catholic Infanta of Spain, and when this highly unpopular initiative failed, he arranged for him to marry the French princess Henrietta-Maria, with consequences no less disastrous for Charles than they had been for Vortiger.

Middleton's play added significantly to existing versions of the Saxon invasion by giving full exposure to the dangerous nature of exogamic marriage: Roxena, Hengist's daughter and Vortiger's second wife, is contrasted with his former wife Castiza, a 'character' name Middleton had previously used in *The Phoenix* and *The Revenger's Tragedy*. In the play's final moments, Castiza is identified with Truth (V. ii. 276), and by extension with the true Church, while Roxena becomes an emblem of Falsehood. Her figuring as the Scarlet Woman of Babylon becomes explicit when she reveals to Vortiger her secret love affair with Hersus, begun before they left Germany (and the only addition to the plot that is wholly and characteristically Middleton's invention).[29] Hersus, after an initial pang of jealousy, helps Vortiger to marry Roxena by persuading him to violate his own wife, to abduct and rape her while she is blindfolded, and then accuse her of unchastity, a device Hersus describes as not only cunning, but also fashionable, 'A spring to Catch a Maidenhead after sunsett' (III. i. 195).[30]

---

[28] John Foxe, *The Acts and Monuments*, I. p. 320, cited Briggs, 'Middleton's Forgotten Tragedy', pp. 488–9; John Ponet, *A Short Treatise . . .* sig. l2v., cited A. A. Bromham, 'Thomas Middleton's *Hengist, King of Kent* and John Ponet's *Shorte Treatise of politike power*', *N&Q* NS 29 (1982), p. 144.

[29] Traditionally Hengist and Horsa were brothers, but Middleton avoids the further complication of incest between uncle and niece which this would have introduced (though this situation is present in *Women Beware Women*). Castiza's father and uncle, the Earls of Devon and Stafford, oppose Hengist and Hersus in such a way as to suggest their possible equivalence, as Vortiger's good counsellors.

[30] Inge-Stina Ewbank explores the meaning of this episode in her article '"O Cunning Texture to Enclose Adultery": Sexuality and Intertextuality in Middleton's *Hengist, King of Kent*', in *Heart of the Heartless World: Essays in Cultural Resistance in Memory of Margot Heinemann* ed. D. Margolies and M. Joannou (London and Boulder, Colo., 1995), pp. 180–94.

In the play's final scene, Roxena dies, crowned with flames that reveal her true nature:

> oh mysticall harlott
> Thou hast thy full due, whom Lust Crownd queene before
> Flames Crowne her now, ffor a trivmphant whore.   (V. ii. 199–201)

Castiza, as Truth, renews her marriage with the kingdom by becoming betrothed to Constantius's brother, the conquering Aurelius Ambrosius.[31] The play's final words serve as a warning against the threat of heresy, and the moral turpitude associated with it:

> As I begine my rule with the distruction
> Of this ambitious Pagan, so shall all
> With his adulterate faith distaind, and soild,
> Either turne Christians, dye, or liue exild.   (V.ii. 286–9)

These lines, along with a substantial number of others, have been cut from the printed quarto of the play, presumably because they were politically provocative. Middleton was inclined to sail close to the wind, as the storm over *A Game at Chess* or the extensive cuts marked on the manuscript of *The Second Maiden's Tragedy* indicate. In *Hengist*, the rightful king Constantius is portrayed as a man of high principles, sharply distinguished from the tyrant Vortiger, who is characterized by his opportunism, ambition, lust and gullibility. Such a separation of the ideal of kingship from the frailties of tyranny would later characterize the rhetoric of the Civil War. In Middleton's version, the legend also registers popular resistance to foreign oppression, though the voice of the people is ignored or despised by Vortiger, and they are defeated by the Saxons.[32]

The sub-plot draws a self-conscious distinction between theatrical experience and real life, as Symon the Mayor insists on watching the travelling players perform before allowing them to act before King Hengist, in case they enact sedition.

[31] The two coronations, of Roxena with flames and of Castiza with the rightful crown, recall the two contrasting ceremonies of homage to the Lady that end Middleton's *The Lady's Tragedy*, also known as *The Second Maiden's Tragedy*, ed. A. Lancashire (Manchester, 1978), at V.ii.13 and 200.

[32] Middleton's sympathetic presentation of the people is discussed by Heinemann, *Puritanism and Theatre*, pp. 138–9, and more recently by S. Chakravorty, *Society and Politics in the Plays of Thomas Middleton* (Oxford, 1996), pp. 124–5.

Sym: a play may be dangerous, I have knowne a greate man poysond in a play
Glov: What haue you Mr Maior?
Sym: But to what purpose many time I know not
Fell: Me thinks they shold destroy one another soe
Sym: No no, he thats poysond, is allwayes made privy too it.     (V. i. 147–52)

Although Symon shows himself more sophisticated than the other artisans in recognizing the play as a representation rather than reality, what ought to have been a crucial distinction is invalidated almost immediately, since the players turn out to be the common thieves they play, and their theft is in earnest. As well as performing a play about deception, they also perform an actual deception, robbing Symon by throwing meal in his eyes and stealing his purse and his silver spoons. The difference established between dramatic representation and reality is thus erected only to be collapsed. The comic moral, like the serious one, reminds the audience that old legends should not be too readily dismissed, and may even carry within them the seeds of truth, or foreshadow coming events. In which case the subsequent history of Charles I's disastrous foreign marriage and his rejection of the will of the people could be seen as bearing out Middleton's exemplum from Anglo-Saxon history.[33]

[33] I would like to thank Professor Martin Biddle and Dr David Stocker for their help with this essay.

121

# Crushing the convent and the dread Bastille: the Anglo-Saxons, revolution and gender in women's plays of the 1790s

## JACQUELINE PEARSON

This essay will examine the intersection of three significant cultural trends of the late eighteenth century which are not normally considered together: the rise in importance of women as producers and consumers of literature; a vigorous British response to the events of the French Revolution and its aftermath; and an increasing interest in Anglo-Saxon history and literature.[1] These trends coincide in a small group of plays of the 1790s, and I shall deal especially with Ann Yearsley's *Earl Goodwin* (begun in 1789, staged in Bristol in 1791 and published in the same year) and Frances Burney's *Edwy and Elgiva* (begun in 1788, and repeatedly revised until its London performance of 1795, and unpublished until the twentieth century).

Mainstream English literature in the sixteenth to eighteenth centuries seems surprisingly uninterested in Anglo-Saxon history. With one partial exception, which I shall examine later, Shakespeare's history plays move

---

[1] For women and literary culture in the period see especially A. K. Mellor, *Romanticism and Gender* (London, 1993). For the impact of the French Revolution on British literature, see R. Paulson, *Representations of Revolution (1789–1820)* (New Haven, 1983); I. R. Scott, 'Things as they Are: the Literary Response to the French Revolution 1789–1815', *Britain and the French Revolution*, ed. H. T. Dickinson (London, 1989), pp. 229–49; *Reflections on Revolution: Images of Romanticism*, ed. A. Yarrington and K. Everest (London, 1993); R. Hole, 'British Counter-Revolutionary Popular Propaganda in the 1790s', *Britain and Revolutionary France: Conflict, Subversion and Propaganda*, ed. C. Jones (Exeter, 1983), pp. 53–69; and *Revolution in Writing: British Literary Responses to the French Revolution*, ed. K. Everest (Milton Keynes, 1991). For the rise of Anglo-Saxon studies, see H. Aarsleff, *The Study of Language in England, 1780–1860* (Princeton, 1967).

straight from the Britain of *King Lear* to the medieval England of *King John*, and other seventeenth- and eighteenth-century dramatists are more likely to find subjects in Roman, Greek, or even Turkish history than in Anglo-Saxon. In the late eighteenth century, and especially the 1790s, however, the Anglo-Saxons again became significant in the cultural agenda.

From the mid-eighteenth century a 'renewed interest in national origins'[2] produced both historical texts like Percy's *Northern Antiquities* (1755) and early Romantic poems creating images of a Celtic, medieval or Anglo-Saxon past.[3] It is not accidental that this movement achieved its climax in the revolutionary 1790s and their aftermath, for it was accelerated by its political usefulness in defining an idealized, stable and virtuous English nationalism in opposition to the disorder in France. Oxford had an endowed Chair of Anglo-Saxon from 1795, Sharon Turner's pioneering *History of the Anglo-Saxons* began publication in 1799, and editions in Old English of the whole of *Beowulf* and of the *Anglo-Saxon Chronicle* first appeared in 1815 and 1823 respectively.[4] Anglo-Saxon themes and settings also became more frequent in poetry, fiction and drama, providing a symbolic vocabulary to define an (of course anachronistic) English nationalism before contamination by the Norman French, or to examine events across the Channel. The Germanic Anglo-Saxon monarchs of history also supplied useful analogies for the Germanic Hanoverian dynasty.

The Whig view of history emphasized the 'freedom' of Anglo-Saxon Britain before the invasion by the Norman French, so that 'Anglo-Saxon . . . political freedom' is contrasted with 'French . . . tyranny'.[5] Conservatives like Burke and radicals like Paine, although they were locked in a bitter ideological struggle over the British Constitution and the French

---

[2] Aarsleff, *The Study of Language*, p. 5.

[3] James Macpherson (1736–1796) published *Fingal. An Ancient Epic Poem*, allegedly by the Celtic bard Ossian, in 1762. Thomas Chatterton (1752–1770) was the author of many poems on Celtic, medieval and Anglo-Saxon themes, and indeed is best known for his forgeries of the work of the alleged medieval poet Thomas Rowley: Anglo-Saxon poems include 'Goddwyn. A Tragedie', 'Cerdick, translated from the Saxon', 'Ethelgar, A Saxon Poem', and 'Kenrick' (all published in 1769: *The Complete Works of Thomas Chatterton*, ed. D. S. Taylor in association with B. B. Hoover (Oxford, 1971), pp. 294–305, 276–9, 253–5 and 274–5).

[4] Aarsleff, *The Study of Language*, pp. 170, 167–8, 164 and 173.

[5] M. Kilgour, *The Rise of the Gothic Novel* (London, 1995), pp. 13–14.

Revolution, to a surprising extent shared a political vocabulary in which the Anglo-Saxons figured liberty and the Norman French oppression (though their attitudes to later history, especially Magna Carta, are very different).[6] While Yearsley accepted this Whiggish history in which the Anglo-Saxons figured a Golden Age when the structures of power were amenable to popular opinion, Burney adopts the more pessimistic history of David Hume, in which 'English culture and institutions began with the Norman conquest',[7] and the retrograde power of vested interests destroys the embryonic constitutional monarchy of Edwy.

The Anglo-Saxons, then, became significant in a continuing discourse on nationalism and revolution: but class and gender were also vital elements in this discourse. For women writers of all political persuasions, the Revolution had, by unsettling traditional hierarchies, reopened for debate their own place in those hierarchies, and they tend to use imagery drawn from the Revolution quite explicitly to discuss gender issues, and vice versa. Radical Mary Wollstonecraft describes a heroine 'bastilled . . . for life' in unjust marriage laws, and conservative Maria Edgeworth fears that women's reading of radical French and German texts will effect a disruptive and undesirable *'revolution in public opinion!'*.[8]

Women writers did not have a monopoly on Anglo-Saxon themes and imagery, but they found them especially useful for a number of reasons. Women were of course excluded from higher education, in which Greek and Latin learning were central: they would therefore always be at a disadvantage in the themes of classical history and literature which held such high status in the dominant culture. Frances Burney was a keen reader of Greek and Roman history and literature in translation, but she always felt an anxious sense of trespassing on male prerogatives unless she made it absolutely clear that she was not transgressing the limits of femininity by reading the learned languages.[9] It is significant that the most popular works by women in the 1790s are what have been called 'Gothic' novels, a consciously counter-classical mode of semi-historical

---

[6] R. Miles, *Ann Radcliffe: the Great Enchantress* (Manchester, 1995), p. 61.

[7] Aarsleff, *The Study of Language*, p. 170.

[8] Mary Wollstonecraft, *Maria; or, the Wrongs of Woman* (1798), in *Mary and the Wrongs of Woman*, ed. G. Kelly (Oxford, 1980), p. 155; Maria Edgeworth, *Leonora* (1806), see *The Novels of Maria Edgeworth*, 12 vols. (London, 1893), III, p. 10.

[9] See, for example, *The Early Journals and Letters of Fanny Burney*, ed. L. E. Troide et al. (Oxford, 1988– ), I, p. 95.

discourse in which women simultaneously described and evaded patriarchal authority.

Classical study might cause anxiety to women anxious to remain faithful to traditional ideologies of gender, but they needed to have fewer inhibitions about working in Anglo-Saxon history. The example of Elizabeth Elstob, one of the first editors of Anglo-Saxon texts, who died in 1756, not only legitimized women's entry to literary discourse through the medium of Anglo-Saxon, but also defined Anglo-Saxon itself as a feminized discipline, 'our Mother Tongue', and therefore entirely 'proper' for scrutiny by 'the FEMALES'.[10]

Neither Yearsley's *Earl Goodwin* nor Burney's *Edwy and Elgiva* is a history play in the fullest sense of the term. Neither is much interested in creating a culture of the past with revealing differences in expectation or world-picture from our own, and although as we shall see Yearsley very briefly considers the problems of reading and writing history, Burney does not. For both, the Anglo-Saxons are only interesting in so far as they provide a vehicle for intense emotion and an oblique way of dramatizing the politics – gender politics as well as global politics – of their own day. Their Anglo-Saxons speak an idiom and display manners virtually indistinguishable from any other contemporary dramatic characters. This can become dangerously comic, especially in Burney's play, whose virtuous characters discourse in the exaggerated idioms of sentimental fiction, creating a sometimes bizarre disjunctive effect, as if Byrhtnoth were to meet Sir Charles Grandison. Contemporary commentators were satirical at the expense of an episode in Act V, when the mortally wounded heroine is brought from behind a hedge, and although the location is 'remote from any dwelling', she has nonetheless managed to find 'an elegant couch' on which she is allowed to expire gracefully.[11] This lack of 'period' feel, though, is by no means unusual in late eighteenth-century drama, and suggests again that the plays' real subjects are the dilemmas of their own day, the historical setting merely an indirect means for examining urgent contemporary issues.

Neither author seems to have read much Anglo-Saxon history. The

---

[10] Elizabeth Elstob, *The Rudiments of Grammar for the English-Saxon Tongue* (London, 1715), p. ii, title-page.

[11] Cited by Peter Sabor in *The Complete Plays of Frances Burney*, 2 vols. (London, 1995), II, p. 77. This edition of the play will be used for references in the text.

major factual source for Burney seems, as I have said, to be Hume's *History of England*. Yearsley, a poor labouring woman, had limited access to books (though she may have known Chatterton's Anglo-Saxon poems[12]): but Burney was fond of history, and began reading Hume in 1768, at the age of sixteen. While Yearsley was aware of how history could be distorted by groups with vested interests for propagandist purposes and consequently distrusted it,[13] Burney tends to take at face value its claims to retail an unproblematic truth.[14]

A more important source for everything but the basic facts is, however, Shakespeare, a vital resource for all women writers of the period. Both plays show constant echoes of Shakespearian tragedy, especially *King Lear* and *Macbeth*. *Edwy and Elgiva* has assassins plainly based on the murderers in *Macbeth*, and reaches a climax specifically based on *King Lear*, with the dying king crying, 'Look there! Look there!' over the body of his queen (V.xxiii.11). Yearsley's *Earl Goodwin* uses its Shakespearian sources more creatively, and functions as a kind of inverted *Macbeth*. Edward the Confessor, in *Macbeth* a marginal figure who represents all the goodness and good kingship missing in the (unEnglish) eponymous hero, appears in Yearsley's play as a 'passive' and weak 'bigot' (p. 4), under the thumb of the Catholic church and little more than a lackey of Norman power. His inability to rule England rightly necessitates and justifies the rebellion of Goodwin, who is no Macbethian traitor but a patriot working for the good of his country. Similarly the play's women characters, Edward's mother Emma and his wife, Goodwin's daughter Editha, represent, unlike Lady Macbeth, positive values of domesticity and loyalty.

Both Burney's *Edwy and Elgiva* and Yearsley's *Earl Goodwin* deal with contemporary issues thinly veiled in Anglo-Saxon garb. Both use historical events, for instance, to express a late eighteenth-century distrust of Roman Catholicism. The role of Catholics within English society was controversial in the period, from the Catholic Relief Act of 1778 to the Emancipation Bill of 1829, most visible in the anti-Catholic Gordon

---

[12] See below, p. 135.     [13] See below, p. 133.

[14] For Burney's early reading of Hume, see, Troide, *The Early Journals*, I, p. 40; for her naivety about historical 'truth', see Troide, *The Early Journals*, I, p. 13. The children of Charles Burney were raised to respect historical truth as unproblematic: a great-nephew preferred history to fiction because histories 'prove what they tell' (E. J. Morley, 'Sarah Harriet Burney, 1770– 1844', *Modern Philology* 39 (1941), p. 138.)

Riots of 1780. Both plays show the power of the (Catholic) church as imperilling nationalism and civil rule, and in both plays the power of the monks is contrasted with secular and (anachronistically but by implication) Protestant government. Dunstan in Burney's play uses the power of the church to further his own ambitions for 'supreme authority' (I.ix.34), and the result is disastrous for England. Goodwin, Saxon England's last hope for survival, is poisoned by a monk to preserve papal authority. In both plays a virtuous, secular, English, monarchy is shown to be morally superior to, but also dangerously at risk from, the forces of multinational Catholicism.

The most important area of contemporary politics that lies behind the thin surface of Anglo-Saxon history in these plays is the French Revolution – as is the case with virtually all English literature of the 1790s. Burney and Yearsley both wrote about the Revolution, openly and indirectly, and in the early 1790s Burney was much preoccupied with its immediate practical consequences, publishing *Brief Reflections Relative to the Emigrant French Clergy* in 1793, the same year in which she married a French emigré, Alexandre d'Arblay, who was to assist her in the revisions of *Edwy and Elgiva*.[15]

Yearsley's play belongs to, in Allene Gregory's terms, the first phase of English engagement with the revolution in France, when the English people were cautiously sympathetic with French aspirations for a more equal society where the arbitrary power of the *ancien regime* and the Catholic church would be replaced by a juster form of government,[16] possibly 'a constitutional monarchy on the British model'.[17] The epilogue of *Earl Goodwin* (not by Yearsley) sympathizes with the 'poor Frenchman' who breaks free from 'slavish, tyrant, priestly fetters' and 'Crushes the convent and the dread Bastile' (p. 91), a revealing juxtaposition. (Another regional working-class writer, James Maxwell, reads the fall of the Bastille as evidence of 'GOD'S Almighty pow'r' sweeping away the 'pollution' of the 'arbitrary' rule of king, 'Aristocracy and Priesthood'.[18]) Yearsley was radical in her political outlook: Burney was not only by ideology and

---

[15] Burney used the Revolution as the background to her last novel, *The Wanderer* (1814); see below, p. 132. For Yearsley's poems on revolutionary themes, see below, n. 28.

[16] A. Gregory, *The French Revolution and the English Novel* (London, 1915), p. 221.

[17] Scott, 'Things as they Are', p. 231.

[18] James Maxwell, *On The French Revolution: a Moral Essay* (Paisley, 1792), pp. 7, 11 and 4.

temperament more conservative, she was also producing the final draft of her play in 1795, after the declaration of war between Britain and France and the execution of the French king and queen in 1793, which decisively alienated much British opinion from the Revolution.

Both plays, then, use images from Anglo-Saxon history to make political points about the French Revolution. While Yearsley is highly critical of George III and in support of the first phase of the Revolution, Burney is more conservative, admiring George III and seeing any challenge to the power of the monarchy as potentially disastrous: in the Prologue to her play, written by her brother Charles, Englishmen are warned to keep 'Church and State from innovation pure' (48). Her epilogue ends by drawing specific analogies with the contemporary political scene. Edwy has brought doom on himself by marrying, in defiance of canon law, his cousin Elgiva and has thus gained the hatred of the fanatical and powerful monk Dunstan. The epilogue presents a coming royal marriage as having all the virtues of that of Edwy and Elgiva without its dangers. Caroline of Brunswick, 'the fair Kinswoman of our Royal Race' (61), is celebrated as a new Elgiva, and her marriage with her cousin the future George IV is welcomed by 'every British heart' (66). (Burney is, of course, hopelessly over-sanguine in her estimate of this marriage. Caroline may have been Elgiva but George was no Edwy, and indeed in his conflict with his father his role was more like that of Edgar in the play, the heir to the throne who takes arms against his royal kinsman.)

Although both plays use history to examine contemporary issues, neither should be seen as programmatically allegorical. In Burney's play in particular different levels of meaning are clearly meant to function simultaneously, sometimes to the detriment of overall coherence. Thus Edwy 'is' Louis XVI, seeing his people rise against him and his beloved wife slandered and attacked. But his distraction also links him with George III, the first phase of whose 'madness', in 1788–1789, coincided so exactly with the genesis of the play. The central male character thus becomes Edwy/George/Lear, driven mad by suffering and the ingratitude of his people: the play both laments the fall of Louis and warns England to value its own rulers. More damaging to the ideological coherence of Burney's play, Dunstan is sometimes an embodiment of a conservative and repressive Catholicism, sometimes of popular radicalism and revolution, both forces which Burney sees as threatening English stability as they have already threatened France, but not identical or even compatible, and so working against a coherent conception of this major character.

Frances Burney (1752–1840), daughter of musicologist Charles Burney, is better known as a novelist and diarist. Her four novels, beginning with *Evelina* in 1778, were highly influential in rendering the novel a respectable and legitimate form for women writers and readers. Burney also, though not so successfully, wrote eight plays. Her comedies are vigorous, well-plotted and actable, though she allowed herself to be persuaded by family and friends that it was unsuitable for a respectable woman to be known as a writer of comedy, and so none was published or performed in her lifetime. Only *Edwy and Elgiva* even got as far as performance, playing for one night and then sinking into oblivion.

Burney imbibed conservative principles in the home of her father. To please him, she accepted in 1786 an appointment as Keeper of the Robes to Queen Charlotte, and until 1791 was part of the royal entourage at Windsor, thoroughly miserable in an environment where she was always lonely but could never be alone. Unable to read or write sustainedly enough to begin a new novel, she turned to plays, and produced a series of tragedies whose real subject is her own misery and the political uncertainty of the day. *Edwy and Elgiva* emphasizes suffering, loneliness, and an intense but frustrated desire for an ordinary domestic life: this, coupled with the fact that its composition proved 'almost spontaneous',[19] suggests its special private meaning for her. Interestingly, all the tragedies of this period deal with early English history – *The Siege of Pevensey* and *Hubert de Vere* are set in the reigns of William Rufus and King John respectively, and the fragmentary *Elberta* is another Anglo-Saxon play which, like *Edwy and Elgiva*, focuses on the difficulties and dangers of achieving domestic happiness in the courts of kings.

I suspect Burney's unusual preoccupation with Anglo-Saxon history had something to do with her ambivalence about the household of the German king and queen where she was both privileged and enslaved. She loved the Queen and the princesses, but she bitterly missed her own family and space for her own work, and she hated the stultifying rituals of court life. *Edwy and Elgiva* implicitly praises the German king and queen

---

[19] Sabor, *The Complete Plays*, II, p. 7; for Burney's plays, see also J. Hemlow, 'Fanny Burney: Playwright', *University of Toronto Quarterly* 19 (1949–50), pp. 170–89; M. A. Doody, *Frances Burney: the Life in the Works* (Cambridge, 1988), esp. pp. 150–98.

and follows the contemporary propaganda of the royals by associating them with family values and the domestic virtues. At the same time the protracted suffering of Edwy and Elgiva also punishes George and Charlotte for their confinement of the writer and her imagination. In this sense at least the play might be read as personally subversive while politically compliant. In her life at Windsor Burney had imagined herself 'confined . . . in the Bastile': even her political conservatism could not prevent rebellious, even treasonable, dreams of 'liberty'.[20]

*Edwy and Elgiva* deals with the end of the reign of King Eadwig, who died in 959. His marriage to his cousin Ælgifu was unpopular because of their consanguinity, and Dunstan in particular opposed the king for his resistance to the authority of the church and to the ecclesiastical reforms he intended. At his command Ælgifu was kidnapped, mutilated and murdered, and Eadwig died in battle, to be replaced by his more tractable brother Edgar. As I have said,[21] Burney got the historical facts from Hume, the dramatic style from Shakespeare. The story, indeed, was relatively well-known in popular literature for women at the turn of the century, appearing in *The Lady's Magazine* for 1772 and *The Lady's Monthly Museum* for 1799. Like Burney's, these accounts focus on the 'inhuman' treatment of Elgiva by the 'crafty bigot' Dunstan whose 'boundless ambition' leads him to seek any means to maintain his 'authority'.[22]

Burney's Dunstan is an unprincipled, ambitious demagogue who foments a popular rebellion against the naive Edwy and the saintly Elgiva. As a result 'the people rise/ In clamrous multitudes, and call for Dunstan' (IV.ix.2–3), and as in France 'the tumult spreads/ From Class to Class', until the result is 'Civil War' against the king (IV.xx.2–3, 6), which brings about a 'revolution' (IV.xix.69) equally damaging to the state, the family and Edwy's mind. Dunstan talks a great deal about 'right(s)' and 'Reason' (e.g. I.ii.34, I.xi.65, II.iv.15, III.v.44, etc.), and the resemblance to French revolutionary rhetoric is surely deliberate. Dunstan's name perhaps reminded Burney of Danton, and the character is deeply coloured by her attitude to the populist revolutionary leader who was executed in 1794, as the play was being revised.

If Dunstan 'is' Danton, the innocent, tortured queen Elgiva, young,

[20] Doody, *Frances Burney*, p. 193.     [21] See above, pp. 124 and 126.

[22] *The Lady's Monthly Museum* 3 (1799), p. 3; *The Lady's Magazine* 3 (1772), pp. 497–8.

beautiful, but victim of a damaging smear-campaign, torn from her husband and brutally murdered, can hardly fail to evoke the image of Marie Antoinette, especially the sentimentalized image of the queen which plays a key role in counter-revolutionary propaganda like that of Edmund Burke, himself an admirer of Burney's work.[23] Edwy too recalls Louis XVI, a young but well-intentioned monarch whose only faults are 'inexperience' and consequent 'credulity' (I.x.1–2), and who is certainly reminiscent of some popular conservative English treatments of the French king.[24] Moreover, Edwy's willingness to let 'the Votes of my united people' (I.ix.92) determine his fate recalls Louis's original support for the Estates General. James Maxwell's 1792 poem, for instance, had ended with the king consenting to the 'noble effort' of the first stage of the Revolution, which he welcomes for preserving the nation's 'rights and liberties' (p. 15).

The box-office failure of Burney's play is understandable. *Edwy and Elgiva* is a powerful, painful play, but it is too private, too static and too repetitive, for effective drama, and it arrives at an emotional climax too early and cannot sustain it for five acts. There is fairly little action in the play, which consists of a number of highly emotional confrontations between Dunstan and Edwy and between Edwy and Elgiva. In contemporary fiction tactics of 'repetition and replication become powerful ways' in which women writers create, explicitly or implicitly, 'women's sense of oppression'.[25] Burney makes these tactics of repetition work more effectively in the novel form and in contemporary settings, and indeed the vacillating Edwy, who loves Elgiva but hurts her, is a parallel but less complex version of the heroes of her later novels, especially Mortimer Delville in *Cecilia* (1782) and Edgar Mandlebert in *Camilla* (1796). The latter novel, which she was writing while revising *Edwy and Elgiva*, emphasizes the ambiguity of its hero by giving him a name derived not only from the hero of *King Lear* but also from the anti-hero of her own tragedy, who betrays his brother as Edgar Mandlebert betrays his foster-sister Camilla by his inconsistent behaviour and unjustified suspicions.

Elgiva likewise resembles the heroines of Burney's novels, especially

[23] For Marie Antoinette in Burke's counter-revolutionary writings see V. Sapiro, *A Vindication of Political Virtue: the Political Theory of Mary Wollstonecraft* (Chicago, 1992), pp. 192–4.

[24] See, for example, *The Lady's Magazine* 26 (1795), p. 141.

[25] E. Ty, *Unsex'd Revolutionaries: Five Women Novelists of the 1790s* (Toronto, 1993), p. xii.

Cecilia, Camilla, and Juliet in *The Wanderer* (1814). Mary Russell Mitford disliked Burney's novels because she 'degrades her heroines in every possible way, bodily and mental'.[26] Certainly in these novels Burney emphasizes the suffering of her heroines, and indeed tends to identify female suffering with female virtue. The same is true in exaggerated form in the play, where the tormented Elgiva becomes an icon of faultless, persecuted femininity, defined indeed by her suffering – 'Sweet Sufferer!' (V.iii.27), 'Royal Sufferer!' (V.viii.11), 'Spotless victim!/ . . . all innocence – all excellence' (V.iii.45–6). In her last novel *The Wanderer* Burney frames the suffering of her idealized heroine directly by the French Revolution: Juliet has, to save her foster-father, been forced to marry a revolutionary officer, but she succeeds in escaping him and fleeing to England. In this 1814 novel, however, Burney is less confident of the evident superiority of Anglo-Saxon society, and Juliet's suffering and humiliation as she attempts to make a living are no less intense than Elgiva's and more realistic.

*Edwy and Elgiva*, then, paints a vivid and disturbing picture of popular insurrection and its destruction of order, true religion, love, innocence and family life. Elgiva is a suffering saint meant to recall Marie Antoinette, Edwy a virtuous but inexperienced young man like Louis XVI, Dunstan a Danton whose demagogy achieves power but kills his own soul. The play thus gives a conservative, even in the case of Antoinette/Elgiva a hagiographical, perspective on the events in France and, through the medium of Anglo-Saxon history, warns the English people of the consequences of French revolutionary politics.

Ann Cromarty Yearsley (1752–1806) is an intriguing figure, a working-class woman poet, novelist and dramatist who, despite her use of a similar history and a similar tragic structure, presents a view of the politics of her age very different from that of the conservative Burney. A milk-woman from Bristol, Yearsley published her first collection of poems in 1785 under the auspices of arch-conservative Hannah More, but quarrelled with her because of her heavily paternalistic attitudes (and, perhaps, political differences). The French Revolution, with its opportunities for class restructuring and a new social justice, attracted and interested her, to the extent that she is personally attacked alongside such

---

[26] *The Life of Mary Russell Mitford*, ed. Revd A. G. Lestrange, 3 vols. (London, 1870), II, p. 62.

radicals as Mary Wollstonecraft, Mary Robinson and Charlotte Smith, in a conservative poem, Richard Polwhele's *The Unsex'd Females* (1798), because she has abandoned 'nature' and her natural place in society for the espousal of a dangerous revolutionary politics (p. 20).

Yearsley's novel, *The Royal Captive* (1795), retells the story of the Man in the Iron Mask, which it uses to attack the *ancien regime* for its institutionalization of class and gender inequalities. The lower classes are sympathetically and believably depicted, and so are some individual aristocrats, but it is clear that abuses can no longer be resolved, as Hannah More believed, on the basis of individual benevolence.[27] Only revolution, however appalling a prospect this might be, can hope to cleanse society and return power to where it rightfully belongs, the people figured in this novel as the true king who has been raised as a peasant.

A similar cautious backing for a revolutionary agenda can be found in Yearsley's Anglo-Saxon play, *Earl Goodwin*. The play aims to defend the *'injured reputation'* of Goodwin, described in the Preface as 'this noble earl', who had been a victim of calumny because history has been written by the very monks he opposed. Yearsley's attitude to historiography is more combative and sceptical than Burney's. Goodwin, the father of Harold and Tostie, feels he has no alternative but to rebel against Edward the Confessor, whose court is dominated by priests and Normans who 'wrest/ The nation's statutes with o'er-wheening pride,/ Daring our hopeless Saxons' (p. 2). The ill-treatment of his daughter Editha by her husband Edward also contributes to Goodwin's rebellion.

Goodwin is conceived as the representative of English ('Saxon') nationalism against the oppressive Normans: he claims, for instance, that 'England speaks by me' (p. 41), and on the eve of battle invokes the 'Great genius of our isle' (p. 35) to provide 'Redress for England' (p. 36). Goodwin's Eurosceptic agenda contrasts with Edward's use of 'Saxon' as a term of contempt (pp. 31 and 44) and his identification of his interests with the Normans and the Vatican rather than with England. Goodwin is also the voice of 'the people' who protest against economic and moral abuses (p. 39). As a result of the popular insurrection led by Goodwin,

---

[27] Hannah More, *Village Politics. Addressed to all the Mechanics, Journeymen, and Day Labourers, in Great Britain, by Will Chip, a Country Carpenter*, 2nd edn. (London, 1792), p. 4, where the solution for the nation's ills is that 'every one [should] mend one' – i.e. himself.

Edward is made aware of the true state of England, and king and people are reconciled, as many Britons – like James Maxwell quoted above, p. 131 – optimistically thought would be the result in France of the fall of the Bastille. So far a limited revolution seems to have paid off: its first phase (the equivalent of the storming of the Bastille) is shown to be not only inevitable but wholly positive.

But the lessons of history teach Yearsley that revolutions do not end with that first phase. Goodwin's faction is deeply divided: Tostie, the 'valiant but ferocious Saxon' (p. 49), ambitious for power and hating 'vile inglorious peace' (p. 49), fights his brother Harold and leaves for the continent, renouncing the 'ties/ Of nature' and family loyalty (p. 51). Moreover, the church is not prepared to lose its power, and the Archbishop of Canterbury orders the murder of Goodwin, who is poisoned by the monk Lodowicke (the historic Godwine died in 1053; Stenton[28] makes no reference to poison). Yearsley's play ends ironically poised for the loss of all that Goodwin has fought for: Harold's short reign and the return of Tostie will leave the field open for the conquest of the Norman William (as the moderates in the French Revolution were to fall before Robespierre and the Reign of Terror).

Yearsley's play adroitly balances two, apparently incompatible, purposes. On the one hand, it gives voice to a working-class English nationalism by defending the English 'Saxon' against 'Norman' French oppression and Roman superstition – not only conservatives in the 1790s sought to 'demonise the "Other"' by 'figuring it as foreign'.[29] On the other hand, *Earl Goodwin* also defends, and perhaps recommends for English emulation, the first stage of the French Revolution. While real personages – Danton, Louis, Marie Antoinette – can be seen below the surface of Burney's play, this seems less true of Yearsley's. Goodwin is no real individual but a perfected, anglicized, leader of a revolution that might have been. Revolution is dangerous, the tide of history may destroy its achievements, and the virtuous moderate is always in danger from extremists of both sides (as the example of the French Revolution was all too vividly to show). But passive acceptance of the *status quo* might be even more dangerous under an autocratic and bloodthirsty government: a bitter footnote to the play attacks 'our *Most Gracious*

---

[28] F. M. Stenton, *Anglo-Saxon England* (Oxford, 1943), p. 418.
[29] Miles, *Ann Radcliffe*, p. 156.

*Sovereign George III'* (p. 90) for an intemperate use of the gallows as an instrument of social control.

In 1789–1791, Yearsley could afford to write sympathetically of the revolution, and even in 1795 in *The Royal Captive* she uses a historical context and historical analogy to attack the arbitrary power of the *ancien regime*. But after the executions of Louis XVI and Marie Antoinette, like many other radicals,[30] she clearly felt the need to distance herself from its excesses, and she wrote poems sympathizing with the 'Ill-fated Louis' and the 'Much injur'd Beauty' the Queen.[31] But these poems have a half-hearted quality and lack the hysterical edge of contemporary conservative writings: even these terrible acts of violence do not for the working-class poet discredit the revolutionary struggle for social justice.

Burney apparently accepts Hume's view that English culture began with the Norman conquest, and her Anglo-Saxons, in the words of the play's Prologue by her brother Charles, live in 'Mystery's gloom and Errors Maze', as did all England between the 'primitive simplicity' of the Celtic church and the Protestant Reformation (lines 16, 15). Yearsley, on the other hand, like other linguistic and political radicals, identifies pre-Conquest culture with 'Anglo-Saxon liberty' and freedom from the 'Norman yoke':[32] with an idealized democratic English nationalism under threat both in the eleventh and the eighteenth centuries.

An important source for this radical view of the Anglo-Saxons is the fragmentary tragedy by a fellow Bristol poet, Thomas Chatterton's 'Goddwyn . . . bye Thomas Rowleie' (1769). Yearsley certainly knew Chatterton's work; her *Poems on Various Subjects* (1787) contains an elegy on him (pp. 145–60). In 'Goddwyn', Chatterton writes in the person of a medieval poet dramatizing an Anglo-Saxon past, and it is likely that, like Yearsley, he was really writing not about the eleventh but about the eighteenth century, with Edward the Confessor's tyranny figuring that of George III, and Godwin and Harold as patriot leaders.[33]

---

[30] See Scott 'Things as they Are', pp. 236–7.
[31] Yearsley, *Reflections on the Death of Louis XVI* (1793), p. 6; *An Elegy on Marie Antoinette of Austria, Ci-Devant Queen of France* (1793), p. 5.
[32] Helen Maria Williams, *Letters Written in France in the Summer of 1790* (1790), cit. G. Kelly, *Women, Writing and Revolution 1790–1827* (Oxford, 1993), p. 37. See also James Ingram's *Inaugural Lecture on the Utility of Anglo-Saxon Literature* (1807), cit. Aarsleff, *The Study of Language*, p. 17.
[33] Taylor, *The Complete Works*, p. 973.

One issue remains: both Burney and Yearsley, keenly aware of the disadvantages faced by women in late eighteenth-century society, make gender a key issue in their Anglo-Saxon plays. In both plays the family is the crucial arena in which its conflicts are played out: this politicization of domesticity is a central feature of women's writing of the 1790s.[34] Women are thus allowed access to the discourses of nationalism and revolution because those discourses are both mirrored and rooted in the family.

Both plays begin by asserting the primacy of family relationships. In *Edwy and Elgiva* the marriage between the central characters embodies the play's most important moral values. 'Domestic' is a key word in the play (e.g. I.ix.8, I.xi.49, III.iv.58, etc.), and Dunstan's worst crime is his assault on the values of domesticity. 'Home' is 'Man's dearest right' (III.iii.40), even for a king, and without 'Equality; which Wedlock solely gives' (III.iv.28) the King cannot carry out his onerous and lonely task. In Burney's play the watchwords of the French Revolution, liberty, equality, fraternity, are feminized and reclaimed for traditional values. Thus freedom means not revolution but 'choice' (I.ix.13) in private relationships, 'Equality' (III.iv.28) the domestic union of husband and wife, and fraternity the virtuous consanguinity of the hero and heroine which only the violent revolutionaries led by Dunstan oppose. The destruction of this marital relationship figures the destruction of civil rule in England: Elgiva's tortured body is also the body of England (or, metaphorically, of revolutionary France).

Yearsley's Goodwin is, like Edwy, the spokesman for domestic values as opposed to the sterile celibacy of Edward and the priests, and their attack on domesticity has disastrous effects both for individual women and for the nation. In *Earl Goodwin* the conflict between a corrupt theocracy and a virtuous secular government is played out by the male characters over a number of female bodies – the body of England who 'shall on her breasts feel iron-footed war' (p. 65), of Queen Emma, forced to undergo the ordeal of red-hot ploughshares, and of Editha, abandoned by her husband because he is persuaded by his confessor that even 'sanctified' marital love 'dissolves the soul,/ And drags her views from heaven!' (p. 4). In a play whose women are both virtuous and 'dare [to] think' (p. 27), the

[34] See Ty, *Unsex'd Revolutionaries*, p. xi; K. Sutherland, 'Hannah More's counter-revolutionary feminism', *Revolution in Writing*, ed. Everest, esp. pp. 36–8.

misogyny of church and king is self-evidently foolish: as a footnote tells us, 'Edward's concepts of female excellence are narrow and resulting from ignorance' (p. 20). Yearsley also indulges in a good deal of Macbethian wordplay over such words as 'manly': Tostie accuses his more humane brother of behaving like a 'woman', but is told by Harold that 'Barbarity' is not manliness but 'Cowardice' (p. 50): indeed 'pity' is more 'manly' than cruelty, and Emma's wisdom is 'more . . . than manly' (p. 60).[35] Both plays chart the disastrous consequences of the breakdown of the family, of the torment both literal and metaphorical of the female body, and of a language that equates manliness with barbarity.

The Anglo-Saxons undergo some strange metamorphoses in these plays, but they prove an important resource for the woman writer. Among other things, they give an effective oblique language for dangerous political material that was by law literally unspeakable in performance: the epilogue to *Earl Goodwin* was cut by order of the Lord Chamberlain, and the lines about the Bastille were excised. The Anglo-Saxons give utopian or monitory images for English political life, may represent a democratic Golden Age or a dark night of superstition and disorder, and provide a language either for criticizing revolutionary France or for sympathizing with the dilemma of the moderates. Perhaps most strangely – although in the light of recent research about the power and independence of Anglo-Saxon women both real and fictional, perhaps not so strangely after all[36] – they provide a gallery of strong and virtuous female characters and a framework for what was of most urgent interest to women writers of the 1790s: the politics of domesticity.

---

[35] This interrogation of words like 'manly' can also be seen in *Eduy and Elgiva* (e.g. I. xi. 28–30).

[36] E.g. C. Fell, *Women in Anglo-Saxon England* (Oxford, 1986); *New Readings on Women in Old English Literature*, ed. H. Damico and A. H. Olsen (Bloomington, 1990); and H. Damico, *Beowulf's Wealhtheow and the Valkyrie Tradition* (Madison, 1984).

# Anglo-Saxon attitudes?: Alfred the Great and the Romantic national epic

## LYNDA PRATT

In 1801 the leading radical poet Robert Southey gave his non-literary friend Charles Biddlecombe his private opinion of two recent publications:

Have you seen Cottles *Alfred?* I do not advise you to buy it – nor the Laureate['s, Henry James Pye's poem of the same name] which is shorter and dearer – in good rhymes and deadlily dull.[1]

The works that he was so very pointedly failing to recommend both had the same title – *Alfred, an Epic Poem.* The first, in which Southey was probably more involved than he cared to admit, was by his loyal friend and early publisher Joseph Cottle, and appeared in 1800.[2] The second, published less than a year later in 1801, was by Henry James Pye, the ex-politician who had held the post of Poet Laureate since 1790.[3] As their identical titles suggest, both poems were epics (though Cottle's work was about twice as long as Pye's), both had as their central, heroic figure Alfred the Great, and both concentrated on exactly the same period in the Anglo-Saxon king's career (his retreat to the isle of Athelney and his eventual defeat and conversion of the Danish invaders). Moreover, there is another, less commendable, similarity between the two texts. From a late twentieth-century perspective, Southey's negative judgement of both seems to have been right. Neither *Alfred* is part of the canon, and Cottle and Pye have, respectively, suffered from either ridicule or total neglect.

Yet, if we return to the late eighteenth and early nineteenth centuries, a very different picture emerges. In 1800–1802, both poems were very

---

[1] *New Letters of Robert Southey*, ed. K. Curry, 2 vols. (New York, 1965), I, p. 246.
[2] J. Cottle, *Alfred, an Epic Poem in Twenty-Four Books* (London, 1800).
[3] H. J. Pye, *Alfred; an Epic Poem, in Six Books* (London, 1801).

widely reviewed and accorded a status and a significance that more recent criticism has overlooked.[4] The pro-government periodical the *Anti-Jacobin Review* devoted over twenty pages spread over three separate issues to Pye's *Alfred* – more space than it gave to any other epic poem of the period.[5] Its analysis concluded by comparing the Poet Laureate very favourably to Homer and prophesying that 'his success will place him in the foremost ranks of the poets of his day'.[6] Cottle's poem also received its fair share of praise. The *British Critic* described it as 'an ingenious and very commendable performance' and the *Gentleman's Magazine* acknowledged the poet's wisdom in choosing to write on 'one of the most fruitful subjects in our own or perhaps in any other language', in other words, on Alfred the Great.[7]

The reviews therefore offer another, much more positive and potentially productive, way of reading, or rereading, Cottle and Pye's epics. They simultaneously demonstrate the benefits gained by placing these poems within their public literary and critical context and also raise a series of crucial questions. Why did Cottle and Pye, two authors who came from totally different social, educational, political and literary backgrounds, who lived in different parts of the country, and who never met or corresponded with one another, almost simultaneously produce epic poems on the same subject? Why should contemporary critics of these poems have assigned an importance to them which later writers have overlooked? And what can a rereading of these two neglected epics tell us about British literature, and indeed British society, in those crucial years at the turn of the eighteenth century?

In writing about Alfred the Great, Cottle and Pye had chosen a historical figure who, by the late eighteenth century, was already an integral part of national history and of a growing, increasingly articulate and articulated national consciousness – a monarch who was part of the

---

[4] *Critical Review* 31 (1801), pp. 160–71 (Cottle's *Alfred*); *Critical Review* 34 (1802), pp. 361–70 (Pye's *Alfred*).

[5] *Anti-Jacobin Review and Magazine* 9 (1801), pp. 232–4, 340–7; *Anti-Jacobin Review and Magazine* 10 (1801), pp. 12–21.

[6] *Anti-Jacobin Review and Magazine* 10 (1801), p. 20.

[7] *British Critic* 16 (1800), p. 614; *Gentleman's Magazine* 70 (1800), p. 975. The author of the latter review lamented the fact that Cottle had not written a 'Life of Alfred' and noted the whereabouts of manuscripts and materials of help to a biographer of the Anglo-Saxon king (*ibid.* p. 975).

national myth. For Cottle and Pye and their contemporaries, Alfred was widely acknowledged as the lawgiver *par excellence*, the father of the British constitution and of the British navy, the reviver and patron of learning and literature, the ideal Christian monarch, an accomplished scholar and poet, and, above all, the founder of the British nation and preserver of its inherent liberties from the ravages of Danish invaders.[8] However, his status as the pre-eminent example of heroic Christian kingship was in fact very much an eighteenth-century phenomenon. The Anglo-Saxon king was quite literally the creation of the age.

Although Alfred had received occasional positive mentions in seventeenth-century literature – the republican Milton had praised him, and the royalists Robert Powell and Obadiah Walker had compared Charles I and Charles II to him – his reputation had been subordinated to that of Edward the Confessor.[9] By the early to mid-eighteenth century this situation had changed and, as Christopher Hill has observed, Edward was 'entirely eclipsed by Alfred'.[10] The reasons for this transformation in Alfred's reputation and significance are complicated and somewhat obscure. Firstly, it might have owed something to the greater availability of material on his life. Secondly, from the accession of George I in 1714, it was undoubtedly connected to the Hanoverian, Protestant succession. The new monarchs eschewed the idea of sacramental kingship promoted by the Stuarts and, as a result, may have been uneasy at taking the saint-king Edward as their role model. Nevertheless, the very real threat posed by Jacobitism required the new dynasty to promote both its legitimacy and its Britishness. One way of doing this was to proclaim their own lineal descent from Alfred. The propaganda potential of this strategy was demonstrated in 1723, when Richard Blackmore dedicated the first attempt at an English epic poem on the Anglo-Saxon king, *Alfred: An Epick Poem in Twelve Books*, to the Prince of Wales's son, *'the Illustrious*

---

[8] Alfred the Great's reputation in the late eighteenth century was succinctly described in *Gentleman's Magazine* 70, p. 975: 'Alfred has been very justly ranked as one of the most shining characters in the pages of our National History; as a legislator, second to none; a warrior, the first in battle; a philosopher, equal to his favourite Boetius; a poet among poets, the restorer of learning, and the patron of science.'

[9] C. Hill, *Puritanism and Revolution. Studies in Interpretation of the English Revolution of the Seventeenth Century* (1958; London, 1990), p. 101.

[10] *Ibid.*, p. 101.

*Prince Frederick of Hanover*.[11] Blackmore's poem, with its description of the childhood adventures and education of Alfred the Great, quite literally offers up the Anglo-Saxon monarch-hero as the ideal educative model for the young Hanoverian prince, the boy on whom the future hopes of Britain itself rest.

Dynastic imperatives aside, Alfred's increasing popularity also owed much to his flexibility as a political and cultural symbol. As the eighteenth century showed, he could be, and was, appropriated by individuals with very different political affiliations. In the 1730s the patriot opposition to Robert Walpole reincarnated him as the ideal Gothic patriot hero, the 'Founder', as the inscription on a statue commissioned by Prince Frederick, now Prince of Wales and a fierce opponent of his father George II and his chief minister Walpole, put it, 'of the Liberties and Commonwealth of England'.[12] By the 1790s, in the aftermath of the French Revolution of 1789 and with the outbreak of war between France and Britain and her allies in 1793, his significance had changed yet again. As the decade leading up to the publication of Cottle and Pye's epics showed, Alfred could be, and was, used as a potent symbol in the patriotic rhetoric of both sides – both those who supported the Revolution and those who opposed it. He was an essential component in the debate on the nature of patriotism and, by extension, on the nature of Britishness itself.

Myths about the Norman yoke and the ancient Anglo-Saxon liberties embodied in Alfred's constitution played key roles in the political theory

---

[11] R. Blackmore, *Alfred: An Epick Poem In Twelve Books* (London, 1723). Its significance is discussed in C. Gerrard, *The Patriot Opposition to Walpole: Politics, Poetry, and National Myth, 1725–1742* (Oxford, 1994), p. 117. Comparisons between members of the house of Hanover and Alfred continued to be made throughout the eighteenth century, though not all were potentially flattering. The anonymous author of an 'Exhortatory Ode to the Prince of Wales, on his entering his thirty-fourth year', warned the future George IV that only if he reformed his dissipated lifestyle would 'A second ALFRED rise in Thee – / The best of earthly kings', *Cambridge Intelligencer*, 29 August 1795.

[12] Gerrard, *Patriot Opposition*, pp. 116–17. Later eighteenth-century fictional works that made use of the Anglo-Saxon king included J. Home, *Alfred. A Tragedy* (Dublin, 1777), E. Rhodes, *Alfred, an historical tragedy, to which is added a collection of miscellaneous poems by the same author* (Sheffield, 1789), and Anon., *Sketch of Alfred the Great; or, the Danish Invasion, a Ballet* (London, 1797[?]). See also above, pp. 11–13.

and discourse of radical writers of the 1790s.[13] The king could readily be invoked by anti-government writers such as the young Samuel Taylor Coleridge as a shining example of a radical definition of nationality:

I must confess, my heart . . . experienced a proud delight when I found that Count RUMFORD was an ENGLISHMAN. The recent rejection of the Bill for the abolition of the Slave-trade, had well nigh cured me of this fond partiality. – The countryman of Alfred, of Milton, and of Sydney, I blushed for my birth-place, and imagined a kind of contamination in the name of Briton. But no! the title shall still be high in honour among the nations of the world – HOWARD and RUMFORD were both BRITONS.[14]

Alfred's flexibility as a political symbol is amply demonstrated by Coleridge's completely unconscious lack of irony in placing the monarch next to his seventeenth-century republican heroes Milton and Algernon Sydney.

Yet Alfred could also be used as the defender of more conservative values. Indeed the exigencies of the age allowed him to be conjured up in support of anti-revolutionary politics. As the anonymous *Letters of the Ghost of Alfred* (1798) explained in its address to the leading opposition politician Charles James Fox and to the lawyer Thomas Erskine (who in 1794 had successfully defended a group of prominent London radicals against the charge of High Treason), the shade of the king had returned to 1790s Britain in order to:

---

[13] Hill, *Puritanism and Revolution*, pp. 98–113. Significantly, Cottle's description of the invading, imperialist Danes as 'Normans' (*Alfred* (1800), p. 211), invokes both the Scandinavian ancestry of the later Norman invaders and the radical version of the yoke theory.

[14] *The Collected Works of Samuel Taylor Coleridge*, Bollingen Series 75: 2 *The Watchman*, ed. L. Patton (London, 1970), pp. 175–6. Coleridge might well have considered writing an epic poem on Alfred the Great. D. Wu, 'Cottle's *Alfred*: Another Coleridge-inspired epic', *Charles Lamb Society Bulletin* NS 73 (1991), pp. 19–20, notes how the Anglo-Saxon king's suitability as subject matter for an epic was proposed to Coleridge by Richard Poole on 3 May 1796, and suggests that the former passed on the idea to Cottle. Coleridge's imprecision in his use of the terms 'Englishman' and 'Briton' was shared by the majority of his English contemporaries, including Cottle and Pye, though greater sensitivity to definitions of national and regional identity would have been observed by his Scottish, Welsh or Irish peers. For the complexities and contradictions involved in eighteenth-century definitions of Britishness, see M. G. H. Pittock, *Inventing and Resisting Britain: Cultural Identities in Britain and Ireland, 1685–1789* (Basingstoke, 1997).

correct the irregular, indecent, and unconstitutional practices of those advocates, who seem to have taken a general retainer for the domestic . . . enemies of the country: – to lay open the wiles and artifices of French revolutionary treason: – to rescue trial by jury from the fallacies and false doctrines, by which factious and seditious men seek to render it, not only a shelter for the worst of crimes, but an engine of destruction to the constitution itself . . . to exhibit, in just colours, the unexampled profligacy of the same desperate party, in extolling, patronizing, and promoting, that horrid and destructive system of revolution and anarchy, which has already proved the most dreadful scourge that ever afflicted the human race, and which threatens to lay the whole fabric of civil society in ruins.[15]

In the *Letters* the past, in the person of Alfred, literally speaks to the present, and the interconnection of the two is made very clear. Alfred becomes once again the heroic defender of the nation, and of the institutions which history attributes to his making. But this time the enemy is not the marauding Danes but a combination of treacherous, unpatriotic British fifth columnists and French revolutionaries. His ghost therefore provides both a series of public rebukes to the radical cause and a potent reminder of the ancient structures that will be lost forever if the radicals are allowed to win. The lesson offered is that the Anglo-Saxon past is not dead and forgotten, but alive and relevant – that patriotic Britons, as the heirs of Alfred, should treat his legacy with respect and defend it against all those who, like the French revolutionaries and internal opponents of the British government, would 'lay the whole fabric of civil society in ruins'.[16]

The message given by radical and conservative writings from the 1790s is that Britons should look to, rediscover and appropriate their own past in order to learn the inherent truths about themselves and their own natures – to reveal what it was to be a true Briton. The process was not

---

[15] Anon., *Letters of the Ghost of Alfred. Addressed to the Hon. Thomas Erskine and the Hon. Charles James Fox, on the Occasion of the State Trials at the Close of the Year 1794, and the Beginning of the Year 1795* (London, 1798), quoted in *Anti-Jacobin Review* 1 (1798), p. 64. This was not the only use of the Anglo-Saxon king in 1790s epistolary propaganda. Five years earlier Sir James Bland Burges had adopted the pseudonym of 'Alfred' and produced a volume entitled *Alfred's Letters; or a Review of the political state of Europe to the end of summer 1792. As originally published in the Sun* (London, 1793). The political significance of the epistolary form in the late eighteenth century is discussed in M. A. Favret, *Romantic Correspondence: Women, Politics and the Fiction of Letters* (Cambridge, 1993).

[16] Anon., *Letters of the Ghost of Alfred* (1798), quoted in *Anti-Jacobin Review* 1 (1798), p. 64.

confined to explicitly political literature. It also informed the writing of history itself. In the Prefaces to his immensely detailed and influential four-volume *History of the Anglo-Saxons*, published between 1799 and 1805, Sharon Turner defended his work upon subjects and manuscripts which some people might regard as barbaric and therefore unworthy. As he explained, his researches into early history were not intended just to please 'the idle curiosity of a dull antiquary'.[17] Instead, if read properly, they offered a picture of the origins of British society and of Britishness – they literally put the reader in touch with his true ancestors:

We roam the most distant oceans, to explore the manners of uncultivated savages, and even the philosopher reads, with interest, every description of their customs and transactions. Why should he then despise the first state, and the improving progress of his Saxon ancestors? This nation exhibits the conversion of ferocious pirates, into a highly civilized, informed, and generous people – in a word, into ourselves. Can it be frivolous to depict the successive steps of this admirable change?[18]

Chief amongst these ancestors was Alfred the Great himself:

Amid this nation, in the ninth century, a man [Alfred the Great] arose who may be compared with the proudest names of antiquity, without disgracing them by his society. Can such a character be unworthy of the contemplation of the reflective?[19]

In Turner's view, and in his reclamation of the Anglo-Saxon past, Alfred both takes his place amongst the great heroes of world history and becomes, as in more explicitly political writings from this period, a potent national symbol. In the late 1790s and the first decade of the 1800s, a period dominated by the rise of Napoleon and by fears of imminent invasion by the French (something briefly and bloodily realized in Ireland in 1798), the Anglo-Saxon king's suitability as national icon was capable of satisfying both an apparent and an urgent necessity.[20] His heroic struggle against the Danish invaders could stand as a symbol for the very topical subject of British resistance against France. Moreover, Alfred's successful defence of his country offered a model to his British descendants.

---

[17] S. Turner, *The History of the Anglo-Saxons*, 4 vols. (London, 1799–1805), II, p. xii.

[18] *Ibid.*, II, p. xii.  [19] *Ibid.*, II, p. xii.

[20] The formation of national identity in this period is discussed in L. Colley, *Britons: Forging the Nation, 1707–1837* (Yale, 1992).

The dilemma facing writers of the 1790s and early 1800s was how to make their contemporary audiences aware of Alfred's true significance. History and political propaganda offered two possible opportunities for achieving this end, but a third, possibly even more potent and culturally significant one, was presented by poetry, particularly by turning Alfred into the hero of a new, national epic poem. The need for a national epic had been articulated by William Hayley as early as 1782. His *Essay on Epic Poetry*, written only some twenty years after the publication of the Celtic heroic poems of Ossian, had claimed that the most interesting subjects for a new epic were to be found in English history, and that 'the great desideratum in English literature' was a truly national epic poem.[21] Although he did his utmost to encourage his fellow poets to produce epics, Hayley very pointedly refused to do so himself. Instead, describing himself as a 'friend to Art' rather than an 'Artist', he conveniently transferred the task of producing the great English epic to his good friend William Mason.[22] Mason did not oblige but other authors did and, by the first decade of the nineteenth century, Hayleyesque complaints about the dearth of native epic poets had been well and truly superseded by comments, complaints and witticisms as to their frequency. As the radical John Thelwall rather self-pityingly observed in the Preface to his own attempt at a medieval epic ('Specimens of the Hope of Albion; or, Edwin of Northumbria', published in 1801), times had changed, and he now found 'the press teeming, and perhaps, the public already satiated with NATIONAL HEROICS, which, when his principal work was first projected, was *a desideratum* in English Poesy'.[23] By 1801 the outpouring was such that the *Poetical Register* actually set aside a separate section for reviews of what it described as 'Epic and Historical Poems'.[24] Indeed, the same year saw not only the publication of Pye's *Alfred*, but also the appearance of two other epics on national themes, John Ogilvie's *Britannia: a National Epic Poem in Twenty Books* and Sir James Bland

---

[21] W. Hayley, *An Essay on Epic Poetry* (London, 1782), p. 96. The epic revival of the late eighteenth century, and Hayley's influence on it, are discussed in S. Curran, *Poetic Form and British Romanticism* (Oxford, 1986), pp. 158–79.

[22] Hayley, *Essay*, pp. 112–16.

[23] J. Thelwall, *Poems Chiefly Written in Retirement* (Hereford, 1801), p. xliii. 'Specimens of the Hope of Albion' was finally published in *ibid.*, pp. 176–202.

[24] *Poetical Register* 1 (1801), pp. 357–9.

Burges's *Richard the First*.[25] It was undoubtedly not coincidental that 1801 was also the year of the Act of Union between Britain and Ireland. This generic glut was somewhat wearily summed up by the anonymous *Monthly Review* of Pye's poem, with the laconic comment 'The Public have lately been presented with a sort of Series of Epic poems'.[26]

Cottle and Pye's works were therefore not unique in terms of their interest in 'NATIONAL HEROICS', but their choice of subject matter was, as the majority of their reviewers observed, especially 'fruitful and patriotic'.[27] Alfred the Great was, after all, a much more savoury hero than the crusading, absentee monarch Richard I. As his presence in the political, historical and cultural consciousness of the period suggests, an epic on Alfred offered a coalescence of a national subject (the Anglo-Saxon king) with a nationalistic genre (the epic), and therefore an end-product which was the cultural embodiment of Britishness. By implication, such a poem also promised to transmute its author into the national epic poet – a British Homer or, indeed, a new Milton. It was from this context that Cottle and Pye's strikingly different epics emerged.

Pye's *Alfred* was published in 1801, a few months after Cottle's. Its author came from a conventional background – that of an impoverished, university-educated gentleman with literary ambitions, a man whose parliamentary career had failed and who had been given the Laureateship as a reward for his loyalty to his political master William Pitt. Pye's poetry reflected his social and political conservatism. Amidst all the political upheavals of the 1790s, the Laureate was solidly on the side of the loyalists. His translation of *The War Elegies of Tyrtaeus, Imitated: and Addressed to the People of Great Britain*, published in 1795, about two years into the war with France, had a threefold dedication: firstly to Marquess Townshend, the father and patron of the militia; secondly to the militia

---

[25] Sir J. Bland Burges, *Richard the First, a poem: in eighteen books*, 2 vols. (London, 1801), J. Ogilvie, *Britannia: a National Epic Poem, in Twenty Books. To which is prefixed, a Critical Dissertation on Epic Machinery* (Aberdeen, 1801).

[26] *Monthly Review* 37 (1802), p. 179 n.*.

[27] Thelwall, *Poems*, p. xliii; *Critical Review* 34 (1802), p. 361. Alfred continued to attract the attention of would-be writers of epic. Although not venturing 'to call his work an epic poem, lest its title should seem to challenge a comparison with others of a more grave and exalted character', Richard Payne Knight used his poem on the Anglo-Saxon king to defend Byron's *Cain, a Mystery* (London, 1821) against charges of blasphemy and to contrast the heroic Alfred with the 'sordid selfishness' of Napoleon Bonaparte: see R. P. Knight, *Alfred; a Romance in Rhyme* (London, 1823), pp. vi, viii and xvi–xvii.

and volunteer corps of Great Britain and Ireland; and finally to Pye's old regiment, the Berkshires.[28] Three years later he followed it up with his *Naucratia; or Naval Dominion. A Poem.*[29] Published in 1798, only a year after the serious naval mutinies at Nore and Spithead, disturbances whose proximity suggests that Pye's praise of British naval power was prompted by patriotic anxiety, this poem was dedicated to George III and concluded with a rousing chorus of James Thomson's 'Rule Britannia'.[30] Thomson's poem had originally had contemporary political applications of its own. It had first appeared in his and Mallet's *Alfred*, a patriot, oppositional masque written for George III's father Prince Frederick in 1740.[31] In the changed, but equally factional, climate of 1790s Britain, Pye selected the Anglo-Saxon king as the hero of his own next major work.

The loyalist, conservative political allegiances of the Laureate's *Alfred* are apparent from its very first page. The poem is dedicated to Henry Addington, who had replaced William Pitt as prime minister in February 1801, and Pye makes it clear that he has taken his obligations both to his patron (Addington) and to his public very seriously, as befits one who is writing on 'a great national subject'. As the 'Dedication' explains:

On one thing alone I pride myself, though I am sorry to say, it is not the pride of some poets of the present day . . . in celebrating the Founder of the Jurisprudence, the Improver of the Constitution, and the Patron of the Literature of my Country, I have endeavoured to appreciate, at their just value, the important blessings we derive from each . . . I am glad to have it observed, that there appears throughout my verses, a zeal for the honour of my country; and I had

---

[28] H. J. Pye, *The War Elegies of Tyrtaeus, Imitated: and Addressed to the People of Great Britain. With some observations on the Life and Poems of Tyrtaeus* (London, 1795). As Pye confessed, the 'chief deviation of these elegies from the original, consists in the application of the exhortations to my own countrymen', (p. 19). A radical up-dating of the genre was provided in the 'War Elegy; better suited to our circumstances than the War Elegies of Tyrtaeus' appended to J. Fawcett, *The Art of War. A Poem*, 2nd edn. (London, 1795), pp. [53]-59.

[29] H. J. Pye, *Naucratia; or Naval Dominion. A Poem* (London, 1798).

[30] *Ibid.*, p. 76.

[31] J. Thomson and D. Mallet, *Alfred: a Masque* (London, 1740), discussed in Gerrard, *The Patriot Opposition*, pp. 135–6. The masque gained renewed contemporaneity in the political conflicts of the 1790s. In its issue of 26 February 1798 the *Anti-Jacobin; or, Weekly Examiner* 16 (1798), p. 122, used an epigraph taken from Thomson and Mallet's *Alfred* as a rallying call to loyalists.

rather be thought a good Englishman, than the best poet, or the greatest scholar, that ever wrote.[32]

The poem that follows is the very epitome of the conservative epic, both in terms of its style and interpretation of the genre, and in the way in which it handles its subject. One of the striking things about Pye's work is that it is almost exclusively focused upon Britain and Britons. At the centre of this epic is Alfred himself. The Anglo-Saxon monarch is the embodiment of the 'ENGLISH HERO': both lord and father of his people, just legislator, educator, great warrior, founder of British commerce and accomplished, patriotic poet.[33] He is totally dedicated to his country, vowing 'To live her guardian, or her martyr bleed', and, in return, receives unquestioning loyalty from all but one of his subjects.[34] This hero is also, as Pye's retelling of the well-known Hanoverian genealogy confirms, the direct ancestor of George III. Or rather, George III is not merely the inheritor of Alfred's British throne, he is also the modern embodiment of all of Alfred's virtues:

> And see, best glory of that patriot race,
> Her monarch [George III], Briton-born, Britannia grace;
> Loved, honour'd, and revered by all, save those
> Who, foes to Freedom, to her friends are foes.
> But foes in vain – for Anarchy's wild roar
> Shall never shake this Heaven-defended shore,
> While Freedom's sons gird Freedom's sacred throne,
> With loyal Faith's impenetrable zone.[35]

The connections are obvious. George III's struggle against revolutionary France is the equivalent of Alfred's against the Danes, and supporting the Hanoverian monarch is identical to fighting for the Anglo-Saxon king. The Alfred story therefore offers a convenient way of historicizing and commenting on the present, providing right-minded, loyalist patriots with the ultimate nationalistic justification for their support of the monarchical, governmental, and social status quo. You too, it promises the loyal subject, can uphold the traditions of your ancestors and

---

[32] Pye, *Alfred*, 'Dedication'.

[33] *Ibid.*, pp. 87–91, 101–4, 126, 132–3 and n..    [34] *Ibid.*, p. 131.

[35] *Ibid.*, pp. 98–9. The *Anti-Jacobin* commented on Pye's 'exceedingly happy' 'allusions to modern times, and modern characters', and directed readers' attention to his portrayal of the 'patriot king', *Anti-Jacobin Review* 10 (1801), p. 15.

participate in the modern day epic heroism of resistance to France. Or, as a less sympathetic reviewer, Southey, put it, the poem is testimony to 'Mr Pye's occasional attempts to put into metre the popular political phrases of the time'.[36] This includes, amongst other things, celebrating the aristocratic, landholding classes on the grounds of their Saxon ancestors' loyalty to Alfred; punishing a traitorous, Anglo-Saxon fifth columnist – the ninth-century equivalent of a late eighteenth-century English Jacobin; and justifying the 1801 Act of Union between Britain and Ireland on the grounds that it recreated a national ideal previously envisaged by the Anglo-Saxon king.[37]

If *Alfred*'s subject matter is given a loyalist slant, its style and conception of the epic genre and the epic poet are equally conservative. The poem is written in rather flat rhyming couplets and contains all the usual characteristics, or cliches, of epic writers – extended similes, catalogues of heroes and of their arms and armour, the odd battle and single combat, and two visions of the nation's future.[38] In places, as reviewers remarked, it also includes translations of scenes from Homer and rather blatant adaptations of Milton.[39] Pye therefore places himself within a well-established literary tradition – a tradition of which he, as Laureate, wishes to be the culmination. His intention, and conception of his own role as epic poet, becomes most apparent in the sixth and final book of the poem. After the climactic battle of Edington a Druid prophesies how:

> There shall, in Time's remote and distant day,
> A voice to Alfred's name devote the lay . . .
> Yet while his tongue shall chaunt, in humble strain,
> The real glories of an Alfred's reign,
> If not by Genius, fired by patriot zeal

---

[36] *Critical Review* 34 (1802), p. 370.

[37] Pye, *Alfred*, pp. 167, 212. He traces the descent of the Wyndhams, Temples and Berties from supporters of Alfred: *ibid.*, pp. 25 and n.; 125 and n..

[38] For examples see *ibid.*, pp. 41–2, 85–104, 144, 167–8 and 235–40. Cottle, from 'a persuasion that the modern writers of epic poetry have been influenced too much by custom', rejected 'machinery, battles, classical allusions, and supernatural agency' from all but the first book of his epic (*Alfred*, pp. i–ii). Southey had rejected similar traditional devices in his first epic poem *Joan of Arc*: see R. Southey, *Joan of Arc*, 2nd edn., 2 vols. (Bristol, 1798), II, pp. 11 and 16–18.

[39] Some of these borrowings are identified in *Monthly Review* 37 (1802), pp. 180–1.

For Freedom's favourite seat, for Albion's weal;
For him, though no perennial laurel bloom . . .
Yet Truth approving, sure may give one flower,
Faint though its tint, and short its transient hour.[40]

The links between this future epic and the well being of Britain are made apparent. Moreover, the druid goes on to suggest that this future bard's 'daring Muse shall soar . . ./Beyond of Grecian song'.[41] In other words that Pye will not merely be the British Homer but that he will actually outdo his great predecessor. As Southey's review sarcastically commented, this was the Laureate's one truly original contribution to the epic:

the inspired druid again strikes the prophetic string, to celebrate . . . what a noble summit to the climax! Mr Pye's publication of Alfred, an epic poem in six books! This is a species of puff for which the writer is certainly entitled to a patent: it is altogether original, never having, to the best of our knowledge, . . . been thought of by . . . any other wit.[42]

Southey's ridiculing of Pye's ambition was not the only point of view. Indeed, what he portrayed as pretentiousness, the conservative, pro-government *Anti-Jacobin Review* saw as praiseworthy patriotism, confidently predicting that, after Pye's death, 'the grateful regret of his countrymen' would ensure that his fame would be 'neither faint nor transient'.[43] Moreover, it deliberately juxtaposed Pye's loyalist epic, and his 'manly and judicious' defence of the 'good Englishman', with a very different type of contemporary heroic literature:

The weak and worthless leader of the 'Isocratists,' who makes 'liberty' a cloak for his envy, and 'truth' a cover for his malignity, will do well to consider it [*Alfred*] seriously before he insults his country a second time by an ostentatious display of the triumphs of her enemies.[44]

*Alfred* therefore offered a model which the unpatriotic poet would do well to learn from. However, as the *Anti-Jacobin* unintentionally hints, at the turn of the eighteenth century the definition of the national poem was not at all clear cut. Pye's conservative epic was not the only option. Indeed, its patriotic platitudes owed a great deal to anxiety over the presence and effectiveness of a generically and politically radical alternative.

---

[40] Pye, *Alfred*, pp. 238–9.     [41] *Ibid.*, p. 239.

[42] *Critical Review* 34 (1802), p. 369.

[43] *Anti-Jacobin Review* 10 (1801), p. 21.     [44] *Anti-Jacobin Review* 9 (1801), p. 232.

For the *Anti-Jacobin*, and other contemporary reviewers, this radical alternative was embodied in the work of Robert Southey, in particular in his *Joan of Arc, an Epic Poem*, published at the end of 1795 and re-issued in a much revised form in 1798.[45] With its French heroine, condemnation of the English hero, Henry V, and its rejection of many of the features of traditional heroic poems, *Joan of Arc* constitutes a full-scale attack on the epic and upon the nationalism latent in the genre.[46] As the *Anti-Jacobin's* review of the second edition pointed out:

> The established rule for the epic, that the subject be national, is, surely, founded on true patriotism. To this rule . . . [Southey] has acted in direct opposition, and chosen . . . the ignominious defeat of the English . . . Is there not a squint of malignity – a treacherous allusion in such a picture? And was it not rather a seditious than a poetic spirit that first contemplated the Maid of Orleans, as the heroine of an English epic?[47]

For this loyalist reviewer, Southey's anti-national epic is the product of, and testimony to, his radical, unpatriotic politics. The foreign subject-matter and self-conscious cultural and political revisionism of *Joan of Arc* may seem to be very remote from the national heroics of Pye's, and indeed Cottle's, epics, but in fact they are intimately connected. Firstly, because the conservative rhetoric of Pye's poem could be read, as the *Anti-Jacobin* pointed out, as a direct response to Southey's radical redefinition of patriotism and of the patriotic epic. Secondly, because Cottle had published *Joan of Arc* and was closely and publicly linked with his radical contemporary.

Cottle's background was very different from Pye's. He was born, and spent all of his long life, in the thriving provincial city of Bristol. Although he did not receive a classical education and did not go to university, he had a passion for reading, selling, publishing and writing

---

[45] R. Southey, *Joan of Arc, an Epic Poem* (Bristol, 1796); the revised second edition was *Joan of Arc* (1798).

[46] In the provocative 'Preface' to his epic Southey acknowledged that 'It has been established as a necessary rule for the Epic, that the subject be national. To this rule I have acted in direct opposition, and chosen for the subject of my poem the defeat of my country' (*Joan* (1796), p. vii). The poem's revisionist agenda and its centrality to British epics of the 1790s are discussed in L. Pratt, 'Patriot Poetics and the Romantic National Epic: Placing and Displacing Southey's *Joan of Arc*', *Placing and Displacing Romanticism*, ed. P. Kitson and N. Roe (forthcoming).

[47] *Anti-Jacobin Review* 3 (1799), pp. 120–1.

books, and a similar attraction towards promising young authors, particularly those who needed his help. In the 1790s he had been responsible for publishing the early works of Southey, and his friends Coleridge and William Wordsworth, and he had also consolidated his own literary ambitions, producing two collections of poetry. *Alfred* was his first attempt at writing an epic poem though, to the increasing despair of his literary friends, it was not to be his last.[48]

Cottle was both publicly and personally identified with Southey and was better informed than most about the controversial nature of the latter's experiments with the epic.[49] Yet his own epic is, at least superficially, not as radical as one might expect. Alfred, unlike the French peasant woman Joan of Arc, is a male, royal, British hero, a monarch 'justly called the great . . . who has ever been esteemed the pride and glory of the English nation', and the defender of national lives and liberties.[50] Indeed, it is very possible that the choice of the Anglo-Saxon king as the hero of the poem acts as a rebuke to Cottle's protege, or, at least, was intended to show Southey that it was very possible to write a new kind of epic on a national subject.[51]

However, *Alfred*'s surface dissimilarity from *Joan of Arc* does not mean that it is identical to Pye's epic. Cottle's portrayal of the Anglo-Saxon king is, in many ways, the total opposite of the Laureate's. This Alfred is torn much more obviously between love of his family and duty to his country. He is a warrior who dislikes battle and who, even when he is at his most hostile to the Danish invaders, urges his troops to be merciful and to treat their enemies as fellow human beings – something which Pye

---

[48] For evidence of his friends' responses to Cottle's *Alfred*, see *Collected Letters of Samuel Taylor Coleridge*, ed. E. L. Griggs, 6 vols. (Oxford, 1956–1971), I, p. 645, and *The Letters of Charles and Mary Anne Lamb 1796–1821*, ed. E. W. Marrs Jr., 3 vols. (Ithaca, NY, 1975), I, p. 236. Cottle's later epics included *The Fall of Cambria* (London, 1809) and *Messiah: a poem* (London, 1815).

[49] Cottle's massive preface to *Alfred; an Epic Poem in Twenty-Four Books*, 2nd edn., 2 vols. (London, 1804), I, pp. ix–l both confirms his literary allegiances and defends himself and his friends against hostile critics. Cottle later capitalized on his friendships with his better-known contemporaries in his *Early Recollections chiefly relating to the late Samuel Taylor Coleridge*, 2 vols. (London, 1837) and *Reminiscences of Samuel Taylor Coleridge and Robert Southey* (London, 1847).

[50] Cottle, *Alfred*, p. 39 n. 3.

[51] Curran, *Poetic Form*, pp. 168–9.

would have undoubtedly found unthinkable.[52] Moreover, Cottle's Alfred is also a kind of proto-Romantic poet, a sensitive appreciator of nature and of the natural world, a man who wanders round the countryside talking to rural folk and listening to their tales 'of misery', and who is as likely to address poems to the moon as to make high-sounding speeches urging his army into battle.[53] In its own way, Cottle's poem is as much a critique of the nationalistic epic as that of his better known radical protege.

Cottle's reaction against the conservative epic is moreover, like Southey's, a very wide-ranging one. His *Alfred* is an attempt to relocate and fundamentally redefine the very nature of epic heroism and of the epic itself – to make the Anglo-Saxon king into the ideal Christian, compassionate hero of a new national, but not nationalistic, epic for a new age. This purpose emerges most clearly in the Preface attached to his poem, a Preface which, by the time of the second edition of 1804, ran to some forty-two pages.[54] As his earlier 'War A Fragment' (1795) had already shown, Cottle was fiercely opposed to warfare. His real difficulty with traditional, classical epics was therefore intimately connected with their reliance upon battles and bloodshed. As the 'Preface' to *Alfred* explained, the argument that epic battles had a 'moral tendency' was, when examined with care, totally untenable.[55] Not merely were these conventional descriptions of conflict often full of cliches, but they also tended to have a 'contrary and pernicious effect' on their readers, debasing, rather than elevating, their minds.[56] But the 'Preface' went much further than this, questioning the very nature of the heroism endorsed and promoted by these traditional epic contests. As Cottle

---

[52] The battle of Edington is described in thirteen lines (Cottle, *Alfred*, p. 348). Alfred continuously reminds his followers that 'A gallant soldier, ever spares the foe/ That asks for mercy' (p. 196). He disowns Sigbert, a follower who ignores a Danish warrior's plea for mercy (pp. 203–4).

[53] For examples, see *ibid.*, pp. 84, 221 and 60–1.

[54] Cottle, *Alfred* (1804), I, pp. ix–l.

[55] *Ibid.*, I, p. xxxvii. 'War A Fragment' was published in Joseph Cottle, *Poems, containing John the Baptist. Sir Malcolm and Alla, a Tale, Shewing to All the World what Woman's Love can do. War, A Fragment. With a Monody to John Henderson, and a Sketch of his Character* (Bristol, 1795), pp. 73–93. The 'Preface' to *ibid.*, pp. [i]–xvi, contains an earlier formulation of his opposition to war and its traditional glorification. Curran, *Poetic Form*, p. 169, describes Cottle's *Alfred* as 'virtually a pacifist epic'.

[56] Cottle, *Alfred* (1804), I, p. xxxvii.

explained, too many heroic poems had been used to glorify men who were unworthy of the name of hero:

The generality of persons almost imperceptibly admire strength and heroism, without nicely examining the justice of that cause which calls them into action, and which alone renders such qualities estimable . . . many *wars* may have been undertaken, and much blood may have flown, from the glowing and unqualified commendation, which writers have sometimes heaped on men, who possessed prowess and intrepidity, but who were strangers to the virtues, which, alone, could rightly direct those powerful engines . . . The sentiment of noble resistance to oppression, and that courage which disdains all perils in vindication of laws, liberties, and national existence, cannot be inculcated too forcibly; but the great danger arises from our liability to transfer these feelings to causes less just, and which partake . . . more of aggression than defence.[57]

His own version of *Alfred* is intended to address this problem, and to correct this bias. The Anglo-Saxon king is, Cottle insists, chosen not simply because he is a national hero but because he is the right kind of national hero – a man of peace rather than of war.

Cottle therefore exposes and repudiates traditional ideas of epic heroism, and the generic baggage of aristocratic single combats, arming scenes and battles which surround them, in favour of a much more democratic, or at least democratizing, heroic form. Unlike Pye, he is not interested in the heroic ancestry of modern-day British aristocrats, or indeed in Alfred as the noble *pater familias* of his nation. Cottle's monarch, like Pye's, acknowledges his duty to his subjects but, unlike the latter's, it is an acknowledgement founded upon personal experience and first-hand knowledge of their sacrifices. Pye's stereotypical British yeomen are replaced by Cottle's brave but suffering peasants. The Laureate's poem concludes with a series of rousing, patriotic platitudes, '"Free be the Briton's action as his thought"', and with a vision of the Anglo-Saxon, and Hanoverian, thrones being 'Rear'd on the base of Liberty and Law'.[58] Cottle's ends with Alfred establishing a much more down to earth compact with his people, the subjects whose loyalty and bravery have helped him retain his throne:

> '. . . Each man whose sword was drawn
> In this his country's cause, and who requires
> A safe and quiet home, shall soon possess,

[57] *Ibid.*, I, pp. xxxvii–xxxviii.     [58] Pye, *Alfred*, p. 243.

> Together with my smiles, a plot of land,
> A cottage that shall every good contain,
> And I will be your Father! I will rule
> In mercy, and my thoughts . . .
> Shall be to serve you, and to make you feel
> Protection and all joy'[59]

Moreover, Cottle's *Alfred* democratizes the epic in yet another, possibly more significant, way – in its style. Pye, as befitted a university-educated Laureate and a prolific translator of classical literature, used an elevated, classically influenced style and language. Cottle used blank verse, avoided classical allusions and cultivated a language which was simple to the point of being prosaic. As he explained in the Preface to the second edition:

In the following Poem, the Reader will find neither classical or scientific embellishments, neither learned references, nor metaphysical illustrations of abstract sentiments. It comes to him without sanction or patronage – with many disadvantages to encounter, and perhaps some prejudices to surmount.[60]

Cottle's contemporaries correctly, and at times hostilely, interpreted his low style as a literary and political statement, one which linked him with the linguistic, poetic and political radicalism of the group of 'modern writers' whose chief was Southey.[61] What *Alfred* does is to employ a more democratic discourse in order to offer a startlingly different version of the national poem to that proposed by Pye. The readers of Cottle's national epic do not need a classical education in order to understand it. Instead

---

[59] Cottle, *Alfred*, p. 453.

[60] Cottle, *Alfred* (1804), I, xlix. He also defended himself against the accusation that his literary style was not 'sufficiently elevated', admitting that he had 'adopted a studious simplicity of phrase', and attacking 'false notions respecting the sublime' (*ibid.*, I, pp. xix–xxiv).

[61] Cottle claimed to 'have associated my efforts with no class of writers' (*ibid.*, I, p. xxiii), but reviewers disagreed with him. The *Monthly Review* 48 (1805), p. 437, linked Cottle with the unconventional practices of certain 'modern writers', by which it meant a group of authors that included Southey, Coleridge and Wordsworth, and that was known for its literary and political unorthodoxy. Several earlier reviewers had also publicly connected Cottle with the Southey circle (*Monthly Magazine* 11 (1801), pp. 603–4, *Monthly Mirror* 11 (1801), pp. 395–6, and, most condemnatory of all, *Monthly Review* 35 (1801), pp. [1]–9). For the political implications of experiments with language in this period, see O. Smith, *The Politics of Language, 1791–1819* (Oxford, 1984).

they need to shed their literary prejudices. What Cottle offers is a fundamental return of the epic to the English vernacular. In its rejection of the classical past and of classical form and language, his *Alfred* shows how the true British epic should be expressed and embodied in the vernacular and, indeed, how the vernacular is the validation of the national epic. His Anglo-Saxon poem is written in Cottle's modern-day equivalent of an Anglo-Saxon language.[62] We are, he insists, politically, socially, culturally and linguistically Alfred's heirs.

Cottle and Pye's choice of Alfred the Great as the hero of their epics is therefore anything but a chance coincidence. Instead it reflects their engagement in the political and cultural debates of their time. The Anglo-Saxon king, in the hands of both writers, is transformed into the British hero of a much needed national poem. Yet, although on identical subjects, what the two poems actually reveal is that at the turn of the eighteenth century there was no consensus about what made either a national epic, or a patriotic poet – that any idea of a coherently structured, unified national cultural consciousness was a myth. The two *Alfred's* are therefore part of their age, not merely in their choice of subject matter and genre but also, at the most basic level, in terms of the opposing ways in which they choose to engage with the task at hand.[63]

---

[62] Southey later claimed that there was no distinction between high and low culture in the Anglo-Saxon language: 'The language of a Saxon thane was not more cultivated than that of the churl on his estate; indeed, the best as well as earliest of our Anglo-Saxon poets was in the lowest condition of freemen, and was employed as a night-herdsman when he composed his first verses. The distinction between the language of high and low life could not be broadly marked, till our language was fully formed, in the Elizabethan age' (R. Southey, *The Lives and Works of the Uneducated Poets*, ed. J. S. Childers (London, 1925), p. 13).

[63] I would like to thank Professor Donald Scragg and Dr Ian Packer for their constructive criticism of an earlier version of this article.

# 'Utter indifference'?: the Anglo-Saxons in the nineteenth-century novel[1]

## ANDREW SANDERS

'What Englishman cares for Saxon or Norman, both brutal invaders, more than for Chinese and Cochine-Chinese'. So Coleridge wrote despondingly to his friend Thomas Allsop in April 1820 with reference to Sir Walter Scott's *Ivanhoe*. He was attempting to contrast Scott's avowedly 'English' novel with the predominantly 'Scottish' fiction produced so far by the 'author of *Waverley*'. The new novel, he insisted, would arouse 'utter indifference' in readers accustomed to subjects seemingly more relevant to the modern age than the feuds of the twelfth century. It was not that potential readers were at fault; the very subject of *Ivanhoe*, the conflict of Norman and Saxon, was, Coleridge held, 'a mere conflict of indifferents . . . minim surges in a boiling fish kettle'.[2] As the original sales and the continued, and sometimes vicarious, popularity of *Ivanhoe* have served to prove, Coleridge was mistaken. Scott had successfully shifted his focus from Scotland to England and from a nation violently maturing in the eighteenth century to one being forged in the twelfth. The impact of the novel was to be both pervasive and lasting. In his study of Scott, John Sutherland has justly, but nonetheless provocatively, written:

*Ivanhoe* . . . asks to be read as a treatise on nationality. There had been 'national

---

[1] I have dealt more extensively with the fiction of Bulwer and Kingsley in chapters 3 and 7 of my book *The Victorian Historical Novel 1840–1880* (London, 1978).

[2] Coleridge to Thomas Allsop (8 April 1820); T. Allsop, *Letters, Conversations and Recollections of S. T. Coleridge*, 3rd edn. (London, 1864), p. 25. Elsewhere Coleridge speaks of 'our utter indifference to the feuds of Norman and Saxon (N.B. what a contrast to our interest in the Cavaliers and Jacobites and Puritans, Commonwealthmen, and Covenanters from Charles I to the revolution'), *Coleridge's Miscellaneous Criticism*, ed. T. M. Raysor (London, 1936).

tales' in plenty before Scott: but *Ivanhoe* was something more – a novel about the making of England. Intermingled with the novel's nationalist themes was an investigation of race. The author of *Ivanhoe* was largely responsible for injecting consciousness of race (and a sizeable dose of racism) into the popular British mind.[3]

This is some way from Mark Twain's extraordinary claim that *Ivanhoe* had been a contributory cause to the American Civil War,[4] but it remains a contentious statement. The enduring international afterlife of the novel is evident enough, however: it was rapidly translated into other European languages; it was to be given a flippant coda in the form of Thackeray's *Rebecca and Rowena* of 1850; it was to be regularly adapted for the Victorian popular stage; it was, thanks to the benign suggestion of Queen Victoria, to form the basis of Sir Arthur Sullivan's grand opera of 1891. It was to be made into florid movies in 1952 (with Elizabeth Taylor as Rebecca) and 1982 (with James Mason as Isaac of York) and it was to be adapted as a blandly medieval television series in the late 1950s with Roger Moore as the title character and as a rather better, but nonetheless freely inventive, television serial in 1996. But to see it as 'injecting consciousness of race . . . into the popular British mind' does seem to require some pause for questioning thought.

As a consequence of its popular impact it could be argued that *Ivanhoe* did not simply influence British, American and European ideas of racial and national identity but the whole development of nineteenth-century historical fiction. It clearly had an immediate impact on historians, most notably on Augustin Thierry's *Histoire de la conquête de l'Angleterre par les Normands, de ses causes, et ses suites* (published in 3 vols. (Paris, 1825), translated into English by William Hazlitt as the *History of the Conquest of England by the Normans*, 2 vols. (London, 1847)). Thierry's thesis certainly stresses the significance of race in history. As he noted in his introduction:

The principle states of modern Europe have at present attained a high degree of territorial unity . . . Yet there is perhaps not one of them which does not still

---

[3] J. Sutherland, *The Life of Walter Scott: a Critical Biography* (Oxford, 1995), p. 229.

[4] In his *Life on the Mississippi* (Boston, 1883), ch. 46, Twain claims that Scott 'made every gentleman in the South a major, or a colonel, or a general, or a judge, before the war', and he saw the novel as 'a curious exemplification of the power of a single book for good or harm'. *Don Quixote*, he believed, had 'swept the world's admiration for the medieval chivalry-silliness out of existence' whereas *Ivanhoe* had restored it.

present the inquirer living traces of the diversity of the races of men which, in the progress of time, have combined to form that population . . . it is a falsification of history to introduce into it a philosophical contempt for all that does not enter into the uniformity of existing civilization . . .[5]

The Norman conquest, Thierry believed, was the last real territorial conquest in Western Europe and therefore to be distinguished from subsequent 'political . . . invasions' which did not entail a transfer of races. Thierry, in common with Scott, was intent on dusting down the old revolutionary idea of the oppressive 'Norman Yoke' for a new post-revolutionary era, and on seeing the modern British class system as a consequence of this racial transference ('the higher and lower classes . . . are in many countries the lineal representatives of the peoples conquering and the peoples conquered of an anterior epoch').[6] The first chapter of *Ivanhoe* had famously seen class in the twelfth century as a matter of diet and language, with a clear distinction between those who tended domestic animals and those who owned and ate them:

There is old Alderman Ox continues to hold his Saxon Epithet, while he is under the charge of serfs and bondsmen . . . but becomes beef, a fiery French gallant, when he arrives before the worshipful jaws that are destined to consume him. Mynheer Calf, too, becomes Monsieur de Veau in like manner; he is Saxon when he requires tendance, and takes a Norman name when he becomes a matter of enjoyment.[7]

As nineteenth-century readers would have been aware, this is not merely a lesson in linguistic archaeology or the history of food, it is a matter of one class imposing words on another in order to define its exclusive rights. Such distinctions and impositions were to remain vivid enough to the increasingly 'class conscious' Victorians.

Nevertheless, *Ivanhoe* and its successors with twelfth-century settings

---

[5] Augustin Thierry, *History of the Conquest of England by the Normans: its causes and its Consequences, in England, Scotland, Ireland and on the Continent*, trans. from the 7th Paris edition by William Hazlitt, 2 vols. (London, 1847), I, p. i.

[6] *Ibid.*, p. xix. For the 'Norman Yoke' theory see C. Hill, *Puritanism and Revolution: Studies in Interpretation of the English Revolution of the Seventeenth Century* (London, 1958), pp. 50–122. See also Sutherland, *The Life of Walter Scott*, p. 230. For the thinness of Norman blood in English aristocratic families see L. G. Pine, *They Came With the Conqueror: a Study of the Modern Descendants of the Normans* (London, 1954).

[7] All citations are from the first editions of Scott's novels (*Ivanhoe* (1819), *The Betrothed* (1825)) published in Edinburgh.

(the so-called 'Tales of the Crusaders') contain, exhibit and explore a more complex and subtle thesis than such a restrictive quotation might suggest. Just as he had done in his earlier 'Scottish' fiction, the 'Author of *Waverley*' was determined to suggest that historic antagonism, whether of race, class or culture, or of all three, was integral to a dynamic historical dialectic. Out of conflict the benevolent inevitability of progress emerges. Much as Culloden and its aftermath had made modern Scotland, so Hastings made England. Scott's Saxons are characterized in the first chapter of the novel by their 'plain, homely, blunt manners' and by their 'free spirit infused by their ancient institutions and laws'; his Normans, by contrast, have a 'high spirit of military fame, personal adventure and whatever could distinguish them as the Flower of Chivalry'. Yet the overall theme of the novel is not a demonstration of contentious difference but an argument in favour of the political advantages of amalgamation. In another of the 'Tales of the Crusaders' (*Ivanhoe* of 1819, *The Betrothed* and *The Talisman* both of 1825) he refers to a happy admixture of English and Welsh blood by means of which 'German sullenness' is tempered by 'the hot blood of the Celt' (*The Betrothed*, ch. 3). *Ivanhoe* and its successors are concerned not simply with intermarriage but with longer term racial and social reconciliation. Ivanhoe may prefer the pure-blooded, blonde, royal Saxon, Rowena, to the dark, Jewish Rebecca, but his marriage is brought about by the intervention of a Plantagenet king and it lays to rest the ghost of Cedric's hopes for a Saxon restoration. King Richard fights with his Saxon subjects at the siege of the Norman stronghold of Torquilstone and at the end of the novel he emerges as the unchallenged and popularly acclaimed king of England. When he reveals his true identity to Cedric, Scott plays on his titles and their significance:

'Know me as Richard Plantagent.'
'Richard of Anjou' exclaimed Cedric, stepping backwards with the utmost astonishment.
'No, noble Cedric – Richard of England! whose deepest interest – whose deepest wish, is to see her sons united with each other . . .' (ch. 42)

In *The Talisman*, Richard is again specifically identified with England itself, for it is the theft of his personal, and, more to the point, national standard which forms the pivot of the novel's plot. In *The Betrothed*, set in the Welsh Marches rather than the Holy Land, the final union of Eveline Beranger and the gallant Damien betokens the union of the races in still divided Britain. It is Rose, the Fleming who is detached from the conflict of Celt, Saxon and Norman, who, in response to an angry Saxon question, has the wisdom to recognize the resolution that the British future holds in store.

'Saxon, Dane and Norman, have rolled like successive billows over the land, each having strength to subdue what they lacked wisdom to keep. When shall it be otherwise?'

'When Saxon and Britain, and Norman and Fleming,' answered Rose, boldly, 'shall learn to call themselves alike the children of the land they are born in.' (ch. 14)

Even in Scott's floundering, but occasionally brilliant, last novel, *Count Robert of Paris*, the dispossessed Saxon hero, Hereward, who had become a member of the Varangian Guard in his exile, is finally restored to his birthright through the good offices of his new friend, the Frankish Count Robert. As late as 1947, G. M. Young could speak of the 'lasting distortion to our concept of medieval history' due to Scott's 'fancy' that Norman and Saxon persisted as 'consciously hostile races'.[8] Young's is an accusation which deserves to be rebutted, or, at the very least, carefully qualified.

The influence of Scott's *Ivanhoe* and the 'Tales of the Crusaders' on subsequent writers of fiction ought in fact to be seen less in terms of race and racial conflict than in terms of a new emphasis on national identity. The novel can be seen as having set the agenda for a good deal of the debate about British nationhood in Victorian fiction. As Scott himself would probably have been the first to acknowledge, 'national identity' required a sense of Britishness rather than exclusive 'Englishness'. When John Sutherland argues that *Ivanhoe* proposes a polygenic theory of race rather than a monogenic one, that is that the novel makes play with the newly current idea that there were separate racial origins for the major ethnic groups, he only does partial justice to the novel's sociopolitical argument.[9] Certain Victorians might indeed have been persuaded by Scott, by Thierry or by other popularizers of anthropological theory that

---

[8] G. M. Young, 'Scott and the Historians' (a lecture delivered in Edinburgh in 1947), republished in *Last Essays* (London, 1950), pp. 17 ff. Young singles out Scott's influence on Thierry for particular criticism, blaming him for 'the notion that Beckett's cause was the cause of Saxon against Norman'.

[9] Sutherland, *The Life of Walter Scott*, p. 229.

the genetic and cultural differences between Saxon, Dane, Norman, Fleming and Celt were more crucial than racial admixture, but others patently were not. The core of this essay's argument is to suggest that 'Anglo-Saxon' historical fiction generally failed to make a significant impact in nineteenth-century England simply because the notion that there was something truly distinctive about Anglo-Saxondom had already foundered on the rock of Britishness. When Tennyson as Poet Laureate valiantly proclaimed in his welcome to the Danish princess, Alexandra, in 1863, that the race that welcomed the royal bride was 'Saxon and Norman and Dane', he was expressing a commonplace which would have been familiar enough to most of his readers. As the author of the *Idylls of the King* was also well aware, the race was likely to have nearly as much Irish, Scottish or Welsh Celtic blood in its veins as it did Teutonic. Some northern English members of the Victorian third estate might have been as democratically assertive as Elizabeth Gaskell's Mr Thornton in claiming that their 'Teutonic blood' was 'little mingled in this part of England' so that they possessed an 'inward strength, which makes us victorious over material resistance, and over greater difficulties still . . . We stand up for self-government and oppose centralization' (*North and South*, vol. 2, ch. 15). But, as the narrative suggests, this seems a somewhat provocative and tendentious justification of bourgeois independence. Yet more provocative, and certainly more comic, is Trollope's Miss Thorne, for whom 'Hengist, Horsa and such like, had for her ears, the only true savour of nobility' (*Barchester Towers*, ch. 22). But then, as Trollope's narrator naughtily points out, Miss Thorne's dotty 'Saxon' games are in fact a tribute to the despised Norman chivalry. In line with the principles established in both *Waverley* and *Ivanhoe*, Victorian writers of historical fiction seem, by contrast, to have been at pains to point not to Saxon survival or Saxon revival, let alone to a residual and ingrained Saxon resentment of Norman oppression, but to the long-term advantages of the Norman Conquest. The England invaded by the Normans, both historians and novelists generally affirmed, was an England already well settled by Danes. The England forged by the Normans was in turn to impose its (to most Victorian commentators) benevolent sway over the rest of the island of Britain and subsequently over Celtic Ireland. Much as the heptarchy had been superseded by a united English kingdom, so the Norman Conquest was viewed as sealing England's, and subsequently Britain's, independent imperial destiny. 'Anglo-Saxondom' had been merely a phase in the making of the United Kingdom and its Empire. To proclaim an exclusive cultural inheritance as the birthright of the unadulteratedly Teutonic English race appeared to many Victorians to be a, dull, perverse and unnecessary exercise.

One especially influential Victorian writer and politician needs to be noticed briefly in this context. On their father's abandonment of his Jewish faith, Benjamin Disraeli's younger brothers had been taken to their christening by their godfather, the eminent historian of the Anglo-Saxons, Sharon Turner (1768–1847). Turner was a close friend of Isaac Disraeli and Benjamin, as Prime Minister, was to honour the friendship in 1874 by appointing Turner's son to the Deanship of Ripon.[10] Benjamin Disraeli's relationship to the Saxon ancestors of the English nation, to their traditions and to their supposed influence on the modern state and its institutions, was to be decidedly ambiguous. In Disraeli's last completed novel, *Endymion* (1880), the elder statesmen, Baron Sergius, declares a principle to which the novelist himself would appear to have assented. Race, Sergius insists, is 'the key of history, and why history is so often confused is that it has been written by men who were ignorant of this principle . . . there is no subject which more requires discriminating knowledge . . .' (ch. 56). This sentiment in part echoes one proclaimed earlier by another of Disraeli's sagacious mouthpieces, that archetypal outsider and man of peculiar genius, Sidonia. Sidonia, first introduced in *Coningsby* (1844), declares in its successor, *Tancred: or, The New Crusade* of 1847:

Is it what you call civilization that makes England flourish? Is it the universal development of the faculties of man that has rendered an island, almost unknown to the ancients, the arbiter of the world? Clearly not. It is her inhabitants that have done this: it is an affair of race. A Saxon race, protected by an insular position, has stamped its diligent and methodic character on the century . . . All is race; there is no other truth. (ch. 14)

Disraeli's very distinctive view of Saxondom may well be derived from his own proud, but slightly diffident awareness of his inherited Jewishness. He is, in his own way, vindicating his distinctively Anglican- (as opposed to Anglo-) Jewishness by stressing the advance of an English Christian civilization rooted in the religion of Israel and by proclaiming his faith in the England to which he and his immediate forbears had committed

---

[10] For Disraeli and Turner see R. Blake, *Disraeli* (London, 1966), pp. 11 and 685.

themselves. In his 'political biography' of his old 'Young England' associate, Lord George Bentinck, published in 1852, he returned yet again to England and to the significance of race in its development. He now appears to be speaking *in propria persona* as a politician with a post-Reform Act 'one-England' Tory programme:

Progress and reaction are but words to mystify the millions. They mean nothing, they are nothing, they are phrases and not facts. All is race. In the structure, the decay, and the development of the various families of man, the vicissitudes of history find their main solution. The Norman element in our population wanes; the influence of the Saxon population is felt everywhere and everywhere their characteristics appear (ch. 18)

This is the England, dominated by the mills and merchants of Manchester, that Coningsby had been urged to see by Sidonia in the first novel of the so-called 'Young England' trilogy. This too is the assertive, manufacturing England created by that representative of the new economic order, the significantly named Oswald Millbank in the same novel. Millbank insists that both he and his enterprise are Saxon. His daughter is named Edith, he proudly informs Coningsby, because it is 'a Saxon name, for she is the daughter of a Saxon' (*Coningsby*, IV, ch. 4). Moreover, Millbank regards his industrial success as a demolition of the unhappy social effects of the Norman Conquest. Bourgeois Saxon endeavour undoes the older aristocratic Norman assumptions of power and cultural sway. The Norman aristocracy, he maintains, has had to be replaced by a 'real' and 'natural' aristocracy of talent. Nevertheless, as he points out, the considerable pretensions of the existing aristocracy should be seen as little more than a 'masquerade'. The real Norman blood, Millbank insists, has long been dissipated:

The real old families of this country are to be found among the peasantry; the gentry too may lay some claim to old blood . . . but a peer with an ancient lineage is to me quite a novelty. No, no the thirty years of the wars of the Roses freed us from those gentlemen. I take it after the battle of Tewkesbury, a Norman baron was almost as rare as a wolf is now. (*Coningsby*, IV, ch. 4)

*Coningsby*, in common with *Sybil* and *Tancred*, is a thesis novel which contains a whole variety of contradictory theses. If Disraeli explores rather than endorses the 'Young England' dream of a return to an England of beef, beer and Catholic hospitality in which peer and peasant live in symbiotic bliss, his toying with the opinions of pushy, anti-aristocratic northern manufacturers such as Millbank must also be seen as an intellectual ploy. Disraeli does not seek to dwell on a lost England but to experiment with present possibilities. Nevertheless *Coningsby* ends, as *Ivanhoe* had ended, with a marriage that seems to unite opposed political, racial and social factions. The alliance of the gentlemanly Coningsby, the heir apparent to Lord Monmouth's money and his political influence, with Edith, the daughter of a rich and would-be radical tradesman, brings together north and south, Saxon and Norman, trade and manners as effectively, if somewhat more arbitrarily, as does the union of Margaret Hale and Thornton in Gaskell's infinitely more subtle and suggestive novel of 1855.

Disraeli's aristocratic friend, sometime political ally, sometime fellow-dandy, and earnest fellow-novelist, Edward Bulwer-Lytton, would certainly have endorsed much of Millbank's attack on the 'masquerade' of 'Norman' blood in the nineteenth century. Bulwer, a gentleman of somewhat dubious and diluted Norman pedigree, who had turned to historical fiction in the mid-1830s as an alternative to his early 'Silver Fork' excursions into high society in the company of dandy heroes with political ambitions, had an equally distinct and informed programme to present to his readers.[11] He too was directly influenced by Scott's 'Waverley' novels and by *Ivanhoe* in particular. It was to Scott, whose fame had already 'attained that height in which praise has become superfluous', that Bulwer's romance *Eugene Aram* was dedicated in 1831, and more than thirty years later he made specific and pointed reference to *Ivanhoe* in an essay on the art of fiction:

the gentle insipid virtues of Ivanhoe are indicated as the necessary link between Saxon and Norman. It is ever to this day. The man who yields to what must be . . . has always, when honourable and sincere, a something in him of an Ivanhoe or a Waverley.[12]

Scott's advantage over the conventional historian, Bulwer maintained, was that as a novelist he had been able to appear as an impartial observer, selecting material and allowing character to develop easily and steadily. The historical novelist could see character moulded by specific historical circumstances and also able both to influence, and be influenced by, a

---

[11] For Bulwer's 'Silver Fork' fiction see A. Aldburgham, *Silver Fork Society: Fashionable Life and Literature from 1814 to 1840* (London, 1983).
[12] Edward Bulwer-Lytton, *Miscellaneous Prose Works*, 3 vols. (London, 1868), III, p. 475.

particular turn of events. He, or she, was thus able to render history immediate to the modern age. As a historical novelist himself, Bulwer was, from first to last, drawn inexorably to periods of transition in which 'gentle insipid virtue' showed itself as a proto-Darwinist, creative 'adaptability' to painful circumstance. It is, of course, significant that so many of Bulwer's novels contain the words 'the last of' in their titles. Where both *The Last Days of Pompeii* (1834) and *Rienzi: the Last of the Roman Tribunes* (1835) had dealt with the matter of Rome, both ancient and medieval, his English novels tend to deal with different kinds of historical crises, crises which the novelist held had determined the nature of the English and British present.

The scheme of composing a novel centred on the Norman invasion of 1066 had, Bulwer claimed in his 'Dedicatory Epistle' to *Harold: the Last of the Saxon Kings* (1848), been long mulled over. The Conquest was, he believed, the crux of English history, but the realization of the project was delayed until an ample scholarly basis had been formed in his mind, in his library and in his notebooks. There was, moreover, a problem with presenting the material to readers unaware of how vital a national issue the Conquest was:

The main consideration which long withheld me from the task, was my sense of the unfamiliarity of the ordinary reader with the characters, events, and, so to speak, with the very physiognomy of a period *ante Agamemnona*; before the brilliant age of matured chivalry, which has given to song and romance the deeds of the later knighthood, and the glorious frenzy of the Crusades. The Norman Conquest was our Trojan War; an epoch beyond which our learning seldom induces our imagination to ascend.

Equally significant is the fact that *The Last of the Barons*, Bulwer's long, worthy and wordy fictional study on the impact of the Wars of the Roses, had been published in 1844. *The Last of the Barons* is set in the troubled and interrupted reign of Edward IV, a monarch presiding over the bloody demise of the old aristocracy and encouraging (in Bulwer's eyes at least) the rise of the industrious and industrial bourgeoisie. At the centre of the story is Nevile (*sic*), the 'last of the barons', fighting for a doomed and exclusive aristocratic cause and symbolically poised between the weak superstitious simpleton, Henry VI, and the middle-class inventor, Adam Warner, respectively the representatives of a decaying age of faith and a nascent age of science. Bulwer was greatly given to such symbolic readings of history, both fictional and factual. His *Harold* required not simply a diagrammatic interpretation of the past but, as he pointed out in the Preface he added to the third edition of the novel, a great deal of systematic research:

I have indeed devoted to this work a degree of research which, if unusual to romance, I cannot consider superfluous when illustrating an age so remote, and events unparalleled in their influence over the destinies of England. Nor am I without hope, that what the romance-reader at first regards as a defect, he may ultimately acknowledge as a merit.[13]

This research is reflected in often laborious descriptions of landscape and townscape, of architecture and cuisine, of customs and costume. The elaborately speculative and archaeological reconstruction of the London of Edward the Confessor in the novel's fourth chapter is as unlikely to divert modern readers as the actual city appears to please the visiting Duke of Normandy ('By the rood and mass, o dear king, thy lot hath fallen on a goodly heritage').

Bulwer's singularly infelicitous style does not exactly ease this task. The attempt to reconstruct a fit manner of speech for his Saxon and Norman characters is, however, more often than not a disaster. Those accustomed to his truly dire opening sentences may well be surprised by the brevity of 'Merry was the month of May in the year of Our Lord 1052', but they will not be disappointed by its awkward successor: 'Few were the boys, and few the lasses, who overslept themselves on the first of that buxom month'. Likewise, the opening account of the fraught encounter of Edward, William and Hilda, a Nordic witch, in the ruins of a Roman villa in the Old Kent Road has a contrived stiltedness about it which probably renders it merely risible to twentieth century ears ('"*Per la resplendar De*, bold dame," cried the knight by the side of Edward, while a lurid flush passed over his cheek of bronze; "but thou are too glib

---

[13] 'Preface to the Third Edition', the New Knebworth edition. (London, 1896), p. 20. Bulwer did much of his research for the novel in the library of its dedicatee, the hospitable Tennyson D'Eyncourt, at Bayons Manor in Lincolnshire. Alfred Tennyson, though he had been much offended by Bulwer's early reviews of his work, and though he remained estranged from his uncle, acknowledged his own debt to *Harold* in his verse tragedy of the same name. Bulwer's Commonplace Books, containing notes made in preparation for composition, are preserved with the Lytton Papers in the Hertfordshire County Record Office.

of tongue for a subject, and pratest overmuch of Woden, the Paynim, for the lips of a Christian matron." '). His turgid but meticulous description of the meeting of the Witena-gemot in Book III is substantially borrowed from Francis Palgrave's *The Rise and Progress of the English Commonwealth* (London, 1832), and the debt is glowingly acknowledged. Throughout the novel, footnotes refer us to contemporary chronicles or to modern historians and editors. Detail is all, and scrupulous attention to sources is proclaimed to be a virtue; but both, alas, do little more than drain the dye out of local colour.

*Harold: the Last of the Saxon Kings* succeeds best, both in its own terms and in terms of a modern reader's likely response to it, as a representation of an England in transition. The Confessor's sentimental sacerdotalism and ineffectual government have sapped the kingdom of energy and independence; his predilection for Norman culture and Norman administrators is seen as having rendered his Saxon subjects largely impotent, and even the upright Harold's last-ditch resistance seems to be a doomed gesture in the face of the inevitable triumph of the ruthless and calculating William. The flame of Englishness, which glows in the prelude to defeat at Hastings is, however, seen as undying. It will be rekindled once the Normans and their ways have been assimilated by the oppressed majority. Defeat at Hastings, Bulwer's narrator insists, is a decisive evolutionary point, one which, to the long-sighted historian, determines a happier future than the myopia of the vanquished might suggest. The Churchillian last paragraph stresses the ultimate triumph of the English inspired by Harold's example:

Eight centuries have rolled away, and where is the Norman now? or where is not the Saxon. The little urn that sufficed the mighty lord [William] is despoiled of his very dust; but the tombless shade of the kingly freeman still guards the coasts, and rests upon the seas. In many a noiseless field, with Thoughts for Armies, your relics, O Saxon Heroes, have won back the victory from the bones of the Norman saints; and whenever, with fairer fates, Freedom opposes Force, and Justice, redeeming the old defeat, smites down the armed Frauds that would consecrate the wrong – smile, O soul of our Saxon Harold, smile, appeased, on the Saxon's land!

Bulwer's Harold is justified not simply by an emphatically sympathetic narrator interpreting how the man matches the historical moment, but also by the long-term view of the steady development of English history. He had outlined his intentions in his 'Dedicatory Epistle':

While I have carefully examined and weighed the scanty evidences of its distinguishing attributes . . . I have attempted . . . to shadow out the ideal of the pure Saxon character . . . marked already by patient endurance, love of justice, and freedom – the manly sense of duty rather than the chivalric sentiment of honour – and the indestructible element of practical purpose and courageous will, which defying all conquest, and steadfast in all peril, was ordained to achieve so vast an influence over the destinies of the world.

Here is a destiny manifest *in* history and justified *by* history. Here also is Saxondom justified in retrospect. Because England, and by extension, Great Britain, had attained world power by 1848, therefore its history must prove right. The Norman Conquest of England has been undone by the conquest of the world by England. The English character, having been proved and tested by defeat, has in turn defeated all comers. Having been unwillingly forced into an alien empire it has responded by building an empire of its own in its own image. Bulwer's *Harold* is a brave attempt at reading historic failure as ultimate success.

Charles Kingsley was a nationalist of a different, if scarcely less confident, stamp. Where Bulwer tended to see historical patterns emerging in a long, secular retrospect, Kingsley saw the evidence of a divine providence, working for the special benefit of the English nation, in an assertively bible-informed contest. As Professor of Modern History at Cambridge in the 1860s he proclaimed that the study of human history was the study of human morals ('as a people behaves so it thrives; as it believes, so it thrives').[14] History was incontrovertibly a process of 'God educating Man', a process which was evident thanks to 'the observation of thousands of minds, throughout thousands of years.'[15] Where these Cambridge lectures touch on the central ideas of *Hereward the Wake* is in their emphatic pro-Teutonism and especially in their faith in the continuity of English customs and institutions. Where Macaulay had stressed the constitutional significance of the Glorious Revolution of 1688, Kingsley insists on a far longer constitutional lineage:

1688 after Christ? 1688 before Christ would be nearer the mark. It [the British Constitution] is as old, in its essentials, as the time when not only all the Teutons formed one tribe, but when the Teutons and Scandinavians were still

---

[14] Kingsley's Cambridge lectures were published as *The Roman and the Teuton* (Cambridge and London, 1864, repr. London, 1884), p. 334.

[15] *Ibid.*, pp. 338 and 340.

united . . . We at least brought the British Constitution with us out of the bogs and moors of Jutland; along with our smock-frocks and leather gaiters, brown bills, and stone axes; and it has done us good service, and will do, till we carry it right round the world.[16]

The folksy stress here is not merely a play with an aspect of mid-century popular democracy (Kingsley had evolved his idea of 'Christian Socialism' in response to the atheistic tendencies in Chartism); it is an indication of the extent to which he sees the modern English as the heirs to a mixed 'Teutonic' tradition. Norman and Saxon and Dane had jointly, not antagonistically, forged the constitution and their mongrel Teutonic descendants were to determine its nineteenth-century development.

*Hereward the Wake, 'Last of the English'* was published in 1866 to mark the eight-hundredth anniversary of the Conquest, but it does not mourn the passing of Saxon England. It rejoices in the providential intermixing of two branches of the great Teutonic race and in the progressive impetus given to a new England. Hereward is the undoubted hero of the piece, but the Conqueror is no mere foreign villain. Both men are united in their northern valour and their northern blood. The foreignness of the Norman invader lies in his veneer of French culture, a veneer which will be gradually stripped away as blood proves itself to be thicker than furniture glue. The large theme of the novel is stated, somewhat ambiguously, in its opening Prelude:

We have gained doubtless, by that calamity [the Conquest]. By it England and Scotland, and in due time Ireland, became integral parts of the comity of Christendom, and partakers of that classic civilization and learning, the fount whereof, for good or for evil, was Rome and the Pope of Rome: but the method was at least wicked; the actors in it tyrannous, brutal, treacherous, hypocritical; and to say that so it must have been; that by no other method could the result (or some far better result) have been obtained – it is not to say that men's crimes are not merely overruled by, but necessary to, the gracious designs of Providence; and that – to speak plainly – the Deity has made this world so ill, that He is forced at times to do ill that good may come?

This is something of a mini-debate over the ways of God to Man, a debate which is also vexed by the Roman ghosts that continually haunted Kingsley's polemics. The chief ambiguity of his statement is, however, explained in his subsequent characterization of William the Conqueror.

---

[16] *Ibid.*, p. 249.

There is a 'manly' generosity in William which is more than mere Frenchified proto-chivalry. When the Conqueror treats Edgar Etheling with particular courtesy in chapter 18, Kingsley's narrator is at pains to explain that:

the descendant of Rollo the heathen Viking, had become a civilized chivalrous Christian knight. His mighty forefather would have split the Etheling's skull with his own axe. A Frank king would have shaved the young man's head, and immured him in a monastery. An eastern Sultan would have thrust out his eyes, or strangled him at once. But William, however cruel, however unscrupulous, had a knightly heart, and somewhat of a Christian conscience; and his conduct to his only lawful rival is a noble trait amid many sins.

Similarly, when Hereward, in disguise, comes face to face with the Conqueror at Brandon, in chapter 30 we are told that he looks into the visage of 'a great man' and feels instinctively that 'it was the face of the greatest man whom he had ever met'.

Hereward himself is a hero in the 'muscular Christian' mould much cultivated by Kingsley. The novel is pointedly dedicated to Rajah Sir James Brooke and to Bishop Selwyn, missionaries and imperialists both, whom Kingsley describes as exhibiting 'that type of English virtue, at once manful and godly, practical and enthusiastic, prudent and self-sacrificing . . .' Hereward is, like King David, another of the novelist's favourite heroes, an occasionally bloodthirsty adulterer, but he is also a man transfigured by his mission inspired by both race and by Heaven. Hereward's largely solitary struggle against the victorious Conqueror is, nevertheless, not exclusively national. His resistance is centred not in Saxon Wessex but in semi-Viking East Anglia. For Kingsley, the 'real' England of the novel is the old Danelaw and the Cambridgeshire Fenland, and Hereward and his fellow guerrillas are representative of Viking blood and Viking tradition. So too, the novelist reminds us, are the Normans. The narrator's self-evident sympathy with restless Nordic energy rather than with settled Saxon complacency again suggests something of his fictional irresolution. Kingsley tends to see the military enterprise of Anglo-Norse England as evidence of the divine mission for the Teutonic tribes. Thus his victorious Normans, also Teutonic in origin, are ultimately to be justified, as are their English subjects. The historical Hereward gained no lasting victory and the cultures of Norman and Saxon were to be fused rather than continually opposed. The fictional solution to this potential dilemma lies in a concentration on the flawed brilliance of the heroic Hereward, and in viewing Hereward's final defeat as a consequence not of military failure but of his own moral shortcomings. David sins with Bathsheba; Hereward with Torfida. Redblooded heterosexuals both may prove themselves to be, but they are also unworthy of the moral responsibility thrust upon them by the national mission entrusted to them.

Eight years after the publication of *Hereward the Wake* Kingsley delivered a series of lectures entitled 'The First Discovery of America'. Here he attempted to expand upon his fixation with the Teutonic vocation to world-rule by drawing America into his expansively impressionist and imperialist argument. In these lectures he also stresses the providential nature of the Norman Conquest without the inconvenience of mentioning Hereward's resistance to the imposition of Norman rule:

England *was* to be conquered by the Norman; but by the civilized not the barbaric; by the Norse who had settled, but four generations before, in the North East of France . . . and . . . with that docility and adaptability which marks so often truly great spirits . . . [they] had become, from heathen and murderous Berserkers, the most truly civilized people of Europe . . . so greatly had they changed, and so fast, that William, Duke of Normandy . . . was perhaps the finest gentleman, as well as the most cultivated Sovereign, and the greatest statesman and warrior in all Europe.[17]

Here again we meet the Darwinian word 'adaptability', though not necessarily in a Darwinian context. Evolutionary processes for Kingsley are exclusively the workings out of God's purposes and, as he reminded his American audience, the lesson to be drawn from a meditation in the ruins of Battle Abbey is that 'God's thoughts are not as our thoughts, nor are His ways as our ways'.

For Kingsley the Norman Conquest was 'the making of the English people'.[18] This may have seemed to be an inconvenient message to some Victorian nationalists, but to others it was the only acceptable way of describing, and inevitably relishing, a great unbroken sweep in British history. Defeat is to be read as victory, culture shock as progressive education, trauma as therapy. In an important sense all of these lessons

[17] Charles Kingsley, *Historical Lectures and Essays* (London, 1880), p. 246.
[18] *Ibid.*, p. 250.

had been implicit in the dialectics of the *Waverley* novels. In shifting his ground from Scotland to England in *Ivanhoe*, Scott had prepared the way for the Anglo-Saxon novels of his Victorian successors and for an agenda which was unlikely to seem a matter of 'utter indifference' to Victorian readers. If pre-Conquest England never seems to have gripped the English novel reader's and novel writer's imagination in quite the same way that, say, the eighteenth century did, this was not simply a matter of finding an eight-hundred year gap more difficult to bridge than Scott's 'sixty years since'. Relative familiarity and the intimate relationship of the present to its immediate origins were, of course, matters of great significance, but the real distraction in dealing with Saxon England lay in the fact that it was exclusively Saxon. A national myth based on early England was simply not pressing and vital enough. Despite both radical and conservative attempts to elevate King Alfred to prime heroic status, Alfred was too distant and too exclusively English. Great Britain did, and does, prefer neutrally 'British' heroes (witness the exclusively eighteenth- and nineteenth-century figures, citizens of a United Kingdom, who have appeared to date on Bank of *England* notes). Problematic nineteenth-century Ireland, even when cast in the role of 'West Britain', was likely to be yet more restless with an exclusively Saxon political pantheon. Even for England, then as now, the choices open to those who seek to adumbrate and delineate an historical 'Golden Age' were multiple.

# The charge of the Saxon brigade: Tennyson's *Battle of Brunanburh*

## †EDWARD B. IRVING, JR

The first modern translation of Anglo-Saxon poetry with much claim to readability and poetic merit was Alfred Lord Tennyson's version of the *Battle of Brunanburh*, a poem from the *Anglo-Saxon Chronicle* for the year 937, celebrating a victory by West Saxons and Mercians over an alliance of Vikings from Dublin, Danes from the kingdom of York, Welshmen and Scots. Tennyson's translation was written probably in 1876 and was first published in 1880 in a volume called *Ballads and Other Poems*.

With its publication, familiarity on the part of general readers with Old English poetry must have expanded suddenly by a quantum leap. Tennyson was by then the famous Poet Laureate whose splendidly bewhiskered caricature in *Punch* was assumed to be recognizable without even needing an identifying label attached, a friend of Gladstone and of members of the royal family. His translation drew widespread attention for the first time to a body of poetry that up until then had scarcely been known except to a few scholars and philologists, whose translations, when they provided any, were pragmatic and likely to seem uncouth and repellent to the average reader.

Tennyson's version, based chiefly on a prose translation provided by his son Hallam,[1] was praised at the time in reviews of the volume that contained it, and has been often praised since. Edward FitzGerald wrote to Hallam Tennyson in 1881 (offering the kind of technical remark one poet makes to another): 'Tell [your father] . . . that, when I saw his version of your "Battle of Brunanburh," I said to myself, and afterwards to others, "There's the way to render Aeschylus's Chorus at last!" unless indeed it

---

[1] Published in *Contemporary Review* 11 (1876), pp. 920–2.

might overpower any blank verse dialogue.'[2] Queen Victoria herself apparently liked it, or at least liked the volume it was in, since in 1882 Tennyson wrote to his publisher Kegan Paul: 'The Queen wants another copy of "Ballads and Poems" bound in Royal blue with Crown, lined with white silk. Please send it to me here.'[3]

Still, in the spirit of objectivity, we should record one early dissenting voice, that of an anonymous critic who hurt the poet's feelings by what appears to be a technical objection to Tennyson's metrics, according to a memoir by H. D. Rawnsley, who was illustrating Tennyson's hypersensitivity to criticism: 'He [Tennyson] said of one man whom, I knew, he loved and honoured dearly, 'I wish he had never spoken of my "Battle of Brunanburh" as reminding him of the "House that Jack Built." '[4]

In this century, Christopher Ricks, editor of the standard edition of Tennyson's poetry, has claimed it to be 'probably the best verse-translation of any Anglo-Saxon poetry'.[5] The distinguished Anglo-Saxonist John C. Pope makes the point that *Brunanburh* is 'perhaps the most familiar of all Old English poems' because of this translation, which he terms 'a brilliant and thoroughly Tennysonian performance', though he adds the slightly ominous qualification 'for good and for ill'.[6] A more recent translator of Old English, Michael Alexander, in his illuminating and thorough study of this translation,[7] though noting and deploring instances of Tennyson's 'excessive musicality and Technicolor diction,' still remarks wistfully 'I now envy Tennyson his exuberance,' a quality that he sees as denied to more muted and cautious modern translators.

I append a copy of Tennyson's translation so that readers can make up their own minds about its qualities. (I have also included a brief sample

---

[2] Letter to Hallam Tennyson, 30 November 1881, in *The Letters of Edward FitzGerald: 1877–1883*, ed. A. McK. Terhune and A. B. Terhune, 4 vols. (Princeton, 1980), IV, p. 459.

[3] *The Letters of Alfred Lord Tennyson: 1871–1892*, ed. C. Y. Lang and E. F. Shannon, Jr., 3 vols. (Oxford, 1981–1990), III, p. 219. Letter dated 31 January 1882.

[4] From a memoir by H. D. Rawnsley, first published in *Memories of the Tennysons* (Glasgow, 1900) and reprinted in *Tennyson: Interviews and Recollections*, ed. N. Page (London, 1983), p. 69.

[5] C. Ricks, *Tennyson* (New York, 1976), p. 292.

[6] John C. Pope, in his commentary on the poem in *Seven Old English Poems* (New York, 1981), p. 55.

[7] M. Alexander, 'Tennyson's "Battle of Brunanburh"', *Tennyson Research Bulletin* 4:4 (November, 1985), pp. 151–61, at p. 159.

of the original Old English, and a specimen of Alexander's modern translation.) Rest assured that I will eventually disclose my own opinion – but first we should take a look at the historical context of Tennyson's version.

*What exactly did Alfred Tennyson know about Old English poetry, and when did he know it?* Anglo-Saxonists have been intrigued by the fact that John Mitchell Kemble of the famous theatrical family was a close friend of Tennyson when they were both undergraduates at Cambridge and fellow-members of the Apostles. Kemble was the nephew of Mrs Siddons as well as the brother of Fanny Kemble – and, an American must add, the great-uncle of Owen Wister, author of the first Western novel, *The Virginian* – though of course best known to medievalists for having brought out an important edition of *Beowulf* in 1833. Tennyson even addressed a sonnet to Kemble, which was published in 1830. I find, however, no real evidence that they continued in such close contact in later years. Tennyson's son Hallam reports a brief journal entry by his father in 1839: 'London. There is no one here but John Kemble with whom I dined twice.'[8] And Kemble died in Dublin at the age of 49 in 1857, almost twenty years before Tennyson composed his translation.

Still, it is of interest to see how Tennyson and his friend Arthur Hallam reacted to 'Black Jack' Kemble's scholarly activities in the Anglo-Saxon field, which began shortly after they all left Cambridge. Hallam wrote to Tennyson in September of 1832: 'The last two days Kemble has been staying here. He has been very lively but is so absorbed in Gothic manuscripts, that however conversation may begin he is sure to make it end in that. If one says 'a fine day John' he answers 'very true, and it is a curious fact that in the nine thousandth line of the first Edda, the great giant Hubbadub makes precisely the same remark to the brave knight Siegfried.'[9] Kemble was at the time working on *Beowulf*, presumably the 'Gothic manuscripts' Hallam mentions. Perhaps Hallam had actually glanced at something Kemble had written, at least enough to be able to make a joke out of it, when later he assures Kemble that he will help him read the proofs of a scholarly article and 'will make with pencil or pen that important alteration of *swylce* for *swylke* on which the destinies of

[8] Hallam Tennyson, *Alfred Lord Tennyson: a Memoir* (London, 1899), p. 142.
[9] *The Letters of Arthur Henry Hallam*, ed. J. Kolb, (Columbus, 1981), AHH to Alfred Tennyson, 13 September 1832, p. 646.

mankind may reasonably be supposed to depend'.[10] In another letter to Kemble dated 18 October 1832, Hallam jocularly urges Kemble to provide some publicity for Tennyson's forthcoming volume of poems with a 'Puff collateral,' asking 'Couldn't you bring it in head & shoulders to illustrate some very ancient passage in an Edda?'[11] In a more sober tone, Hallam wrote to their mutual friend Richard Trench (who himself in later life became a noted philologist and was credited with suggesting the idea of the *Oxford English Dictionary*): 'I rejoice to hear he [Kemble] is spoken of in the highest terms by our best Saxon scholars for real learning and capacity for the subject.'[12]

In November 1833 Kemble wrote an affectionate and jokey letter to Tennyson, telling him: 'I rejoice to say *Beowulf* is out,'[13] to which Tennyson dutifully replied 'I am heartily glad you have got *Beowulf* out.'[14] Another friend, Stephen Spring Rice, wrote to Tennyson from Oxford, after Kemble had been given an appointment there on the strength of his edition: 'Kemble [Anglo-Saxon *Lecturer* to the University] sends you to fill up your leisure hours a folio Saxo-Grammaticus . . . to be jammed into the bowl of your pipe.'[15] It is sad to realize, however, that this banter was going on at the very time that Tennyson was about to receive the news of Arthur Hallam's sudden death abroad at the age of twenty-two. Most readers would agree that Tennyson's greatest poem was his long meditation on that death, *In Memoriam A.H.H.*

It seems certain, in any event, that Kemble discussed *Beowulf* and other Anglo-Saxon poems with Tennyson. We even have a fragment of Tennyson's translation of a few lines of *Beowulf*, found in his unpublished notebook of 1830–31, done while he was still an undergraduate.[16] But the evidence does not indicate that Kemble's friends themselves ever studied the language in any depth, or thought that his working on it was to be taken with grave seriousness, as perhaps working on the classics

---

[10] *Ibid.*, AHH to Kemble, 15 March 1833, p. 738.    [11] *Ibid.*, p. 667.

[12] *Ibid.*, 3 April 1833, p. 744.

[13] *The Letters of Alfred Lord Tennyson*, ed. Lang and Shannon, Kemble to AT, 27 November 1833, I, p. 98.

[14] *Ibid.*, AT to Kemble, early December 1833, I, p. 100.

[15] *Ibid.*, Stephen Spring Rice to AT, 27 November 1833, I, p. 99.

[16] *The Poems of Tennyson*, ed. C. Ricks, (London, 1969), p. 1235. All quotations from Tennyson's poems are from this edition. The text of Tennyson's *Beowulf* translation (of lines 258–63) is printed by Alexander, 'Tennyson's "Battle of Brunanburh"', p. 161.

might have been taken. The field was still distinctly marginal. But Tennyson did at least know that the field existed and was taken very seriously by one of his friends.

His contact with Anglo-Saxon matters was not renewed, however, until some forty years later, when the mature Tennyson became deeply interested in English history and wrote a series of rather unsuccessful historical plays, including the play *Harold*, which deals with the Norman Conquest. He seems to have translated *Brunanburh* at the same time he was doing some research and working on *Harold*. Tennyson's research included visiting the Tapestry at Bayeux and the battlefield at Hastings, reading the Norman *Roman de Rou* and Freeman's *Norman Conquest*, and carefully studying a historical novel by Bulwer-Lytton.[17]

He wrote a sonnet while visiting Hastings, 'Show-Day at Battle Abbey, 1876,' which was prefaced to the play *Harold*. I quote a few lines of it to show Tennyson's distinctly pro-Saxon view of the battle. I do not know whether representing William the Bastard as a cuckoo's egg was a conceit original with the poet.

> A garden here – May breath and bloom of spring –
> The cuckoo yonder from an English elm
> Crying 'with my false egg I overwhelm
> The native nest:' and fancy hears the ring
> Of harness, and that deathful arrow sing,
> And Saxon battleaxe clang on Norman helm.
> Here rose the dragon-banner of our realm:
> Here fought, here fell, our Norman-slandered king.[18]

One scholar writes of the nature of his interest in history: 'Like Sir Walter Scott and later historical novelists, he was attracted by points of change, when nations and cultures were forged in the aftermath of conflict', and she goes on to say: 'His interest in Brunanburh is typical of his impulse to explore the decisive moments of the national past'.[19] Tennyson

---

[17] This information is contained in a letter Tennyson wrote to the Earl of Lytton (Bulwer's son) on 21 December 1876 (*Letters of Alfred Lord Tennyson*, ed. Lang and Shannon, III, p. 139).

[18] Ricks, *The Poems of Tennyson*, p. 1234.

[19] L. Ormond, *Alfred Tennyson: a Literary Life* (New York, 1993), p. 178. Henry Kozicki sees an interest by Tennyson in 'historical beginnings and pristine valor' in the three historical plays, in the translation of *Brunanburh*, and in the poem 'The Revenge' of 1877 (*Tennyson and Clio* (Baltimore, 1979), p. 166).

apparently felt only a little personal involvement in the events of 1066. When the American poet and scholar Longfellow wrote to congratulate him on *Harold*, Tennyson replied: 'You ask "What old ancestor spoke through you?" I fear none of mine fought for England on the Hill of Senlac, for, as far as I know, I am part Dane, part Norman'.[20]

Tennyson's translation clearly reflects some preconceptions about that national past, especially about the character of the Anglo-Saxons themselves. As we know, English scholars in the early part of the nineteenth century tended to be patronizing about the Anglo-Saxons and their literature. Sharon Turner's remarks are especially dismissive. Turner dislikes the periphrastic style, the constant variation typical of the verse, and calls the structure of *Brunanburh* 'artless,' remarking that in the poem 'we see poetry in its rudest form, before the art of narration was understood.'[21] He quotes a few of the simpler trochaic verses we will examine shortly and states, in his patronizing way: 'To produce this rhythm seems to have been the perfection of their versification . . . When their words would not fall easily into the desired rhythm, they were satisfied with an approach to it' (212). But then we should bear in mind that Turner did not even bother to comment on the magnificent last third of *Beowulf*, the dragon-fight, claiming it to contain 'some further adventures, which are not of equal interest with the former' (181). In similar tones, J. J. Conybeare, in a work published in 1826, mentions the 'extreme jejuneness and barbarity' of the famous lists of tribes in *Widsith* and describes *Deor* as 'a species of rude song'.[22]

In 1838, however, in a review of several works on Anglo-Saxon, including Kemble's *Beowulf*, a review that Tennyson might very well have read, since he had considerable correspondence with the author of it, the American poet Longfellow had a more appreciative view of the poetry.[23] Although he begins badly, calling the Anglo-Saxons 'brave, rejoicing in sea-storms, and beautiful in person, with blue eyes and long, flowing hair'

---

[20] *Letters of Alfred Lord Tennyson*, ed. Lang and Shannon, III, p. 141; 14 Jan 1877.

[21] Sharon Turner, *The History of the Anglo-Saxons*, 3rd. edn., 3 vols. (repr. Paris, 1840), pp. 166–7. For an excellent survey of the history of criticism of Old English literature, see D. G. Calder, 'Histories and surveys of Old English literature: a chronological review,' *ASE* 10 (1982), pp. 201–44.

[22] *Illustrations of Anglo-Saxon Poetry*, ed. W. D. Conybeare (London, 1826); the first quotation is from p. 10, the second from p. 239.

[23] Longfellow, review in *North American Review* 47 (1838), pp. 90–134.

(p. 95), unlike the early scholars Longfellow is a poet and he recognizes poetry. He picks out for praise, for example, Byrhtwold's great speech in *The Battle of Maldon* – 'What a fine passage this is!' (p. 114). And as a poet, he is impressed though puzzled by the unfamiliar metrics: 'it had line-rhymes and end-rhymes; which being added to the alliteration, and brought so near together in the short, emphatic lines, produce a singular effect upon the ear. They ring like blows of hammers on an anvil.' (This last phrase may be well be one that Tennyson remembered when he came to write his play *Harold*, as we will see.) Longfellow also prints a translation of *Brunanburh*, commenting: 'What a striking picture is that of the lad with flaxen hair, mangled with wounds; and of the seven earls of Anlaf, and the five young kings, lying on the battle-field, lulled asleep by the sword!' (If you look at line 74 of Tennyson's translation, you may find his 'mangled to morsels' possibly echoing Longfellow's 'mangled with wounds' – neither phrase really justified by the original.)

But Longfellow was at odds with his time. More typical, though obviously they constitute a ludicrous extreme, are the notorious remarks on Anglo-Saxon literature made by the French critic Hippolyte Taine, whose history of English literature was widely known in England; a translation of it was current in the early 1870s.[24] Taine saw the Anglo-Saxon poets as strangely alien bards, with a distinct Neanderthal cast to them:

They do not speak, they sing, or rather cry out. Each little verse is an acclamation, which breaks forth like a growl; their strong breasts heave with a groan of anger or enthusiasm. (I, p. 53)

At one point, he in fact quotes from a prose translation of *Brunanburh* by Sharon Turner, and then exclaims:

Here all is image. In their impassioned minds events are not bald, with the dry propriety of an exact description; each fits in with its pomp of sound, shape, coloring; it is almost a vision which is raised, complete, with its accompanying emotions, joy, fury, excitement. (I, p. 54)

Then he quotes the lines (they are lines 25 to 30 in Tennyson's version) about the sun's progress across the sky, commenting:

---

[24] H. Taine, *Histoire de la littérature anglaise* (Paris, 1863), trans. H. van Laun as *History of English Literature* (Edinburgh, 1871). The quotations are from van Laun's second edition (Edinburgh, 1873).

Four subsequent times they employ the same thought, and each time under a new aspect. All its different aspects rise simultaneously before the barbarian's eyes, and each work was like a shock of the semi-hallucination which exalted him. (I, p. 54)

Some may indeed wonder whether the French critic is actually looking at the poem before us. We may remember that W. H. Auden once called Tennyson the stupidest English poet, but one would hope he had sense enough to reject this grotesque view of Anglo-Saxon poets. Yet I must believe that the idea that the Anglo-Saxons were truly primitive – even if *delightfully* primitive – had been planted firmly in his mind, probably not by Taine, but by the prevailing culture that Taine seems to reflect.

The best evidence for this may be found in the play *Harold*. I quote a little of it, a dialogue between First Thane and Second Thane.

> FIRST THANE. What's Brunanburg [*the poem*]
> To Stamford-Bridge? a war-crash, and so hard,
> So loud, that, by St Dunstan, old St Thor –
> By God we thought him dead – but our old Thor
> Heard his own thunder again, and woke and came
> Among us again, and mark'd the sons of those
> Who made this Britain England, break the North.
> [*then First Thane begins chanting:*]
>> Mark'd how the war-axe swang,
>> Heard how the war-horn sang,
>> Mark'd how the spear-head sprang,
>> Heard how the shield-wall rang,
>> Iron on iron clang,
>> Anvil on hammer bang –
> SECOND THANE. [*correcting him*] Hammer on anvil, hammer on anvil.
> Old dog, Thou art drunk, old dog!

What a very peculiar introduction this is to the old poetry. You will observe how it is associated with hardness, loudness and crashing, with Thor's thunder, and with incoherent drunkenness, and the chanted verses seem to me to be a parody of Anglo-Saxon compositions. 'Iron on iron clang, / Anvil on hammer bang' indeed. The subtle poet of *Beowulf* would have shaken his head at the sound of that. And here you will recall, as Tennyson may have recalled, Longfellow's remark that the Old English lines 'ring like hammers on an anvil'. Tennyson's lines certainly do. His effects are crude and obvious, and grossly over-determined: if you use

181

alliteration as a structural principle, you do not also need rhyme or anaphora, but this fragment stacks them all atop each other.

Yet Tennyson is a master of sound-effects, credited with one of the best ears of any English poet; it's not possible that he doesn't know what he is doing, or that he is simply incompetent. Must we not conclude that he here intends to create appropriately primitive poetry, – though perhaps here hedging a bit by associating it with drunkenness?

Later in the play *Harold*, just before the Battle of Hastings, King Harold asks if his men have managed to get any sleep. Leofwin says they have, and continues:

> LEOFWIN.      They are up again
> And chanting that old song of Brunanburg
> Where England conquer'd.
> HAROLD. That is well. The Norman, what is he doing?
> LEOFWIN. Praying for Normandy;
> Our scouts have heard the tinkle of their bells.
> HAROLD. And our old songs are prayers for England too!

In this scene, apparently borrowed from Bulwer's novel, *Harold the Last of the Saxon Kings*, the noisy old English war-songs seem to be set in positive contrast to the wimpish tinkling bells of the priest-ridden Normans. In 1849, Thomas Babington Macaulay had remarked: 'The polite luxury of the Norman presented a striking contrast to the coarse voracity and drunkenness of his Saxon and Danish neighbours'.[25] Indeed, these rough but lovable English do their praying through chanting their powerful and primitive songs. In Bulwer, the prayers of the English seem frankly pagan. There Normans are singing a 'monastic hymn' while the Saxon camp is loud with 'shouts of drink-hael and was-hael, bursts of gay laughter, snatches of old songs . . . [which] still spoke of the heathen time when War was a joy, and Valhalla was the heaven'.[26] This is of course pretty much Romantic nonsense: the Anglo-Saxons had been Christians for many years – longer than the Normans, in fact. Tennyson seems rather to be shadowing forth some Victorian opposition, where hearty English Protestants are placed against sly and evil continental Catholics, both embattled on the field of Hastings.

---

[25] Vols. I and II of *The History of England* appeared in 1849; the quotation is taken from a later edition (Boston and New York, 1899), I, p. 11.

[26] *The Works of Edward Bulwer-Lytton*, 30 vols. (New York, 1901), IX, p. 531.

This is a heavy weight of significance carried both by the play *Harold* and by Tennyson's conception of 'Brunanburh'. It has always seemed odd to Old English scholars of this century that this poem is made to carry this burden. Those of us who have grown old in the teaching of elementary Old English may think of *The Battle of Brunanburh* as a poem that is tidy but not especially exciting in any poetic sense, nonetheless a very useful one to have your students read early, mainly because it is completely conventional, a rich mass of clichés that students will need to learn in order to read such highly formulaic poetry. If we feel the need to provide students with truly exciting war-songs, we can turn to *The Battle of Maldon* or, even better, the fragmentary *Fight at Finnsburg* or perhaps to some of the stirring speeches in *Beowulf*.

Furthermore one prevailing view of *The Battle of Brunanburh* has been that it is exactly the kind of war-song that would be composed by someone who had never been near a battlefield, something penned at leisure by a talented monk back in the palace bureaucracy who was chiefly concerned with stressing the political significance to the Wessex royal house of this victory. His poem offers virtually no real detail of the actual fighting but treats the participants in scorecard fashion as either exulting winners or humiliated losers, and stresses, as bureaucrats do, the statistics of the event: ITEM five kings killed, ITEM seven earls eliminated, ITEM one king's son left abandoned by his father, ITEM two enemy leaders run away in disgrace, etc.

To be fair to *Brunanburh*, however, we should see it as it is, and not as what it is not. It is surely not the primitive war-song Tennyson thought it was, but it does have genuine importance as one of the earliest documents in English to show any real sense of nationalism or patriotism, and it expresses such feelings strongly and well.[27] The poet carefully praises Mercians along with West Saxons, and sets their firm alliance in contrast to the appalling disintegration of the invading forces. A nation is being born here, in a swelling surge of triumphant recognition of the fact. Early, and more authentic, heroic poetry ordinarily shows little

---

[27] For defences (on different grounds) of the poem's artistry, see T. Lawlor, 'Brunanburh: Craft and Art', *Literary Studies: Essays in Memory of Francis A. Drumm*, ed. J. H. Dorenkamp (Wetteren, Belgium, 1973), pp. 52–67, and D. W. Frese, 'Poetic Prowess in *Brunanburh* and *Maldon*: Winning, Losing, and Literary Outcome', in *Modes of Interpretation in Old English Literature: Essays in Honour of Stanley B. Greenfield*, ed. P. R. Brown, G. R. Crampton and F. C. Robinson (Toronto, 1986), pp. 83–99.

understanding of historical context, nor can its memory move back more than a generation or two. But the literate *Brunanburh* poet understands enough history to recognize that his own English ancestors once swarmed just as hungrily over Britain as the recent invaders swarmed over the field at Brunanburh – the crucial difference, isn't it, is that We Won and These Guys Lost. There may well be certain congruences here with the feelings of Victorian Englishmen and women, at an exciting time of imperial expansion, even though (or maybe because) Tennyson had never been near a battlefield either. In introducing his prose translation, in fact, Hallam Tennyson calls the poem 'this fine old English national war-ode'.[28]

If we turn from content to the style of the poem, we find that it is a little hard now to remember that in 1876 any sample of Old English still seemed fresh and new to readers unfamiliar with much Old English verse (certainly so to the Tennysons). We have the advantage of having read *Beowulf* and some of the elegiac poems, where the style is put to much more demanding poetic use. Scholars now are likely to think of *Brunanburh*'s particular style as one of deliberate archaizing; the poet has made a decision to celebrate a contemporary event in the heroic language of the old days, which he has pulled out of some cold-storage file and reconstituted fairly well.[29] Indeed, in his study of Tennyson's translation, Michael Alexander calls the poem 'the epitaph as well as epitome of the old heroic verse,' having particularly in mind its overabundance of poetic diction.[30] Still, when Alexander comes to the actual translation of the poem, he confesses real admiration for the original. 'The feature of *Brunanburh* which most impressed and eluded me in translating it,' he remarks, 'was its sustained syntactical control: clichés everywhere, the whole magnificent' (p. 158). I'm sure that Tennyson sensed some of this magnificence, though perhaps without fully understanding its nature.

Alexander notes Tennyson's use of archaic words: you will observe such ancient and obsolete past tenses as 'brake', 'glode', 'hapt' and 'gat', as well as the mysterious 'war-glaive'. But of course this is a quite different kind of archaism than what the Anglo-Saxon poet attempted: it is a modern's attempt to suggest the antiquity of all this poetry – indeed of the very

---

[28] Hallam Tennyson's comment appeared in the *Contemporary Review* 11 (1876), p. 920.

[29] See my article, 'The Heroic Style in *The Battle of Maldon*', *SP* 58 (1961), pp. 457–67, for a description of how this might be done.

[30] Alexander, 'Tennyson's "Battle of Brunanburh"'.

language itself – by preserving a few selected fossil forms for display. Hallam and Alfred Tennyson found some of this archaism ready-made in Edwin Guest's opinionated *History of English Rhythms*, which had come out in 1838.[31]

Guest's book deserves a little mention. After ill-tempered scoldings of Rask, Grimm, Thorpe and other early scholars, Guest offers a translation with notes for what he calls *The Brunanburh War-Song*, a title which explains Tennyson's references to the poem as a war-song. He calls Brunanburh 'a battle, that involved more important interests, than any that has ever yet been fought within the Island. It was indeed a battle between *races*: and had England failed, her name might have been lost for ever . . . The song, which celebrated the victory, is worthy of the effort that gained it.'[32] Modern historians surely would not 'play the race card' and might be unlikely to cast the battle's importance in such extreme terms; but perhaps Guest drew his impression chiefly from the poem's own rhetoric of superlatives.

In his pursuit of the archaic, Guest rather cryptically refers to swords as 'hammer-glaives' and a ring-giver as 'beigh-giver', preserving the Old English word *beah* 'ring'. Tennyson keeps the glaives but we can be grateful he drops the beighs. A few words and phrases of Guest's translation survive intact into the elder Tennyson's version: for instance, the curious use of the word 'spoiler' for 'hettend' (usually translated as 'enemy') in line 20 of Tennyson's translation; the inevitable 'fallow flood' (61); and 'the grey beast, the wolf of the weald' (110).

In such ways, Tennyson tries to preserve some flavour of alterity, but he also makes some important changes. One change – a way of making it seem more familiar to readers – is to divide the poem up into sections or strophes, following the classical models Tennyson and many in his audience knew so well. Old English poetry ordinarily runs non-stop without such breaks. Henry Morley in the second edition of his *English Writers* mentions German theorists like Karl Müllenhoff who had proposed in 1861 an original strophic form for Germanic verse; Tennyson might have heard of this hypothesis, now discarded.[33] The effect of the

---

[31] E. Guest, *A History of English Rhythms*, 2 vols. (London, 1838). Vol. II contains the translation and discussion of *Brunanburh*.

[32] Guest, *A History of English Rhythms*, II, p. 60.

[33] H. Morley, *English Writers*, 2nd edn. (London, 1888), II, pp. 27–31.

division into strophes in our text is to imply more elaborate planning on the part of the poet, or at least a different kind of planning. At its best the strophe form sets off or underlines important contrasts that were clearly in the mind of the original poet (e.g. the difference between the way the defeated enemies go home and the way the victorious West Saxons go home, as in sections XII and XIII), but sometimes it seems ham-handed and unnecessarily distracting. Some simple unnumbered paragraphing, such as we see, for instance, in Tennyson's own poem *Ulysses*, might have done as well; and indeed this is what modern editors of Old English are likely to introduce, as a less ostentatious way of guiding readers.

From whatever faint memories he may have had of Kemble's conversations, and with the help of his son Hallam and presumably also of Walter Skeat who provided notes for Hallam's version, Tennyson doubtless had a good idea of what Anglo-Saxon sounded like, and his translation is clearly imitative of some of the basic rhythms of the original. One basic rhythm is set up by the trochaic beat most evident in the Sievers Type A verse which in *Beowulf* makes up about 45 per cent of the verses. These verses may be seen in the sample of the original text in the Appendix: *eorla dryhten, sweorda ecgum, bordweal clufon, hord and hamas*, and you can see Tennyson imitating these verses closely in 'glory in battle', 'slew with the sword-edge,' 'brake the shield-wall', and so on. I count well over 85 per cent of the short lines in his translation, more than 90 per cent if we include many of the lines in the longer groups that end his sections, as belonging to this A type or a close variant of it – creating a monotonous hammering effect which is not at all in fact the sound of Old English verse.

The reader would be right to challenge me instantly: how do I know what Old English verse sounded like? I don't, but I am sure it was far more varied in its rhythmical movements than Tennyson's translation – look at his section XI, for instance, for a long run of verses precisely identical in rhythm. Old English verse never displays such monotony. And look again at the Old English sample: for instance, at the verses, usually Sievers Types B and C, which do not begin with heavy stresses but with unimportant words and syllables. The feel of Old English rhythm is better conveyed in the sample of Alexander's translation in the Appendix. A harp originally accompanied and probably punctuated the recitation of Old English verse in some way now unrecoverable by us, but the appropriate instrument for Tennyson's version would be the kettle-drum.

These are the boisterous and rollicking rhythms of an oncoming generation of poets – Rudyard Kipling, Robert W. Service and Vachel Lindsay, none of them much in fashion today (except among American 'cowboy poets'). We do have many accounts of the way Tennyson liked to read his own poetry to visitors, usually in a loud, highly dramatic way and for hours at a time. Actually, what one remembers from his translation of *Brunanburh* is its heavy higgledy-piggledy double-dactylic rhythm, not typical of Old English, but exactly the same rhythm he had used in his 'Charge of the Light Brigade' composed twenty-two years earlier:

> Cannon to right of them
> Cannon to left of them
> Cannon in front of them
> Volley'd and thunder'd.[34]

The rhythm of Anglo-Saxon *Brunanburh* had been converted into a 'war-song' rhythm already heard long before by Tennyson as appropriate to the subject.

But all this is only to say that Tennyson's translation distorts the original. All translations do that. The classic remark is that of the classical scholar Richard Bentley on Alexander Pope's translation of the *Iliad*: 'It is a very pretty poem, Mr Pope, but you must not call it Homer' – as if Pope did not realize that his great version was not Homer, but was an Augustan poem that eighteenth-century readers would understand and enjoy. And so Tennyson wrote for his own Victorian audience. His version of *Brunanburh* must have told thousands of readers that there was some quite exciting and rather different-sounding verse to be discovered back in the dim English past (though it also sounded comfortably modern). Further understanding of its nature would have to await better tools with which to study it.

But now I would like to close on an upbeat by asking not what Alfred Tennyson did for Anglo-Saxon but what Anglo-Saxon did for Alfred Tennyson. His late poems show much interesting experimentation in metre, the use of dialect and general register.[35] The 'Northern Farmer' poems in Lincolnshire dialect are one example. One should remember

---

[34] Ricks, *The Poems of Tennyson*, II, p. 510.

[35] On the style of these late poems, see W. D. Shaw, *Tennyson's Style* (Ithaca, 1976), pp. 70–2, and A. W. Thomson, *The Poetry of Tennyson* (London, 1986), p. 248.

that at the same time Gerard Manley Hopkins was independently working with archaic language, stress metre and heavy alliteration.

Tennyson's greatest achievement in this new style was unquestionably influenced by his contact with Anglo-Saxon verse: it is 'Merlin and the Gleam,' a cryptic summary of his literary career written in 1889 when the poet was eighty years old. This poem uses a more supple variant of the *Brunanburh* metre, but now infused with deep personal feeling – and that makes all the difference. Let the poet speak for himself, and appropriately have the final word:

> And broader and brighter
> The Gleam flying onward,
> Wed to the melody,
> Sang through the world;
> And slower and fainter,
> Old and weary,
> But eager to follow,
> I saw, whenever
> In passing it glanced upon
> Hamlet or city,
> That under the Crosses
> The dead man's garden,
> The mortal hillock,
> Would break into blossom;
> And so to the land's
> Last limit I came –
> And can no longer,
> But die rejoicing,
> 'For through the Magic
> Of Him the Mighty,
> Who taught me in childhood,
> There on the border
> Of boundless Ocean,
> And all but in Heaven
> Hovers the Gleam.'[36]

---

[36] I would like to thank Cecil Lang for a helpful reference, Jerome Denno for securing material, and the library staff of the University of Utah and Brigham Young University for aiding a newcomer in the Victorian thickets.

## THE BATTLE OF BRUNANBURH

1. The Old English text, lines 1–10a.[37]

Her Æþelstan cyning,      eorla dryhten,
beorna beahgifa,     and his broþor eac,
Eadmund æþeling,     ealdorlangne tir
geslogon æt sæcce     sweorda ecgum
ymbe Brunanburh.     Bordweal clufan,
heowan heaþolinde     hamora lafan,
afaran Eadweardes,     swa him geæþele wæs
from cneomægum,     þæt hi æt campe oft
wiþ laþra gehwæne     land ealgodon,
hord and hamas.

2. Tennyson's translation.
   I
   Athelstan King,
   Lord among Earls,
   Bracelet-bestower and
   Baron of Barons,
   He with his brother,           5
   Edmund Atheling,
   Gaining a lifelong
   Glory in battle,
   Slew with the sword-edge
   There by Brunanburh,          10
   Brake the shield-wall,
   Hewed the lindenwood,
   Hacked the battleshield,
   Sons of Edward with hammered brands.

   II
   Theirs was a greatness          15
   Got from their Grandsires —
   Theirs that so often in

---

[37] Text from *The Anglo-Saxon Minor Poems*, ed. E. V. K. Dobbie, ASPR 6 (New York, 1942); this is based on one *Anglo-Saxon Chronicle* manuscript, Cambridge, Corpus Christi College 173.

Strife with their enemies
Struck for their hoards and their hearths and their homes.

III
Bowed the spoiler,                                            20
Bent the Scotsman,
Fell the shipcrews
Doomed to the death.
All the field with blood of the fighters
Flowed, from when first the great                            25
Sun-star of morningtide,
Lamp of the Lord God
Lord everlasting,
Glode over earth till the glorious creature
Sank to his setting.                                         30

 IV
There lay many a man
Marred by the javelin,
Men of the Northland
Shot over shield.
There was the Scotsman                                       35
Weary of war.

V
We the West-Saxons,
Long as the daylight
Lasted, in companies
Troubled the track of the host that we hated,                40
Grimly with swords that were sharp from the grindstone,
Fiercely we hacked at the flyers before us.

VI
Mighty the Mercian,
Hard was his hand-play,
Sparing not any of                                           45
Those that with Anlaf,
Warriors over the
Weltering waters
Borne in the bark's-bosom,
Drew to this island:                                         50
Doomed to the death.

VII
Five young kings put asleep by the sword-stroke,
Seven strong Earls of the army of Anlaf
Fell on the war-field, numberless numbers,
Shipmen and Scotsmen.                                    55

VIII
Then the Norse leader,
Dire was his need of it,
Few were his following,
Fled to his warship:
Fleeted his vessel to sea with the king in it,          60
Saving his life on the fallow flood.

IX
Also the crafty one,
Constantinus,
Crept to his North again,
Hoar-headed hero!                                        65

X
Slender warrant had
*He* to be proud of
The welcome of war-knives –
He that was reft of his
Folk and his friends that had                            70
Fallen in conflict,
Leaving his son too
Lost in the carnage,
Mangled to morsels,
A youngster in war!                                      75

XI
Slender reason had
*He* to be glad of
The clash of the war-glaive –
Traitor and trickster
And spurner of treaties –                                80
He nor had Anlaf
With armies so broken
A reason for bragging

That they had the better
In perils of battle                                    85
On places of slaughter –
The struggle of standards,
The rush of the javelins,
The crash of the charges,
The wielding of weapons —                              90
The play that they played with
The children of Edward.

### XII
Then with their nailed prows
Parted the Norsemen, a
Blood-reddened relic of                                95
Javelins over
The jarring breaker, the deep-sea billow,
Shaping their way toward Dyflen again,
Shamed in their souls.

### XIII
Also the brethren,                                     100
King and Atheling,
Each in his glory,
Went to his own in his own West-Saxonland,
Glad of the war.

### XIV
Many a carcase they left to be carrion,                105
Many a livid one, many a sallow-skin –
Left for the white-tailed eagle to tear it, and
Left for the horny-nibbed raven to rend it, and
Gave to the garbaging war-hawk to gorge it, and
That gray beast, the wolf of the weald.                110

### XV
Never had huger
Slaughter of heroes
Slain by the sword-edge –
Such as old writers
Have writ of in histories –                            115
Hapt in this isle, since

Up from the East hither
Saxon and Angle from
Over the broad billow
Broke into Britain with                                   120
Haughty war-workers who
Harried the Welshman, when
Earls that were lured by the
Hunger of glory gat
Hold of the land.                                         125

3. For comparison, a section of Michael Alexander's contemporary translation, corresponding to Tennyson's VIII and IX. This is much closer
   than Tennyson's version to the varying rhythms of Old English verse,
   and keeps a pattern of two alliterating stresses in each line.

   With a scant retinue
   The prince of the Northmen was put to flight
   By stark need to the stern of his craft:
   The long ship drove out across the dark waters;
   The king slipped away, saved his life.
   The old king likewise came away also,
   The grey-haired campaigner, Constantine, fled
   To the North he knew.

# Lady Godiva

## DANIEL DONOGHUE

In 1857, for Prince Albert's thirty-eighth birthday Queen Victoria gave him 'a gilded silver statuette of a nude Lady Godiva, side saddle on her horse'.[1] Today we cannot be certain of the motivation behind the gift: was it a private token with erotic overtones between a wife and husband? Was it political, with Godiva's figure signifying Victoria's lifelong and heroic self-sacrifice for her subjects' common good – a woman who forsook the private role society expected of the weaker sex in order to assume a public duty? Was it political in a marital sense, a sign of wifely submission to Albert, whose official title that very year had been announced as 'Prince Consort', permanently labelling him as the queen's social and political inferior?[2] Was its appeal simply aesthetic? Whatever the motivation, Victoria's choice of a gift is an indication of the extent to which the Godiva legend had become domesticated by the nineteenth century. In an age that romanticized the medieval past (as other contributions to this volume demonstrate), Lady Godiva was a household name.

It is still a household name. I am convinced that the name 'Godiva' is more widely recognized around the world than that of any other Anglo-Saxon. The greatest irony of her post-medieval notoriety is that the historical Godiva was a pious and respectable countess who almost certainly never made the horseback ride through Coventry that legend attributes to her. Alfred the Great or the Venerable Bede, because of their unquestionable accomplishments, may be more deserving of the title of

---

[1] S. Weintraub, *Victoria: an Intimate Biography* (New York, 1987), p. 239. The statuette was designed by Emile Jeannest, now in the Armoury of Windsor Castle.

[2] The year before Victoria had given him '. . . a picture of myself, in uniform, on horseback.' Queen Victoria's Journal, quoted by Sarah, Duchess of York, with Benita Stoney, in *Victoria and Albert: Life at Osborne House* (London, 1991), p. 123.

the world's most famous Anglo-Saxon, but in contrast to what the *Beowulf*-poet tells us about *dom*, fame doesn't always go to the most deserving. Fame is more like the fickle goddess in Chaucer's dream vision, *The House of Fame*.

Anglo-Saxonists have shied away from studying the historical Godiva because there is something suspiciously tawdry about her popularized, post-medieval reputation; and besides, the pre-Conquest evidence is very slight. On the other hand, literary and cultural historians of later periods seem content to accept her legend as self-explanatory, without looking at the historical woman. This paper begins to redress this imbalance by discussing the cultural reception of Godiva from the early Middle Ages through the Victorian period and up to today, with some speculation on the relevance of her story to recent film criticism.

The extent of Godiva's name-recognition around the world today is hard to overestimate. In casual surveys I have conducted for several years, my informants tell me that Godiva is known in countries as far away as Malaysia, India, China and Japan, not to mention all of Europe and North and South America. Archival research shows that she has been celebrated by everyone from Dr Freud to Dr Seuss; she has been adopted as the patron saint of groups as diverse as tax protesters, advocates for women's rights and nudists; she has been the subject of paintings, sculpture, ballads, poems, novels, plays, movies, pop songs, even an opera. The quality of these works spans the spectrum from the tasteless to the refined, but in almost every retelling Lady Godiva is an exemplary figure: beautiful, virtuous, and unclothed.

Although my informal surveys show that her name is well-known, the details of her legend seem to be fading from memory. Older people seem to know more about the circumstances of her ride; younger ones seem just to know that she rode naked on a horse. Most of my undergraduate students, for example, have no idea that she lived in England, let alone Coventry, and nearly all think she lived in a later century, usually the sixteenth century or later. An important lesson from my survey is that – at least in North America – Godiva has become unmoored from her historical origins. She is simply known to be European from a time when people rode horses. Most of my informants cannot believe that Godiva's scandalous ride could happen in a period as unexciting and undecadent as pre-Conquest England.

The current pronunciation of Godiva, with the accent on the second syllable is perhaps the first obstacle to recognizing her Anglo-Saxon origin. It sounds more Italian than English. Her name in Old English is Godgifu (a compound with primary stress on the first syllable), which means 'good gift'.[3] She lived at the end of the Anglo-Saxon period, flourishing from about 1040 to 1067, her presumed date of death.[4] The earliest historical records, including the *Anglo-Saxon Chronicle* and William of Malmesbury, consistently speak of her as a beautiful woman, generous to monasteries and devoted to the Virgin Mary. In 1043 she and her husband Leofric founded a Benedictine monastery in Coventry, and according to William of Malmesbury, they endowed it with such wealth that the very walls seemed too narrow to contain it.[5] We know she was fairly wealthy: she had extensive land holdings in several counties, and the town of Coventry was one of her possessions. She used her wealth to support a number of other religious houses across Mercia and beyond. We can surmise that she came from a distinguished family not only because of her marriage to Leofric but also because her brother may have been Thorold of Bucknall, sheriff of Lincolnshire.[6] If the legend of her ride had not overtaken her, we would know very little about Godgifu, except perhaps that her marriage made her one of the more important women of her age, certainly not as powerful as the earlier lady of the Mercians, Æthelflæd, or her older contemporary Queen Emma. But even if they overshadow Godgifu, the contemporary and near-contemporary sources

---

[3] Compare the women's names Eadgifu and Æthelgifu; it is less likely that the name means 'gift of God'.

[4] J. C. Lancaster, *Godiva of Coventry* (Coventry, 1967), is the most recent compilation of historical data on Godiva, for the date of death, see page 32 and the list of obits on Plate I, Oxford, Bodleian Library, Douce 139, fol. 1v. Much of the following discussion draws from her review of the historical record. Other compilations are F. Bliss Burbidge, *Old Coventry and Lady Godiva* (Birmingham, 1952), and K. Häfele, *Die Godivasage und ihre Behandlung in der Literatur* (Heidelberg, 1929).

[5] The full passage is 'Erat id in diocesi Cestrensi cenobium a magnificentissimo comite Lefrico et uxore Godifa constructum tanto auri et argenti spectaculo, ut angusti viderentur ipsi parietes æcclesiarum thesaurorum receptaculis, miraculo porro visentium oculis', *Willelmi Malmesbiriensis Monachi Gesta Pontificum Anglorum*, ed. N. E. Hamilton, Rolls Series 52 (1887; London, 1964), pp. 309–10.

[6] 'Ego Godiua comitissa diu istud desideraui': *Codex Diplomaticus Aevi Saxonici*, ed. J. Kemble (London, 1846), p. 128. The charter is a forgery, but it may accurately record the relation between Thorold and Godgifu. See P. H. Sawyer, *Anglo-Saxon Charters* (London, 1968), no. 1230.

(however slight) show her to be one of the more wealthy and generous women at the end of the Anglo-Saxon period.

Her husband Leofric assumed the title of Earl of Mercia under Cnut and held it until his death in 1057, during the reign of Edward the Confessor. Significantly more is known about him. He was an important figure in the shifting balance of power during the last decades of Anglo-Saxon England, in the machinations that took place in determining the succession to the throne, and in other military and political events of the time. Shortly after Edward the Confessor's accession to the throne, for example, he joined the other two earls, Godwine and Siward, in a punitive expedition to Winchester to deprive Queen Emma (Edward's mother) of control over the royal treasury. The *Chronicle* describes Leofric as 'very wise in divine and temporal matters; that was a benefit to all this people'.[7] In addition to his donations to monasteries, his reputation for piety is based on a vision attributed to him, which is recounted in a short piece of Old English prose, *The Vision of Leofric*. When Godgifu died (perhaps ten years after Leofric) she was buried, according to William of Malmesbury, near her husband in the porch of the church in Coventry Abbey.

The first chroniclers to mention her ride were Roger of Wendover (d. 1236) and Matthew Paris (d. 1259), both of whom were monks at St Albans in the thirteenth century. In other words, the first versions of the ride are attested more than 150 years and several chroniclers after Godgifu's death. Contemporary and less distant accounts, such as the *Anglo-Saxon Chronicle*, John of Worcester, Symeon of Durham, William of Malmesbury, Henry of Huntingdon, Roger of Hoveden, and Walter of Coventry make no reference to it. Matthew Paris's version (which closely follows Roger's) recounts the story in surprisingly rich detail:

This countess, piously wishing to deliver the city of Coventry from a burdensome and shameful servitude, often entreated the count her husband, with earnest prayers, under the favour of the Holy Trinity and the Holy Mother of God, to deliver the town from that servitude. And when the count rebuked her for

[7] *An Anglo-Saxon Chronicle from British Museum, Cotton MS, Tiberius B. iv*, ed. E. Classen and F. E. Harmer (Manchester, 1926), anno 1057: 'se wæs swiðe wis for Gode ond eac for worulde, 'þæt fremode ealre þisre ðeode'. Translation from *The Anglo-Saxon Chronicle: a revised version*, ed. D. Whitelock, with D. C. Douglas and S. I. Tucker (New Brunswick, N.J., 1961).

persisting in pointlessly asking for something harmful to him, he resolutely forbade her to approach him on this subject again. She, on the contrary, prompted by female obstinacy, exasperating her husband incessantly with her request, at last extorted this answer from him: 'Mount,' he said, 'your horse naked, and ride through the town's marketplace, from beginning to end, with the people gathered, and upon your return you will be given what you ask.' In response the countess said to him, 'And if I bring myself to do so, will you give me permission?' The count replied, 'I will'. Then the countess Godgifu, beloved by God, on a certain day as it was arranged, mounting her horse naked and loosening the hair and tresses of her head, covered her whole body except her beautiful legs; and when she had finished her journey, not seen by anyone, she returned with joy to her husband, who took this as a miracle. Count Leofric, releasing the city of Coventry from the prior servitude, confirmed the charter thence made with the sanction of his own seal.[8]

The earliest versions contain the essential elements which have been repeated up to the present day: Godiva desires to release the town from an oppressive tax; her unsympathetic husband gives a seemingly impossible condition to fulfil; she accepts it as a literal condition and exacts the promise from him; she rides, with long hair covering most of her body, unseen by anyone; her husband relents and lifts the taxes.

Leofric's pious reaction to her ride – *hoc pro miraculo habentem* – is itself only slightly less miraculous than the mysterious way she was able to ride through the town unseen, *a nemine visa*. In either Matthew's Anglo-

---

[8] 'Hæc autem comitissa religiosa villam Coventrensem a gravi servitute ac turpi liberare affectans, sæpius comitem virum suum magnis precibus rogavit, ut Sanctæ Trinitatis, Sanctæque Dei Genetricis intuitu, villam a prædicta absolveret servitute. Cumque comes illam increparet quod rem sibi dampnosam inaniter postularet, prohibuit constanter ne ipsum super hac re de cætero conveniret. Illa e contrario, pertinacia muliebri ducta, virum indesinenter de petitione præmissa exasperans, tale responsum extorsit ab eo: "Ascende", inquit, "equum tuum nuda, et transi per mercatum villæ, ab initio usque ad finem, populo congregato, et cum redieris quod postulas impetrabis". Cui comitissa respondens, ait, "Et si hoc facere voluero, licentiam mihi dabis?" Ad quam comes, "Dabo", inquit. Tunc Godgyva comitissa, Deo dilecta, die quadam, ut prædictum est, nuda equum ascendens, crines capitis et tricas dissolvens, corpus suum totum præter crura candidissima inde velavit, et itinere completo, a nemine visa, ad virum gaudens, hoc pro miraculo habentem, reversa est. Comes vero Leofricus, Coventrensem a præfata servitute liberans civitatem, cartam suam inde factam sigilli sui munimine roboravit.' *Flores historiarum*, ed. H. R. Luard (London, 1890), anno 1057. The phrase *e contrario, pertinacia muliebri ducta* is an addition by Matthew, replacing Roger of Wendover's less judgmental *vero nihilominus constans in proposito*.

Norman or Leofric's Anglo-Saxon society, Godiva's action would have amounted to a public shaming of her husband, because she puts her body on public display, which under law was her husband's private possession. Any doubt about the spuriousness of the legend should evaporate in light of some of the more egregious anachronisms in this account, such as the fact that eleventh-century Coventry was less a town than a farming village scarcely big enough for a market; or that because Godgifu owned Coventry outright, she presumably could remit local taxes at any time without Leofric's permission. Matthew's and Roger's interpretation of Godiva is shaped by Anglo-Norman law and Anglo-Norman customs, under which the rights of women to own and dispose of property were circumscribed. Upon marriage, the woman's husband would assume control of all property.[9] The late appearance of the story, the erroneous description of Coventry as a market town, and the assumptions about Leofric's exclusive rights to change the taxes are enough to doubt the story's authenticity.

Later historians such as Higden in the fourteenth century, Holinshed in the sixteenth and Dugdale in the seventeenth largely repeat the earliest version or simply allude to it as though it was well known. So we can assume that fairly early the story had entered the general culture and had been accepted as historical fact. Its popularity can be traced, I think, to some contradictory elements in it. Godiva is a blend of sin and saintliness. Her ride smacks of scandal, but her motivations are heroic. She is an erotic figure, but not a seducer. Although naked, she preserves her modesty under her hair and by riding unseen. She is a noble woman who sympathizes with the common people. She emerges from the privacy of her home to risk public censure. Her advocacy borders on defiance of her husband's authority, yet she submits to him in the end. Finally and perhaps most significantly, though the citizens of Coventry are kept from viewing her, the reader is directed to observe her long hair and beautiful legs as she disrobes, mounts and rides across town. In all of these contraries – scandalous but virtuous, naked but modest, defiant but submissive, watched but unwatched – the moral half exculpates the immoral half, so the reader can indulge in the erotic spectacle. In a word, the legend legitimizes voyeurism; and without voyeurism the legend would never have gained popularity. Every age after the thirteenth

---

[9] See C. Fell, *Women in Anglo-Saxon England* (London, 1984), p. 149.

century has retold the story using the norms of privacy, eroticism and transgression of its own time.[10]

Up through the nineteenth century the story is repeated regularly in histories and in literature. A ballad from the end of the sixteenth century gives the crucial conversation between Leofricus and Godiva in the following stanzas:

> 'Command what you think good, my Lord;
>   I will thereto agree
> on that condityon, that this towne
>   in all things may bee ffree.'
>
> 'If thou wilt stripp thy clothes off,
>   & heere wilt lay them downe,
> & att noone-daye on horsbacke ryde,
>   starke naked through the towne,
>
> 'they shalbe free for euermore.
>   If thou wilt not doe soe,
> more lyberty then now they haue
>   I neuer will bestowe.'

This ballad was reprinted at least three times in the eighteenth century, and is quoted here from Thomas Percy's *Reliques of Ancient English Poetry* (1765).[11] It is a version that portrays Leofric as a villain, a characterization that will grow from the sixteenth century onwards, in contrast to Godiva's simple virtue. Note too that Leofric seems to urge her to make the ride insofar as it becomes literalized as a 'condityon' for lifting the taxes: 'If thou wilt stripp thy clothes off . . . they shalbe free for euermore'. The Leofric of the earlier versions clearly does not want Godgifu to ride naked through Coventry and assumes that she would never submit herself to such public humiliation. His offer is an *impossibilia*, the rhetorical equivalent of denying her request. (Compare Dorigen in *The Franklin's Tale*, who promises to give herself to Aurelius

---

[10] For recent studies of voyeurism in medieval literature, see A. C. Spearing, The *Medieval Poet as Voyeur: Looking and Listening in Medieval Love-Narratives* (Cambridge, 1993). See also note 16.

[11] *Percy Folio*, ed. J. W. Hales and F. J. Furnivall, 3 vols. (London, 1867–1868), III, pp. 473–7. About 1750 it was also printed as a broadsheet entitled *Coventry made free by Godina, countess of Chester. To the tune of, Prince Arthur died at Ludlow, &c.* The authorship has been attributed to Thomas Deloney, who died in 1600.

only after the rocks disappear from the coast of Brittany, an *impossibilia* which he takes literally.) The Leofric of the ballad, however, proposes to lift taxes only if his wife puts her body on public display, as if there were a causal link between the two.

An interesting account in the 1569 *Chronicle* by Richard Grafton, a native of Coventry who may have had access to a local version now lost, speaks of a 'streight commaundement' that forbade any citizen from looking 'vpon a great paine', so that Godiva was able to return to Leofric, 'her honestie saued, her purpose obteyned, her wisedome much commended, and her husbands imagination vtterly disappointed'.[12] This version turns Leofric's *impossibilia* into a condition and makes him a villain as in the ballad. Not only is 'his imagination vtterly disappointed' that she accepted his condition and made the ride in the first place, but also that she returned without being seen. There is no hint that he might feel dishonour or relief that her shame was averted. On the contrary, the description of his imagination as 'vtterly disappointed' carries the suggestion that he took pleasure in the prospect of his wife's public humiliation.

In addition to the edict forbidding the townspeople to look when Godiva rides, the period up to 1800 saw another, related addition to the plot: the figure who defies the edict and sneaks a peek. The edict is important because it unambiguously marks the act of looking as a transgression and invites it at the same time. It also, in effect, declares the public spaces of Coventry private; the streets and marketplace become an extension of her private chamber. In the earlier versions of the story, the feat of riding unseen is attributed vaguely to God's intervention, a miracle that preserved her from shame. The newly added scapegoat figure is miraculously blinded or struck dead for defying the edict. In the earliest versions he is anonymous, then identified as a tailor and given a name, Peeping Tom.[13] In fact, the Godiva legend provides the origin for

---

[12] *Chronicle, or History of England* (1569); reprint ed. Sir Henry Ellis (London, 1809), pp. 147–8. On the possiblity of the other source as a chronicle written by Geoffrey, a thirteenth-century prior of Coventry, see Lancaster, *Godiva of Coventry*, pp. 47–8. In his *Antiquities of Warwickshire* (London, 1656), William Dugdale quotes a brief Latin passage from an otherwise unknown 'Chron MS Galfr. Pr. de Cov.', p. 100.

[13] The earliest references to a peeping figure are in the mid-seventeenth century (Lancaster, *Godiva of Coventry*, pp. 53–4). The first reference to a tailor and to the phrase 'Peeping Tom' comes at the end of the eighteenth century (Burbidge, *Old Coventry and Lady Godiva*, p. 52).

the phrase 'Peeping Tom', which has become inseparably linked to voyeurism.[14] Given the official edict just mentioned, a scapegoat punished for his transgression is not a surprising addition. The edict foregrounds the sense of transgression, but the guilt and punishment are transferred to Peeping Tom, which allows the reader to gaze with impunity on the spectacle. With the addition of this character, the story was ready for its reception in the Victorian period.

Fascination with Godiva reaches a peak with the Victorians. She moves from a local to a national hero, paradoxically at a time when historians had established that the legend had no basis in history. The legend was disseminated in a number of ways. The Victorian period was (after the Middle Ages) the great age of encyclopedias, and the entries for Godiva no doubt contributed to her popularization. Even though most declare the legend apocryphal, the entries go on to devote far more space to it than to the historical record. It was a way of debunking the story while reinforcing it in the popular imagination, a pattern that encyclopedias today still follow. The vacillation between history and legend can be seen, for example, in the poems of Leigh Hunt and Tennyson, both of whom refused to believe that the story was fiction in spite of authoritative pronouncements to the contrary. Aside from the numerous literary retellings, a good gauge of Godiva's Victorian popularity are the dozens of paintings and sculptures – far more than from any other period.[15]

Although all things medieval enjoyed a renewed popularity in the Victorian period, the sustained attention to Godiva is extraordinary. Perhaps nothing can adequately explain her phenomenal popularity, but in the Preface to the medieval volume of his *History of Private Life*, Georges Duby hints at one likely cause. After characterizing Emmanuel LeRoy Ladurie's *Montaillou* and its depiction of women given to curiosity, spying and gossip, he quotes from it: 'Not until our own day and the advent of more bourgeois societies enamoured of private life did this female espionage diminish or at any rate decline somewhat in the face of

---

[14] The *OED* entry for 'peeping', *ppl. a²*, says of the word: 'Now usu. applied to a prying person, esp. with connnotations of prurience; one who obtains gratification from furtively observing women not fully clothed or the sexual activity of others; = *voyeur*'. Thirteen of the fourteen citations after 1796 concern 'peeping tom'.

[15] For a comprehensive list and discussion, see R. A. Clarke and P. A. E. Day, *Lady Godiva: Images of a Legend in Art and Society* (Coventry, 1982).

repression'. Duby goes on to question whether it is even 'legitimate (not merely pertinent) to speak of private life in the Middle Ages, to transfer to such a remote era the idea of *privacy*, which first emerged in the nineteenth century in England, at that time the society that had progressed furthest in the establishment of a "bourgeois" culture?'. One can speak of privacy in the medieval period, he concludes, but it must be understood in its cultural context.[16]

Duby's contrast between Victorian England and the Middle Ages is not just a convenient coincidence. There is a deeper connection between the two. What makes the Godiva story so arresting is that it places on public display what is most private. Her transgression is not accidental, but quite deliberate, and is instigated by her husband, who has legal rights over her body. In earlier centuries her ride would be a violation of decent behaviour, of course, but nakedness would have less shock value at a time when privacy was a privilege enjoyed by relatively few. The spying, moreover, is primarily male not female espionage. If, as Duby and others have argued, Victorian England was the first society where privacy was widely established among the middle class, then the public display of nakedness could become spectacularly scandalous. Godiva's nakedness would seem that much more shocking; the need for a scapegoat figure to insulate the reader from guilt would become more urgent; and the relation between the virtuous and scandalous aspects of the story would grow increasingly polarized.

Other social conditions of Victorian England added to the story's potential appeal. It was a time of anxiety in the face of rapid industrialization; a time when the working class suffered exceedingly (heavy taxes being part of the burden), and when middle class women grew increasingly frustrated at the role society expected them to fulfill. The opening lines of Tennyson's famous poem explicitly mention some of these themes:[17]

---

[16] G. Duby, ed. *A History of Private Life: Revelations of the Medieval World*, trans. A. Goldhammer, 2 vols. (Cambridge, Mass., 1988), II, p. ix. I am indebted for this reference to Sarah Stanbury, 'The Voyeur and the Private Life in *Troilus and Criseyde*', *Studies in the Age of Chaucer* 13 (1991), p. 141. See also her 'The Virgin's Gaze: Spectacle and Transgression in Middle English Lyrics of the Passion', *PMLA* 106 (1991), pp. 1,083–93.

[17] See C. Christ, 'The Feminine Subject in Victorian Poetry', *ELH* 54 (1987), pp. 385–401.

> I waited for the train at Coventry;
> I hung with grooms and porters on the bridge,
> To watch the three tall spires; and there I shaped
> The city's ancient legend into this.

Here the train, the engine of industry, is set against the backdrop of the medieval steeples, which evoke an idealized time when a single heroic act could set right a social wrong; the poet mingles with grooms and porters, thus showing how he, like Godiva, sympathizes with the common people. And his poem celebrates a woman who builds 'herself an everlasting name' by defying social codes and masculine authority. So the social ills of industrialization, the oppression of the working class, and the limitations imposed on women are invoked as the context for Tennyson's retelling of Godiva's heroic ride.

Beyond these social concerns, however, is the erotic imagery of the poem. The reader is invited to indulge in the eroticism without guilt, which has been transferred to a Peeping Tom figure, 'one low churl, compact of thankless earth'. His eyes shrivel and fall out before they can see her body, but his punishment enables the reader to continue gazing with a clear conscience as she rides on 'clothed in chastity'. The transference of guilt extends even to the deserted streets, where even architectural details become voyeurs:

> The little wide-mouthed heads upon the spout
> Had cunning eyes to see: the barking cur
> Made her cheek flame: her palfrey's footfall shot
> Light horrors through her pulses: the blind walls
> Were full of chinks and holes; and overhead
> Fantastic gables, crowding, stared.

Although the walls are 'blind', the 'chinks and holes' conceal *and* enable furtive viewing, which add to her 'horrors' and heighten her sense of shame. Participating vicariously in this transgression the reader becomes a voyeur to the extent that one wonders whether Tennyson's Godiva is the champion of the oppressed, or just another object of male desire. This ambivalence recalls the contraries mentioned earlier: is she virtuous or scandalous? A heroic agent or a manipulated object? In either case, at the end of the poem she returns dutifully to her husband, thus restoring patriarchal values after her defiant ride.

Her story was not just retold. It was reenacted for many years in the

Godiva procession in Coventry, which was first recorded in 1678 and has continued into the twentieth century, with the woman playing Godiva tactfully hired from another town. A Coventry tourist guide gives the following description of the procession as it was seen some time before 1826:

> The next object of attraction is the renowned
>
> LADY GODIVA,
>
> mounted on a white horse, with rich housings and trappings. On each side of this celebrated personage rides the City Crier and Beadle, whose coats present a singular appearance, being in conformity with the field of the Arms of Coventry, half green and half red, divided down the centre. On the left arm each wears a large Silver Badge, wrought with the Elephant and Castle.
>
> The Female representing the fair patroness of Coventry is usually habited in a white cambric dress, closely fitted to the body, and a profusion of long-flowing locks, decorated with a fillet or bandeau of flowers, and a plume of white feathers, generally complete her dress and ornaments.[18]

Here she is the picture of femininity, reminiscent even of a bride in virginal white, protectively sandwiched between male figures of civic authority, where their positioning seems to regulate the spectacle's evocation of female sexuality. The processions were enormously popular with as many as 20,000 people attending, including Dugdale, Leigh Hunt and others who later wrote about the legend.

One aspect of Godiva's popularity in Victorian England that seems curious today is the ease with which references to her are de-eroticized, as though her public nakedness was only an incidental detail. The novelist Anna Jameson, for example, mused, 'If I were Queen of England, I would have [Lady Godiva] painted in Fresco in my council chamber' as an inspiration for heroic public-mindedness. And in rebuking herself for succumbing to family pressure not to write a poem against tariffs on grain Elizabeth Barrett compared herself negatively against Godiva's defiant act against taxes. A recent book by Dorothy Mermin entitled *Godiva's Ride*, which recounts these incidents, uses the self-sacrificing image of Godiva as an organizing metaphor for her discussion of women authors in England from 1830 to 1880. The legend, she writes, 'miraculously unites display and modesty, courage and safety, political

---

[18] *The History of the Coventry Show Fair with an Account of Lady Godiva and Peeping Tom, and a Description of the Grand Procession* (Coventry, after 1842), pp. 10–11.

205

engagement and family life'.[19] The writers she discusses are attracted to the heroism of Godiva's ride because

[w]omen writers often figure imagining, writing, and publishing as a kind of solitary travel, like Godiva's ride through the streets of Coventry, into a new realm of experience, an imaginatively transformed world. The heroines of Charlotte Brontë's, Gaskell's, and Eliot's first published novels, *Jane Eyre*, *Mary Barton*, and *Adam Bede* – the books that made them famous – and of *Villette*, which incorporates Brontë's actual experience of fame, undertake journeys that expose them to insult and contempt and culminate in a trial or other scene of self-display and each emerges, like Godiva, with her virtue intact and acknowledged.[20]

Mermin's observation of the way the legend 'miraculously unites display and modesty' interestingly recalls Leofric's reaction to Godiva's ride in the earliest versions: *hoc pro miraculo habentem*. The analogy is loose: while Godiva's 'self-display' exposes her to shame, she is not the victim of insult and contempt. What I find remarkable in the Victorian writers Mermin studies is the suppression of the erotic elements of the Godiva story. Their interpretation seems to dwell on her self-sacrifice, her movement from the private to the public, her courage and virtue. The nakedness has become metaphorized into a notion of social exposure. What is curious about this deflection of the erotic element in previous versions of the legend is that although history has many women who were virtuous, self-sacrificing and public-minded, only one has earned this reputation by disrobing. It is precisely *because* of the erotic dimension in the Godiva spectacle that the legend grew popular, and strategies that deflect attention exclusively to the virtuous aspects of the story still derive their emotional energy from the suppressed sexuality. To invoke Godiva as a symbol of courage is to invoke Godiva as erotic display. It is the unarticulated centre around which the fascination revolves.

The dissemination of the Godiva story in the nineteenth century made it part of the cultural landscape in the twentieth. Many of my casual informants cannot remember when they first heard the story: it seems as though it has always been around. And they seem to know different parts or different versions: some seem to know about Coventry or the tax or

---

[19] D. Mermin, *Godiva's Ride: Women of Letters in England, 1830–1880* (Bloomington and Indianapolis, 1993), pp. xvi, 20.
[20] *Ibid.*, p. 21.

Peeping Tom, and others do not. My students for the most part know only that she is a European from an earlier century, famous for a horseback ride. To a great extent the twentieth century has trivialized the legend, perhaps because familiarity with Godiva has made her ride no longer a scandal but a minor transgression easily forgiven. The heroic element has diminished along with knowledge of the legend's details. Even so, its popularization still comes with an ideology. It is still available as a metaphor for deep-seated cultural values concerning the male gaze and the body as an object of desire.

Godiva's trivialization can be measured in the pop songs written about her. At least nine recordings have Peeping Tom or Godiva in their titles.[21] Hollywood has even got into the act: a 1955 movie starred Maureen O'Hara as Lady Godiva and introduced a young Clint Eastwood as the 'first Saxon'.[22] The self-assured pose on a famous brand of chocolates (now the most widely circulated image of Godiva) continues the trivialization, where the nakedness is audacious, not scandalous. The eroticism is more innocent and consumer-oriented. As if to complete the domestication of her image the Godiva Chocolatier, originally a Belgian company, was recently acquired by the Campbell Soup Company, an American corporation best known for its wholesome canned soups.

Although the trivialized Godiva is more widely known in the twentieth century, the transgressive and violent elements of the legend are still available for writers to revive. Alberto Moravia, for example, re-writes it as a short story told from the point of view of a woman whose husband fantasizes about her as Lady Godiva.[23] Repulsed by the notion, she finally succumbs to a bribe to get her to ride, just once, naked on a horse. She does so for him late one night, but the horse wilfully rears up and kicks him in the head, killing him. In the husband's character Leofric

---

[21] 'Lady Godiva's Operation', by Velvet Underground *White Light/White Heat*; 'Herr Godiva', by Died Pretty *Every Brilliant Eye*; 'Peeping Tom', by Artie White *Tired of Sneaking Around*; 'Peeping Tom Tom Girl', by Marisela Norte *Norte/Word*; 'Peeping Tom – The Maytals', *The King Kong Compilation*; 'Hey, Lady Godiva', by Dr Hook and the Medicine Show *Dr Hook and the Medicine Show;* 'Lady Godiva', by Peter and Gordon *A World Without Love*; 'Peeping Tom', by Tommy Smith *Peeping Tom*; 'Lady Godiva', by Paul Jones *Paul Jones Sings Songs from the film 'Privilege' and Others*.

[22] Directed by Arthur Lubin. In 1951 Joan Collins made her film debut in Frank Lander's 'Lady Godiva Rides Again'.

[23] Alberto Moravia, *Lady Godiva and Other Stories*, trans. Angus Davidson (London, 1975).

and Peeping Tom have merged and receive the punishment originally reserved for the voyeur. As in the legend, the punishment is administered without human agency yet carries with it a sense of transcendent justice.

The association between voyeurism and violence is provocatively explored in Michael Powell's 1960 film, *Peeping Tom*. Although not a commercial success, film critics have singled it out as one of the first explorations of the voyeuristic potential in cinema itself. Linda Williams, for example, comments, 'Along with [Hitchcock's] *Psycho* (also 1960), it marked a significant break in the structure of the classic horror film, inaugurating a new form of psychological horror'.[24] In it a deranged man murders a series of women as they pose for his camera, which records their terror as they die. The gaze, far from being passive, detached and harmless, is sadistically aggressive and possessive. The 'new form of psychological horror' identified by Williams is the shifting of the point of view to that of the deranged killer, so the voyeur-as-film-viewer adopts the perspective of the voyeur-as-killer. The identification between the two is one-sided: there is little corresponding association between the women victims and Godiva or between the victims and the viewer.

How has the legend come to split into two contrary strands: the superficially erotic Godiva as she is popularly known and marketed and the Peeping Tom element, with its aggressive gaze and potential for violence? It helps to think of Tennyson's enormously popular poem as a watershed moment in the history of the Godiva legend.[25] More than any other telling of the story his poem articulates the binary opposites I have mentioned: scandalous/virtuous, defiant/submissive, erotic/modest, seen/unseen, private/public, heroic agent/manipulated object, male/female. But in setting up the binaries, Tennyson may have done his job so well that shortly after the poem's publication in 1842, the story was

---

[24] L. Williams, 'When the Woman Looks' in *Re-Vision: Essays on Feminist Film Criticism*, ed. M. A. Doane, P. Mellencamp, and L. Williams (Frederick, Maryland, 1984), p. 90. An element of Powell's cinematic project that seems to be absent in the Godiva legend is 'the narcissistic mirror that the cinematic apparatus holds up' to the woman victim, who in looking at the camera lens sees herself as an exhibitionist (p. 93).

[25] Before a copy of Tennyson's *Poems* of 1842 even reached America, 'Godiva' was printed in the journal *Brother Jonathan* and spread from there to news sheets. See J. O. Eidson, *Tennyson in America: his Reputation and Influence* (Athens, Georgia, 1943), p. 40 note 21. For the poem's reception in England, see E. F. Shannon, Jr., *Tennyson and the Reviewers: a Study of his Literary Reputation and the Influence of the Critics upon his Poetry 1827–1851* (Cambridge, Mass., 1952), pp. 60–9.

reinterpreted in ways that selectively privileged the positive term in these polar opposites, so that Elizabeth Barrett could, for instance, invoke Godiva as a model of courage to champion the rights of the working class and Leigh Hunt could proclaim her 'Sweet saint' and 'guiltless Eve'.[26] Peeping Tom figures less and less prominently. It seems as though ostracizing him exorcizes the story's transgressive elements. Perhaps the exorcism was only illusory, but if so it has been remarkably successful down to today, when Godiva is commonly thought of as blameless and beautiful and Tom can be reintroduced as naughty and opportunistic.

Even Sigmund Freud, who presumably learned a Victorian version of the story, maintains the bifurcation between Godiva as virtuous and Peeping Tom as deviant. He cites the legend in a paper on the development of the psychogenic disturbance of vision in the context of sexual scopophilia: 'The beautiful legend of Lady Godiva tells how all the town's inhabitants hid behind their shuttered windows, so as to make easier the lady's task of riding naked through the streets in broad daylight, and how the only man who peeped through the shutters at her revealed loveliness was punished by going blind. Nor is this the only example which suggests that neurotic illness holds the hidden key to mythology as well.'[27] In elevating the story to the status of a myth, Freud suggests that we read it, especially the Peeping Tom character, as an allegory of the 'neurotic illness' scopophilia. Interestingly but in conformity with many Victorian retellings, he does not associate Godiva's public display with exhibitionism, the reflex of scopophilia.

That the legend lends itself so well to film criticism and psychoanalysis is not entirely coincidental. Consider the parallels between the medieval legend and twentieth-century cinema: Coventry's Peeping Tom sits in a darkened room, gazing anonymously through an aperture on a woman whose body is made a public spectacle. In some versions the peeping figure was a tailor, equipped with an awl to bore a hole through the wall;

---

[26] See the reference to Barrett in Mermin, *Godiva's Ride*, p. 20. Leigh Hunt's 'Godiva' was first published in *The New Monthly Magazine* in March, 1850. It is in *The Poetical Works of Leigh Hunt*, ed. H. S. Milford (London, 1923), pp. 78–9. He also published a hagiographic essay 'Godiva' in 1819 (well before Tennyson's poem), reprinted in his *Indicator* (London, 1822), pp. 166–70.

[27] See 'The Psychogenic Disturbance of Vision' in *The Standard Edition of the Complete Psychological Works of Sigmund Freud*, 24 vols., trans. J. Strachey et al. (London, 1953–1974), XI, p. 217.

his eye assumes the position of the camera lens and the cinema viewer. His one-way gaze reduces her to an object, and, in the terms of film criticism, 'carries with it the power of action and possession'.[28]

In this regard it is helpful to contrast Tom's solitary viewing with a more familiar medieval experience of public display, the religious procession. If one considers just the carrying of a religious artifact (such as a crucifix) as an object of veneration through a town, a number of contrasts spring to mind: the displayed body is that of a man – a dead man – and is not eroticized. But what is more significant in this context (since the object could as well be a saint's relic, the host, a statue or some other religious item) is the nature of the viewing. It is collective, not individuated, with everyone aware that everyone else's gaze is directed to the same object in a ritualized, collective activity. Godiva's ride is the obverse of the religious procession in several important respects: though she is revered by the townspeople, they honour her by *not* looking when her procession passes by, and thus the only way to view the object of veneration is anonymously and secretly; and unlike a religious object, Godiva is aware of herself as a public display. Her sense of shame is foregrounded.

Another officially sanctioned spectacle for which Coventry was famous was its Corpus Christi drama. A trade guild cycle of ten plays, two of which survive, was not only staged in the town but drew audiences from as far away as London. Dugdale (who as a boy was schooled for five years in Coventry) describes in his *Antiquities of Warwickshire* (1656) how the pageants 'had Theaters for the severall Scenes, very large and high, placed upon wheels, and drawn to all the eminent parts of the City, for the better advantage of Spectators'.[29] The collective viewing of the pageant, with each wagon passing from one viewing spot to the next within the city, again contrasts with the surreptitious viewing of a Peeping Tom figure, an element of the story first recorded in Dugdale's lifetime.[30] An anonymous source recorded in 1866 sketches a more sinister association between Godiva and sacred processions preserved in local traditions going

---

[28] E. A. Kaplan, 'Is the Gaze Male?' in *Women and Film: Both Sides of the Camera* (London, 1983), p. 31.

[29] Dugdale, *Antiquities*, p. 116.

[30] Lancaster, *Godiva of Coventry*, p. 54, quotes from a City Annal written by Humfrey Wanley, which in part reads: 'one desirous to see the strange Case lett downe a Window, & looked out'. See also Burbidge, *Old Coventry and Lady Godiva*, pp. 51–4.

back to the Reformation, when 'A naked Woman on horseback was introduced to ridicule the Sacred Host'.[31] She is followed by a Peeping Tom figure popping his head out of what could be a pageant wagon ('a kind of house drawn on wheels'). If this story has any truth behind it, clearly the citizens of Coventry exploited the differences between the collective gazing of religious processions and the illicit gazing invited by Godiva's ride, between the sanctioned and the forbidden. The subversion could only work if the participants were aware of the differences in the nature of the gaze. Another indication of the popular association between the Godiva procession and biblical drama is the apparent folk etymology from an anonymous protest note affixed to a church in Coventry in 1495, which spells her name 'goode Eve'.[32] The Eve in medieval drama (which would still be an annual event at this time) is perhaps the only other officially sanctioned instance of a woman represented in a state of undress.

The parallels between the Godiva legend and cinema are striking enough that we can read the dynamics of one against the other. Many of the elements of the legend – including the spectacle of the eroticized body and the transgressive gaze – are common terms in recent film criticism. In a much-quoted essay, Ann Kaplan poses the question, 'Is the Gaze Male?' and proceeds through a psychoanalytical reading of what she calls the 'complex gaze apparatus' and 'dominance-submission patterns' to answer her question in the affirmative. Reading the Godiva legend as myth, as Freud suggests, would also lead us to affirm that the gaze is male. It even names him. As a proto-cinematic legend, it illustrates the possessive power of the male gaze with a specificity no less than the

---

[31] Recounted in M. D. Conway, 'Lady Godiva at Home', *Harper's Monthly Magazine* 33 (1866), p. 627. Burbidge, *Old Coventry and Lady Godiva*, p. 52, quotes the same passage, which he attributes to Mr Tomkinson, a churchwarden at St Michael's Church, in 1876. The account goes on to describe how one year the man playing Peeping Tom died on leaving the house, so that in future years no one could be found to play the part; 'hence Peeping Tom has ceased to be part of the procession'.

[32] Quoting from the *Coventry Leet Book*, Lancaster, *Godiva of Coventry* (p. 50), prints the verses, the first four lines of which are:

> Be in knowen & vnderstand
> This Cite shuld be free & nowe is bonde.
> Dame goode Eve made it free;
> & nowe the custome for woll & the draperie.

A number of other sources spell the name 'Godeva'.

camera lens. In defying the edict and gazing at her, Tom usurps the role of Leofric, who as her husband legally possesses her body and who controls the conditions by which the ride will be carried out, down to the issuing of the edict. The sexual nature of Tom's gaze is clearly marked in his punishment of being struck blind, a substitute for castration at least as old as Sophocles.[33] To say the gaze is male is not the same as saying that only a man can adopt it. Although it is not 'literally' male, Kaplan explains, 'to own and activate the gaze, given our language and the structure of the unconscious, is to be in the "masculine" position. It is this persistent presentation of this masculine position that feminist film critics have demonstrated in their analysis of Hollywood films.'[34] The 'male' gaze is a construct that any film viewer, woman or man, is induced to adopt.

If the pleasure of voyeurism is part of the appeal of both the legend and cinema, another pleasure comes from an identification with the object of the gaze. The desire to gaze is matched by the desire to be viewed, as Freud and others have noted.[35] The process of identifying with Godiva-as-viewed is evident in the remaking of her image in popular culture. To illustrate it one can do no better than to turn to the marketing strategies of Godiva chocolates, which aims its advertising at women in upper income and education brackets in magazines like *Bon Appetit*. Not only is the object of the gaze constructed as female in the legend and in cinema, but it too is available for cross-gender identification.[36] As a cultural myth, one of the remarkable strengths of the Godiva legend is that in the dynamics of the voyeuristic gaze both positions, the gazer and the object of the gaze, invite identification by the reader/viewer. And each position, though clearly marked as male and female, is available for cross-gender identification.

The sense of guilt in Peeping Tom and the sense of shame in Godiva have diminished to the extent that they are tantalizing, not taboo. By

---

[33] The appropriateness of the 'talion punishment' of Tom's blindness is the purpose behind Freud's invocation of the Godiva myth.

[34] Kaplan, 'Is the Gaze Male?', p. 30.

[35] See for example Freud's discussion of 'scopophilia and exhibitionism, in the language of the perversions', *Instincts and their Vicissitudes; the Standard Edition*, XIV, p. 129.

[36] In *Men, Women, and Chain Saws: Gender in the Modern Horror Film* (Princeton, 1992), Carol J. Clover argues for cross-gender identification with the young woman who survives in 'slasher' films (p. 51).

contrast the paintings and sculptures of Godiva before the twentieth century show her either with a downcast gaze in a posture of shame or modesty (usually with her body bent over, her shoulders slouched in resignation), or (less often) with her gaze upward as if inspired by a higher purpose.[37] The downcast posture shows a self-consciousness of being looked at and a sense of shame. The chocolate-marketing image of her, however, shows her sitting erect, the hair flowing in profuse elegance, and her look straight ahead, as if her position as the object of the gaze is a matter of indifference.

To the extent that Godgifu's post-Conquest reputation rests on the fiction of her ride, Godiva is not even a suitable topic for this collection. She has evolved from a respectable Anglo-Saxon countess, to a local celebrity, to a national hero, to an international marketing and pop icon detached from Anglo-Saxon England. Her story has persisted so well over the years because of the contradictory elements mentioned earlier (scandalous/virtuous, defiant/submissive, erotic/modest, seen/unseen, private/public, heroic agent/manipulated object, male/female) but also because it captures so well the dynamics of the gaze. But if the story has proved so appealing and durable why does it seem to be fading today? The parallels to cinema may point the way to an answer. As cinema has gained in popularity over the years it seems to have taken over the cultural work once done by the Godiva legend. By 'cinema' I do not mean any particular film or group of films, but rather the medium itself. Film critics, especially since Kaplan, have repeatedly shown that cinema functions through the imposition of the same 'male gaze apparatus' first made famous by the Godiva legend. Now that cinema has grown so popular, the gaze apparatus does not need a legend to articulate its values; they are now conveyed indirectly. Or to adjust Marshall McLuhan's dictum, the medium is the legend. The year 1995 marked the one hundredth anniversary of the first public viewing of a moving picture, a century that has seen the increasing trivialization of the Godiva legend.

---

[37] For example, 'Mr F. G. Stephens, the art critic, writes of [an 1878 sculpture] as "the stately and beautiful statue in marble of Godiva disrobing, letting the last white garment of her sacrifice glide downwards to her feet", and describes her as so "gravely passionate and intensely pure – she thinks less of her nakedness than of her reward". Her face has that far-away look of unconsciousness which the face of such a woman bent on so great a deed of self-forgetfulness, would have.' Quoted from A. Woolner, *Thomas Woolner R. A., Sculptor and Poet: his Life in Letters* (New York, 1917).

The final loss of the legend in future years may bring relief to some and regret to others, but in either case we can marvel at the fame of an obscure Anglo-Saxon noblewoman whose fictionalized deed assumed the role of cultural myth.[38]

[38] I would like to thank the participants of the Third G.L. Brook Symposium, the Harvard Doctoral Conference, and audiences at Smith College and the 1993 International Society of Anglo-Saxonists conference at Oxford for their comments and suggestions on earlier versions. Special thanks go to Alexandra Reid-Schwarz for help with archival work.

# The undeveloped image: Anglo-Saxon in popular consciousness from Turner to Tolkien

## T. A. SHIPPEY

A recent volume of essays, edited by Allen Frantzen and John Niles, has as its title *Anglo-Saxonism and the Construction of Social Identity*.[1] It is the purpose of this essay to argue that Anglo-Saxon studies, if not Anglo-Saxonism, have been affected increasingly over the last two centuries by the destruction, or rather the repression, of social identity for one particular group: a repression the more ironic for having been practised on the group which, in another recent opinion, that of Adrian Hastings,[2] in fact gave the initial model for all later 'constructions of nationhood' – the English.

My argument starts with a comment made in an earlier work by Allen Frantzen, his 1990 study, *Desire for Origins*. Almost at the end of this, Frantzen remarks that his book has been based on the premise 'that the place of Anglo-Saxon studies in modern intellectual life is marginal'.[3] Given the evidence that Frantzen adduces, there can be little doubt that this premise is correct. Two points might however be added to it. One is that this marginality ought to be surprising rather than taken for granted (an argument pursued below). The other is that if anything Frantzen's summation is an understatement. Within academia, especially American

---

[1] *Anglo-Saxonism and the Construction of Social Identity*, ed. A. J. Frantzen and J. D. Niles (Gainesville, Fla., 1997).

[2] A. Hastings, *The Construction of Nationhood: Ethnicity, Religion and Nationalism* (Cambridge, 1997).

[3] A. J. Frantzen, *Desire for Origins: New Language, Old English and Teaching the Tradition* (New Brunswick, N.J., and London, 1990), p. 224.

academia, 'marginal' may well be a fair description. Outside academia one might feel that 'non-existent' or perhaps 'invisible' would be more truthful: Anglo-Saxon history and Anglo-Saxon England, in so far as there is any popular awareness of them at all, are in suggestive ways regularly taken as being not 'marginal' so much as 'off the page'. Perhaps the most obvious signal is the traditional numbering of English kings as taught in every British and American school and university. William I, the Conqueror, whose date of accession almost everyone still knows, may have regarded himself as the legitimate successor of Edward the Confessor, but his claim has been silently ignored or regarded as irrelevant. In every history in the English-speaking world the first Edward, Edward I, reigned from 1272 to 1307. His Anglo-Saxon predecessors Edward the Confessor and Edward the Elder, no matter how wide their realm or how successful their rule, are quite literally felt 'not to count'. They are not part of the history of Britain, or England, or of the state as it currently exists.

Indeed one might go further than this and claim that within popular consciousness, even educated popular consciousness, there is no connected awareness of the Anglo-Saxon origins of the current state at all. If one were to ask a randomly-selected group of educated people to name three pre-Conquest kings, I suspect that the result would be a certain memory of Alfred the Great (burning the cakes), of Harold at Hastings (falling with the arrow in his eye), and perhaps of Ethelred the Unready, with his memorable if by now entirely comic nickname. The rest, Offa and Penda, Edwin and Oswald, Athelstan and Edgar and Edmund Ironside, have all simply vanished. Many Anglo-Saxon names are in any case regarded as inherently comic, sounding to modern ears either vulgar or impossible: Egbert and Oswig, Brithnoth and Uthred. The reason, of course, is that they are either misspelled or mispronounced, as in all the four examples just given. However, misspelling of Anglo-Saxon names is the rule even on national monuments (like the list of former abbots carved in stone at Glastonbury), and the vagaries of the modern spelling system have left all but specialists with no idea how the far clearer Anglo-Saxon spelling system should be read. In every way, pre-Conquest history is marked off as alien and discontinuous: nothing to do with *us*.

It might be said that this attitude, while regrettable to those who do take an interest in the period, is after all not remarkable. Frantzen goes on directly from the premise quoted above to add that there is an 'equally obvious premise', namely 'that, with the exception of a small number of hallowed names and titles, the literature and history of earlier ages are themselves routinely dismissed.' But once again, while this is generally true, and academically true, in popular awareness there are significant exceptions which go beyond a few 'hallowed names and titles.' Much earlier in his book (p. 9) Frantzen had noted that E. D. Hirsch's *Cultural Literacy: What Every American Needs to Know* (Boston, 1987) 'contains not a single reference to Anglo-Saxon culture' – no King Alfred, no Venerable Bede, no *Beowulf* even. Yet it does list in its index both 'King Arthur' and 'Norse myth', as subjects every literate person should be able to recognize. Hirsch here does no more than record the facts, which actually go a good deal beyond the class of 'cultural literates'. If one considers mass-market films alone, the Arthurian story has been responsible in 1995 for *First Knight* (a flop, but not for lack of subject recognition), and in 1991 for the much more successful *The Fisher King*. The amount of learned and even scholarly reference within the latter is itself remarkable,[4] but the main point is that the film needed to explain very little, even to a mass audience: its director could assume (clearly correctly) that everyone had heard of the Holy Grail, and had at least a mental outline of the myth of Fisher King and Waste Land. Meanwhile earlier well-known films included *Excalibur* (1981), *Camelot* (1967) – an image to which politicians can still successfully appeal – and *Monty Python and the Holy Grail* (1975). Literary re-writings of the Arthurian cycle meanwhile appear almost too frequently to count. Again, this is not an academic phenomenon: Arthur's is not a name 'hallowed' only by university syllabuses, but one which continues to mean something or other to the culture at large.

Medieval material can, then, live on perfectly well even in the present educational circumstances. A case perhaps even more relevant to and more contrastive with the oblivion that has overtaken Anglo-Saxondom is that of 'the Vikings'. The image of the Viking (as opposed to his contemporary the Anglo-Saxon) has remained clear and powerful right up to now. A recent essay in Andrew Wawn's collection, *Northern Antiquity*, makes the point with almost comic force.[5] Vikingness is used as a routine aid to product recognition in every way from the selling of sardines to the

---

[4] See R. Osberg, 'Pages Torn from the Book: Narrative Disintegration in Terry Gilliam's *The Fisher King*', *Studies in Medievalism* 7 (1995), pp. 194–224.

[5] R. Boyer, 'Vikings, Sagas and Wasa Bread', *Northern Antiquity: the Post-Medieval Reception of Edda and Saga*, ed. A. Wawn (Enfield Lock, 1994), pp. 69–81.

production of baby-clothes, from body-builders' gyms to professional American football teams. Bearded faces under horned helmets stare out from tins and packets in every supermarket. Meanwhile, if one returns to the matter of films, examples include the successful Kirk Douglas epic *The Vikings* from 1958, and *The Long Ships* from 1964, the latter derived (at admittedly long remove) from one of the best historical novels ever written, Frans Bengtsson's three-volume work in Swedish, *Røde Orm* (English translation published 1957 with the same title as the film). But good historical novels on a Viking theme, if not as common as Arthurian works, are relatively frequent, from Walter Scott's *The Pirate* (1822) and Rider Haggard's *Eric Brighteyes* (1891) on through W. G. Collingwood's two 'sagas of the Northmen in Lakeland', *The Bondwoman* and *Thorstein of the Mere* (1896 and 1895, but in print again from Llanerch Press a hundred years later in 1991), to Bengtsson's *The Long Ships* and Jane Smiley's *The Greenlanders* of 1988.

The contrast with Anglo-Saxon themes is obvious at every level. If one considers films, there was a film starring David Hemmings called *Alfred the Great* (1969), but it is virtually unobtainable. If one considers public image, there is none: even on the level of horned helmets, no one has any shared cultural image to attach to 'Anglo-Saxon'. If one turns to historical novels, it is not quite the case that there are none on Anglo-Saxon themes, but one might argue that those which do exist seem in almost every case to be 'exceptions which prove the rule' of non-recognition. Thus Scott's only venture in the direction of Anglo-Saxonness is the wildly anachronistic *Ivanhoe* (1813), set in the late twelfth century, and having as its theme the subsuming of both Saxon and Norman in a new English identity, part of Scott's more general theme of the shaping of a new British identity: Anglo-Saxons are presented only to be left behind, like the gluttonous Athelstane and the blindly reactionary Cedric. In the nineteenth century, the two major historical novels on Anglo-Saxon themes both have the word 'last' in their subtitles: Bulwer-Lytton's *Harold: Last of the Saxon Kings* (1848) and Charles Kingsley's *Hereward the Wake: Last of the English* (1866).[6] Once again, Anglo-Saxon history only gets 'on to the page' at its moment of termination.

---

[6] For commentary on these, see Andrew Sanders, *The Victorian Historical Novel 1840–1880* (New York, 1979), chs. 3 and 7, and further Sanders's essay, pp. 157–73, above.

In this century there is no more than a straggle of titles, and such works as there are, even in children's literature, show a tendency to deflect their interest on to the Anglo-Saxons' more interesting and accessible enemies, the Vikings. The historian Hope Muntz produced *The Golden Warrior: the Story of Harold and William* (1950), but as its sub-title shows, this is another 'terminal' novel. Alfred Duggan wrote two novels on Alfred and on the Confessor, *The King of Athelney* (1961) and *The Cunning of the Dove* (1960), as well as one on Cerdic and the founding of Wessex, the excellent and sardonic *Conscience of the King* (1962): they have just (1999) been reprinted. A strange work appeared in 1983 called *The Way of Wyrd*, by Brian Bates: its hero might be described as an Anglo-Saxon Carlos Castaneda. If one thinks finally of modern responses to *Beowulf* (a work which does count as one of the 'hallowed titles' and which is listed in Hirsch's *Dictionary of Cultural Literacy* (New York, 1988), even if not in his major argument), they too are mostly distinguished by successful eccentricity or respectful failure. The best and best-known of them is certainly John Gardner's *Grendel* (1971), but as its title makes clear this functions above all as a rejection of the epic. Michael Crichton's extremely strange and highly Scandinavianized *Eaters of the Dead* is back in print (London, 1976), but of course only as testimonial to the success of *Jurassic Park*.[7] By contrast W. H. Canaway's careful and scrupulous retelling of the story, *The Ring-Givers* (London, 1958, rep. by Penguin), has long been unavailable. As a general rule one could say that the only continuingly successful imaginative works using Anglo-Saxon material in the past two centuries (*Ivanhoe*, *Grendel*, and perhaps *Hereward*) have been those which subsumed or rejected it.

This situation is so familiar that it may seem to need no explanation. Yet, as has been said above, Vikings and Norse mythology, and King Arthur and Celtic mythology, still find ready admirers and consumers. Surely it would be only reasonable, indeed by comparison with other European countries only normal, for English readers of the present day to privilege their own native tradition enough at least to make it competitive with related ones. But that is what they have not done. The

---

[7] *Beowulf* has also retained a certain presence in science fiction, as one can see from two relatively recent works, *The Legacy of Heorot* and *Beowulf's Children*, both by the team of Larry Niven, Jerry Pournelle and Steven Barnes (New York, 1987 and 1995 respectively). Crichton's *Eaters of the Dead* has also just (1999) been released as a film, *The 13th Warrior*.

surprising nature of this becomes more marked if one considers, as one should, that with the gradual rediscovery of the old Northern languages and cultures, extending from the sixteenth to the nineteenth centuries, there were in fact several ways in which one might have expected Anglo-Saxon studies to break through and become part of 'cultural literacy', or popular awareness, or at the lowest level (like horned helmets on sardine tins) just general mental furniture. I would suggest indeed, that if one looks back at the middle of the last century, there were by about 1850 at least four routes by which 'Anglo-Saxonism', or 'Anglo-Saxonness', seemed poised to make its mark.

The first of these was religious. Perhaps the earliest motivation for collecting Anglo-Saxon manuscripts and materials was the urge to establish the dignity and independence of the Church of England, a process begun by Archbishop Parker with the assistance of Foxe, Bale, Lambarde, Nowell, Joscelyn, and others.[8] The falsity of the argument over Old English proto-Anglicanism may seem reason enough for this route not to have been followed. But if on the other hand one considers the genuinely immense achievements of the Anglo-Saxon Church – the greatest historian of the medieval West in Bede, the importance for the biblical text of Alcuin, the conversion of Germany by Willibrord and Boniface (né Wynfrith) – it does seem surprising that the Church of England has shown so little interest or national pride in them. Even more surprising is the lack of commemoration of English saints, well evidenced as many of them are and some of them retaining, like Cuthbert and Botolf, strong if superstitious local feeling. Yet Dunstan and Wulfstan, Edmund and Guthlac, Wilfrid and Swithin, have dwindled to being town-names, burial sites, church dedications: it is not only pre-Conquest kings who have dropped out of history.[9]

---

[8] For which see *Anglo-Saxon Scholarship: the First Three Centuries*, ed. C. T. Berkhout and M. McC. Gatch (Boston, 1982), esp. the essays by M. Murphy, 'Antiquary to Academic: the Progress of Anglo-Saxon Scholarship', pp. 1–17, and T. H. Leinbaugh, 'Ælfric's *Sermo de Sacrificio in Die Pascae*: Anglican Polemic in the Sixteenth and Seventeenth Centuries', pp. 51–68.

[9] One might note the contrast with the mid-nineteenth-century situation. Anglo-Saxon themes are prominent among those listed by T. S. R. Boase, 'The Decoration of the New Palace of Westminster, 1841–1863', *Journal of the Warburg and Courtauld Institutes* 17 (1954), pp. 319–58, and one fresco, William Dyce's *The Baptism of King Ethelbert*, received the central place above the throne in the House of Lords.

The second route by which one might have expected Anglo-Saxon England to retain a certain cultural presence also appeared early, but continued to enjoy great prominence well into the nineteenth century. This is the legal route, based on the idea of Anglo-Saxon law as the foundation of both the British and the American constitutions. It has been well documented by Christopher Hill, in his famous essay on 'The Norman Yoke', and further extended (if at the same time made more sinister) by Clare Simmons's book *Reversing the Conquest*.[10] The belief that trial by jury and bi-cameral Parliament went back to King Alfred and 'our Saxon forefathers' was widespread throughout the eighteenth century, as the studies cited show. A further point, powerfully stressed by both Frantzen and earlier Reginald Horsman,[11] is that these views were also highly acceptable to the framers of the American Constitution, in particular Thomas Jefferson, who put Anglo-Saxon (of which he wrote a grammar) on the curriculum of the University of Virginia, so that those who learned it 'will imbibe with the language their [i.e. the Anglo-Saxons'] free principles of government' (Frantzen, *Desire for Origins*, p. 206). But this entire argument has been so long out of fashion that it is no longer even familiar.

Having mentioned Jefferson's grammar, I can remark that the third available route into popular consciousness was via language study. The story of this is very much part of the history of English Studies, and has accordingly also been well charted.[12] Many readers (especially those in Britain) will be well aware that it remains a live issue, with continuing hostility between those who see Anglo-Saxon (or Old English as it is professionally known) as a vital part of the discipline, and those who see it, like pre-Conquest kings and pre-Conquest saints, as essentially 'off the page', no longer connected or relevant to the present. What we may be less aware of is that the argument has been going on, in essentially the same form, for at the very least seventy-five years, time for three

---

[10] C. Hill, 'The Norman Yoke', in his *Puritanism and Revolution: Studies in Interpretation of the English Revolution of the Seventeenth Century* (London, 1958), pp. 50–122; and C. Simmons, *Reversing the Conquest: History and Myth in Nineteenth-Century British Literature* (New Brunswick and London, 1990).

[11] See Frantzen, *Desire for Origins*, pp. 15–19 and 203–7, and R. Horsman, *Race and Manifest Destiny: the Origins of American Racial Anglo-Saxonism* (Cambridge, Mass. and London, 1981), ch. 1.

[12] See D. J. Palmer, *The Rise of English Studies* (London, 1965), chs. 6 and 7.

generations of scholars to grow old and die in.[13] Most of the argument has been energy wasted. If Anglo-Saxon studies had remained powerful elsewhere, students and colleagues would have been readier to concede its linguistic importance (as with Jefferson). Without that, attempts to anchor Old English in literary studies alone have lacked conviction. Nevertheless, it remains strange that the best-evidenced early vernacular literature of Europe should have attracted so few defenders outside a narrow profession.

Yet the most surprising and therefore the most revealing truncation of a once-powerful sense for 'Anglo-Saxonness' remains the racial one. This is now, to English speakers, effectively unknown, but echoes of it, from the nineteenth century, can still be heard in the political discourse of France. In French, the adjective *Anglo-Saxon* – usually modifying such nouns as *perfidie* or *égoisme* – is a way of saying 'British and American in unison'. In the last century (as is amply shown by Horsman in the work cited above) this 'Anglo-Saxonism' was a major part of British and even more of American political rhetoric from about 1814 onwards. Politicians routinely appealed to the brotherhood, or cousinship, of 'the two great families of the Anglo-Saxon race', or invited their American audiences to congratulate themselves that 'our fathers were Englishmen'.[14] This sentiment is now so completely forgotten as to appear bizarre. Nevertheless for a while 'Anglo-Saxon' was in America a wholly positive adjective, free of the political discontent attached to the word 'British'. It is a sign of the change that has taken place that it now survives only in the acronym WASP (White Anglo-Saxon Protestant), and that this is a term now only ever used in a hostile or derogatory way.[15]

How, one is left wondering, could Anglo-Saxon studies have managed to fritter away four such potent advantages? Whatever one might think of the truth or morality of any one of them, they should at least have been collectively able to retain some toe-hold on popular awareness: enough at

---

[13] See, for example, the British Board of Education Report on *The Teaching of English in England* (London, 1921), where hostility to Anglo-Saxon is already fully formed, esp. pp. 218 and 286.

[14] See Horsman, *Race and Manifest Destiny*, p. 95.

[15] This is conceded by Frantzen and Niles, *Anglo-Saxonism and the Construction of Social Identity*, in the editors' 'Introduction', p. 2, although they add that though the term is derogatory, it is 'generally in a good-humored way'. It is unlikely that this excuse would be offered for other derogatory racial epithets.

least (surely) to outweigh the charms of Snorri Sturluson's *Prose Edda*, a thirteenth-century text written in a difficult language in a remote island whose population is still less than that of Bradford. Yet 'Norse myth' is a part of 'cultural literacy', and Anglo-Saxon is not. The fact cries out for some coherent explanation.

The main purpose of the paragraphs above has been to argue that what we take to be a natural if regrettable state is in fact a significant absence. To explain that absence it seems necessary to me to point to another absence, no less significant, but even more widely regarded as part of the natural order of things. This is the absence, for England alone, of marks of national identity regarded as routine by all other nations, and strongly present in the other 'sub-nations' of the United Kingdom. To detail this absence would require consideration of matters not normally a part of academic or political discourse, in particular the embarrassments and anomalies surrounding the participation of England teams in professional sport. Here I can only record that while England does have a national flag (St George's Cross, red on white) and a national day (St George's Day, April 23rd), till recently the former was rarely seen[16] and the latter is still never observed. Meanwhile and with an awkwardness increasingly felt, England still has no national anthem distinct from the United Kingdom's 'God Save the Queen', once more unlike Wales, Scotland, and even united Ireland.[17] These absences in the areas of popular observance and international sport are, however, mirrored in academia, as one can see from the book recently edited by Eric Hobsbawm and Terence Ranger, *The Invention of Tradition*. This points out in detail how relatively recent and deliberately manufactured are the symbols which now mark out Scotland in particular (kilts and tartans and bagpipes, largely the result of skilful

---

[16] The commemorative plaque at Wembley Stadium, which displays the flags of the nations which won the World Cup, shows for 1966 (when England won) the Union Jack of the United Kingdom, not the Cross of St George. Such a lapse would be inconceivable for a Welsh or still more a Scottish team.

[17] Wales has long had its own anthem, 'Land of my Fathers'. In recent years (as 'Britishness' has faded) Scotland has adopted 'Flower of Scotland', while in 1998 the Irish Rugby Football Union commissioned an anthem to replace the awkwardness of using the Irish Republic's 'Soldier's Song' for teams including Protestant Ulstermen. England (and Northern Ireland) remain anomalies.

promotion by Walter Scott, among others),[18] and contains essays also on 'The Hunt for the Welsh Past', on the invention of colonial tradition in India and Africa, and one by David Cannadine on 'The British Monarchy and the Invention of Tradition.' The absence is once again any mention of England. The index provides extensive references to Wales and Scotland and Ireland, and one can find also France and Germany, Bangladesh and Pakistan and even Mongolia. But, just as at Wembley Stadium (see note 16 above), England is not there. And, just as with Hirsch's *Cultural Literacy*, while King Arthur is indexed, King Alfred is not. There is no sign of any English or Anglo-Saxon tradition ever having been invented at all. Hobsbawm indeed noted 'the neglect . . . of any problems connected with English nationalism' in a later work, but the neglect has only just been brought into historical focus, and to some extent repaired, by Adrian Hastings's *Nationhood* – the academic equivalent, one may say without intended impertinence, of the increasing phenomenon of English faces painted defiantly red-and-white at Wembley or Twickenham.[19]

This lack of concern for marks of English identity can of course be seen two ways, as a result of repression by others, or of oppression of others. The fading of English nationalism correlates well with the relentless imposition of the English language first on Celtic speakers and then across the world, while the equation of England with Britain (which goes back to Bede)[20] is often taken as insulting by Scots especially. The readiness to dispense with the common tokens of identity can also be seen (to borrow a phrase from Linda Colley, whose book *Britons: Forging the Nation 1707–1837* details the currents and cross-currents of political assimilation) as 'a powerful demonstration of English confidence'.[21] In

---

[18] See H. Trevor-Roper, 'The Invention of Tradition: the Highland Tradition of Scotland', *The Invention of Tradition*, ed. E. Hobsbawm and T. Ranger (Cambridge, 1983), pp. 15–41.

[19] See E. Hobsbawm, *Nations and Nationalism since 1780* (Cambridge 1990), p. 11, and Hastings, *The Construction of Nationhood*, p. 6. Hastings makes it clear that he is writing as an Englishman, though his book is based on lectures given to a Northern Irish audience in Belfast. He sees it as an answer to a group of theorists of nationalism including Hobsbawm, Ernest Gellner and Benedict Anderson.

[20] See Hastings, *Construction of Nationhood*, pp. 36–9.

[21] L. Colley, *Britons: Forging the Nation 1707–1837* (New Haven and London, 1992), p. 15. Colley uses the phrase to describe Defoe's self-mocking poem *The True-Born Englishman*, which boasts already of the 'mongrel' nature of the English, a claim often

this view the 'invention of tradition' for the Scots, Welsh and Irish might be taken as a mere sop to the self-esteem of groups whose active co-operation was necessary (as Colley points out) for so much of the business of Empire.[22] By pointing to the sequence of absences above I do not mean to claim 'victim-status' for the unfortunate English. What I do mean to suggest is that in the process of English linguistic victory and political domination something got lost: one part of the loss was Anglo-Saxon England.

The thesis I am propounding is then a simple one. My two points above are, first, that the Anglo-Saxon world, unlike the Viking world or the Arthurian one, has no presence at all in modern life; and second, that while England has succeeded in imposing its language especially on much of the rest of the world to an extent far greater than that of any other national group, it has in the process largely forfeited officially recognized national identity.[23] And the thesis is that these two points are related. I suggest that the developing and potentially powerful image of Anglo-Saxon origins was sacrificed during the nineteenth century to the needs of an Imperial and a British, not an English ideology. Englishness became an unwelcome political stance within the 'three kingdoms' of Britain and Ireland, as tending to exclude the non-English among Queen Victoria's subjects. At the same time, the 'invention' of Scottish, Welsh and Irish tradition was encouraged as compensation for progressive loss of independence and erosion of the Celtic languages. Meanwhile, in America Anglo-Saxonness, once embraced with pride, became a threat to the new American unity of mass immigration and faded out of the national rhetoric. These political currents explain why England failed to retain or develop a flag, anthem, national symbology etc., even in an era of violent

repeated in modern times (see below). Colley's point is that only the self-assured can afford to satirize themselves, a claim less true now than then.

[22] That it was a mere sop is suggested by the habit of subsuming British history into 'Histories of England', as noted by David Cannadine in 'British History as a "New Subject": Politics, Perspectives, and Prospects', *Uniting the Kingdom? The Making of British History*, ed. A. Grant and K. J. Stringer (London, 1995), p. 16.

[23] This statement has to be further nuanced by noting very powerful and articulate feeling for Englishness in poetry, from Blake to Rupert Brooke, and also (as with 'Mother Russia' within the USSR in 1941) in times of crisis: see Hastings, *Construction of Nationhood*, pp. 62–3.

European nationalism; and why England also, perhaps uniquely among European nations, failed to develop an origin myth. This in its turn explains why Anglo-Saxon origins, even in the educated or culturally literate mind, remain a blank: nothing happened before 1066. English history as conventionally taught, one might say, begins significantly with a forfeiture of identity in the cause of greater unity.

This thesis can be supported by considering a series of significant withdrawals, or changes of course, which took place with reference to Anglo-Saxonism during the nineteenth and twentieth centuries. The first of these is historical. When Sharon Turner brought out the third edition of his *History of the Anglo-Saxons* in 1820, he could say with truth that twenty-one years earlier, when the first volume of the first edition appeared, 'the subject of the Anglo-Saxon antiquities had been nearly forgotten by the British public': so much so, indeed, that Turner admits that he was led to the subject only by admiration of 'the Quida, or death-song, of Ragnar Lodbrog', not an Anglo-Saxon antiquity at all.[24] But by 1820 *Beowulf* had been edited, James Ingram's *Saxon Chronicles* were about to appear in 1823, and a wave of further text-editing was already being planned. Turner might well have felt that he had rescued the subject for the attention of 'the British public'. And so, in a way, he had. In the first half of the century one can see the recovery of Anglo-Saxon history being assimilated to intense national pride, and made a part of continuing identity. So, most obviously, Thomas Arnold, Sr, in his 'Inaugural Lecture' as Regius Professor of Modern History at Oxford in December 1840, insisted that Anglo-Saxon history was modern because it was part of continuing national life: and by national he very definitely meant English, not British. He told his Oxford audience that 'our history clearly begins with the coming over of the Saxons', and denied any other than a general human connection with 'the Britons and Romans'. Expanding on this theme, he declared:

We, this great English nation, whose race and language are now overrunning the earth from one end of it to the other, – we were born when the white horse of the Saxons had established his dominion from the Tweed to the Tamar. So far we can trace our blood, our language, the name and actual divisions of our country, the

---

[24] Sharon Turner, *A History of the Anglo-Saxons comprising the History of England from the Earliest Period to the Norman Conquest*, 3rd edn., 3 vols. (London, 1820), I, p. v.

beginnings of some of our institutions. So far our national identity extends, so far history is modern, for it treats of a life which was then and is not yet extinguished.[25]

But Arnold's triumphalist rooting of Englishness in the Saxons soon met opposition. His equation of 'blood' and 'language' offered an easy way for 'Britishness' to be recovered, for after all it was clear from contemporary experience that not all those who spoke English considered themselves to be English. Francis Palgrave's moderate and sensible *Rise and Progress of the English Commonwealth*, of 1832, accordingly had a section titled 'Britons not extirpated by the Anglo-Saxons', and tried to argue for good measure that the invaded but surviving British had actually spoken 'a dialect closely allied to the Anglo-Saxon . . . long before the arrival of the last invaders'.[26] Increasing linguistic knowledge soon made Palgrave's pre-philological thesis about language untenable. But similar pressure towards Britishness was felt by even such an ardent Germanicizer and able philologist as J. M. Kemble. In his *The Saxons in England* of 1849 he too tried to argue that there had been Saxons in England long before the traditional dates of invasion (so that the invaders became more native, so to speak), and that one could tell the presence of 'Keltic blood' in the modern population by 'the personal appearance of the peasantry in many parts of England'.[27] A generation later, Edward Freeman was perhaps the most aggressive nationalist of all the Victorian historians, arguing fiercely for continuity between Anglo-Saxon and modern England and against the 'fatal habit of beginning the study of English history with the Norman Conquest'.[28] Just the same, Freeman too had to make concessions to Britishness. In his *Old English History for*

[25] Thomas Arnold, *Introductory Lectures on Modern History, with the Inaugural Lecture*, in *Arnold's Works*, 4th edn. (London, 1849), pp. 23–4. Arnold's phrase 'from the Tweed to the Tamar' excludes respectively Scotland and Cornwall from 'we'.

[26] Francis Palgrave, *The Rise and Progress of the English Commonwealth: Anglo-Saxon Period*, 2 vols. (London, 1832), I, p. 27. The dialect is 'Belgic': Palgrave assumed that the language of part of modern Belgium (Flemish) descends directly from the language of Caesar's Belgic tribes.

[27] J. M. Kemble, *The Saxons in England: a History of the English Commonwealth till the Period of the Norman Conquest*, 2 vols. (London, 1849), I, pp. 11 and 21.

[28] E. A. Freeman, *The History of the Norman Conquest of England, its Causes and its Results*, 6 vols. (Oxford, 1867–1879), Preface to 1st edition.

*Children* of 1869, with its revealing simplifications, he reminds his child audience not to equate past and present:

I do not think I need to tell any of you that the whole island of Great Britain, as well as Ireland and the smaller islands about them, now forms only one Kingdom. Queen Victoria is Queen over all of them . . . We are all now friends and fellow-countrymen, whether we live in England, Scotland, Ireland, or Wales. But it was not so always.[29]

Freeman's pupil, J. R. Green, modified his teacher's statements even further in the direction of assimilation of conquered and conquering races; and while he thought the English had arrived in scattered groups he was quick to see the 'early fusion of such folks in three great kingdoms And recognition by the three kingdoms of a national unity'.[30]

The point of the paragraph above is not to say that these early historians were wrong, still less to open up the question of how much 'Keltic blood' there may or may not be in the modern English population. It is to indicate a kind of defensiveness in the writing of Anglo-Saxon history, springing from contemporary tensions. The trend reaches its apogee perhaps in Winston Churchill's popular and significantly titled *History of the English-Speaking Peoples* (London, 1956), which begins with Julius Caesar (who presumably never so much as encountered an English speaker), and moves through Anglo-Saxon history at rapid pace in a first volume firmly entitled 'The Birth of Britain'. Meanwhile, as time has gone by it has become something of a modern cliché to deny that there were ever any Anglo-Saxons at all. Thus in recent years the historian Geoffrey Elton, writing on *The English*, begins by calling them 'a gathering of various tribes and non-tribal bodies willing to be so described' and their common name 'an accident'.[31] One understands what he means: but of which Dark Age proto-nation (Scotland, Denmark, France) could one not say the same thing? Elton also completely ignores the language question, which did mark off all Anglo-Saxons at some early

---

[29] E. A. Freeman, *Old English History for Children* (London, 1869), p. 21.

[30] Successive sub-headings for ch. 4 of J. R. Green, *The Making of England*, 2 vols. (London, 1881). The 'three kingdoms' of the quotation are Wessex, Mercia and Northumbria, but one feels that East Anglia may have been missed out to make a neater parallel with England, Scotland and Ireland (Wales is a principality).

[31] G. Elton, *The English* (Oxford and Cambridge, Mass., 1992), p. 1. On p. 2 Elton cites Wormald, below, on the 'remarkably precocious sense of common "Englishness"', but stresses 'the absence of any practical reality behind the idea'.

date not only from the British but also from even their closest relatives on the Continent. Reginald Horsman takes the matter a stage further by saying flatly:

In reality there was never a specific Anglo-Saxon people in England. A number of tribes from northern Germany began to settle in England in large numbers in the fifth century; they were not a homogenous group of 'Anglo-Saxons', and they did not completely replace the Celtic tribes already living in England.[32]

It is clear enough that Horsman is not reporting his own research here, but setting down what he regards as established opinion; and he too ignores the language question.

A further factor in the growing unwelcomeness of 'Anglo-Saxonism' stemmed not from British but from European politics. Linda Colley has shown how 'Britishness' was forged above all by war, and specifically by continuing war with France.[33] During the nineteenth century, however, France was replaced as the main threat to the United Kingdom by newly united Germany. This caused increasing unease as to whether 'Saxons' in particular could be properly British, and led to a kind of philological war over the issue of whether the English were really, at bottom, Germans transplanted, or perhaps and eventually much more acceptably, honorary Scandinavians. The German side was for a while very strong, as one can see from the quotation already given from Thomas Arnold,[34] or even more from the works of John Mitchell Kemble, such a fierce German partisan that he actually wrote and published one of his major works in German, and wrote to Jacob Grimm (though it is not at all clear what he meant) that 'God meant something by it when he sent the North-albingians to Britain'.[35] This argument was, however, swept aside during

---

[32] Horsman, *Race and Manifest Destiny*, p. 4.

[33] Colley, *Britons: Forging the Nation*, pp. 17–18, 23–5 and *passim*.

[34] Arnold goes on in his Inaugural lecture, *Arnold's Works*, pp. 26–8, to give a very wide definition of 'the German race' as including not only the English but also the Spanish and Portuguese: 'half of Europe, and all America and Australia, are German more or less completely'. Statements like this would soon lose charm as a united Germany became a political reality under Bismarck. At the very least 'German' and 'Germanic' would become sharply distinguished.

[35] J. M. Kemble, *Über die Stammtafel der Westsachsen* (Munich, 1836). For the letter to Grimm, see *John Mitchell Kemble and Jakob Grimm: a Correspondence 1832–1852*, ed. R. A. Wiley (Leiden, 1971), p. 188.

the middle years of the nineteenth century by the view that the English were really and at bottom Scandinavians.

The thesis took its origin from the 'Gothic Renaissance' of the eighteenth century, was reinforced by Icelanders like Grímur Thorkelín and Thorleifur Repp, and then rammed home by people like George Stephens, the passionately anti-German Copenhagen professor and runologist, Samuel Laing, the Orcadian translator of the *Heimskringla*, and Sir George Dasent, translator of the sagas.[36] It was a thesis particularly welcome to Lowland Scots, who could thus find themselves an ancestry at once non-Gaelic but non-English.[37] Horsman cites a reviewer in the *Edinburgh Review* responding to Laing's 'passionate defense of the Scandinavians as the supreme Teutons', and arguing that all Teutons, whether 'Saxon or Scandinavian', ought to be proud of each other.[38] But when Horsman writes, 'In his impartial feeling for Teutons, this reviewer went further than most Englishmen of the 1840s toward granting others parity with the Anglo-Saxons', he misses the point. The reviewer was almost certainly Charles Neaves, an Edinburgh judge and of course a Scot:[39] as a Scot he becomes pro-Scandinavian, as a member of the Unionist Establishment he can afford to be tolerant of Saxons, in fact promoting British unity from the other side. Carlyle, another Lowland Scot, put the Scandinavian thesis more fiercely with his insistence that:

From the Humber upwards the Speech of the common people is still in a singular degree Icelandic; its Germanism has still a peculiar Norse tinge.[40]

---

[36] For these figures, see the continuing work of Andrew Wawn, respectively: (Repp and Thorkelín) *The Anglo Man: Thorleifur Repp, Philology and Nineteenth-Century Britain*, Studia Islandica 49 (Reykjavik, 1991); 'George Stephens, Cheapinghaven, and Old-Northern Antiquity', *Studies in Medievalism* 7 (1995), pp. 63–104; 'Samuel Laing, *Heimskringla*, and the "Berserker School"', forthcoming in *Scandinavica*; and 'The Victorians and the Vikings: George Webbe Dasent and *Jómsvíkinga saga*', *Proceedings of the Ninth Biennial Conference of the British Association of Scandinavian Studies, April 1991*, ed. J. Garton (Norwich, 1992), pp. 301–15.

[37] For a detailed account of the strange origins of this thesis, see Wawn, *The Anglo Man*, pp. 107–15.

[38] Horsman, *Race and Manifest Destiny*, p. 67.

[39] I owe this point and reference to Clare Simmons, who kindly commented on a draft of this paper. For the identification, see *The Wellesley Index to Victorian Periodicals*, ed. W. E. Houghton, 5 vols. (London and Toronto, 1966–1989), I, p. 494.

[40] Thomas Carlyle, *On Heroes, Hero-Worship and the Heroic in History* (London, 1841), but cited here from Horsman, *Race and Manifest Destiny*, p. 63.

But the same wish to believe in Scandinavian origins affected even the determinedly English arch-priest of patriotism, Charles Kingsley, who said in 1849 that the late Anglo-Saxon state was both rotten and effeminate: the 'Anglo-Saxon (a female race) required impregnation by the great male race – the Norse introduction of Northmen by Edward paving the way for the Conquest'.[41]

Behind all this there may have been a feeling that the Anglo-Saxons were, after all, losers. They had lost at Hastings, and to the French at that, an unwelcome start to Imperial destiny. Better to redefine the Normans as non-French, i.e. Scandinavians, and see Hastings as an episode in a civil war. The underlying uncertainty and urge to self-glamorization may be seen as well as anywhere in Rider Haggard's extremely popular novels *King Solomon's Mines* (London, 1885) and its sequel *Allan Quatermain* (London, 1887). A major character in these is Sir Henry Curtis Bart., the very type of muscular English gentleman, whose innate rather than inherited superiority is repeatedly demonstrated in scenes where he fights hand to hand, with an axe and a made-in-Birmingham mail coat, against spear-wielding Masai or unknown tribes of the African interior. But *is* he an English gentleman? When he is first introduced in *King Solomon's Mines* he reminds Quatermain of 'ancient Danes . . . who, I take it, were a kind of white Zulus', a thought seemingly confirmed by Sir Henry's 'Danish blood'. In the great battle in chapter 14, Sir Henry reverts to 'his Berserkir forefathers':

There he stood, the great Dane, for he was nothing else, his hands, his axe, and his armour all red with blood, and none could live before his stroke.

But though he is a Dane in battle, when Sir Henry gets married at the very end of the sequel to an African princess (of course a *white* African princess) his son is 'a regular curly-haired, blue-eyed young Englishman in looks . . . I hope I may be able to bring him up to become what an English gentleman should be'.[42] Englishmen are really descended from

---

[41] Cited from *Charles Kingsley: his Letters and Memories of his Life*, ed. Fanny Kingsley, 2 vols. (London, 1877) by Horsman, *Race and Manifest Destiny*, p. 76.

[42] Sir Henry's 'racial ideal' quality was pointed out from these quotations by Velma Bourgeois Richmond in her paper at the April 1994 *Old English Colloquium* at Berkeley, 'Historical Novels to Teach Anglo-Saxonism to Young Edwardians'. I am indebted to the author for sight of the paper and permission to use it, although her discussion of Sir Henry does not appear in the published version of her paper, with the same title, in

the Vikings, then (an attitude which has taken hold). But if the English are really Danes (and winners), there is naturally that much less attention given to the Anglo-Saxons (the losers).

Finally, and in the background, one should note the creeping rise of anti-German feeling. At the time of the Franco-Prussian war of 1870, Clare Simmons points to the usual 'Teutonizers' – Carlyle, Freeman, Max Müller, Bulwer-Lytton – either gloating over French defeat or expressing strong solidarity with the Prussians. But she also shows increasing popular alarm over Prussian aggression (it had after all been turned on Denmark six years earlier to the rage of the 'English as Scandinavians' propagandists like Stephens).[43] This political current too put 'Anglo-Saxonism' on the defensive.

With hindsight, one may feel that it was a mistake for English historians ever to use the term 'Anglo-Saxon' at all. It is not a native term, and seems to have been invented by early Continental historians writing in Latin. Its few uses in Old English seem to be learned calques from *Angli Saxones*, a term which (as the *OED* notes in its extensive entry under 'Anglo-Saxon') ought to be taken adverbially, as 'English Saxon', not conjunctively, as 'Angle + Saxon'. The use of the term by historians from 1610 onwards (and originating once more in translation from Latin) has combined with memories of Bede to create a general impression that the Anglo-Saxons were always some sort of a mixture, thus making room for the later British story of increasing union to be 'read back', as Patrick Wormald puts it, into earlier ages. But as Wormald also points out, the extraordinary fact, especially by contrast with Continental Europe, is that even West Saxons like King Alfred always called their language *englisc*, and often appealed to the concept of *Angelcynn*.[44] It was reflections like this which made Freeman, for instance, protest against the 'confused and unhappy nomenclature [which] hinders many people from realizing that

Frantzen and Niles, *Anglo-Saxonism and the Construction of Social Identity*, pp. 173–201. I should add that Haggard, in his capacity as 'editor' of *King Solomon's Mines* (London, 1885), feigns unease about 'un-Englishing' Curtis and suggests Quatermain's 'white Zulus' were really 'Saxons'.

43 C. Simmons, 'Anglo-Saxonism, the Future, and the Franco-Prussian War', *Studies in Medievalism* 7 (1995), pp. 131–42.

44 P. Wormald, 'Bede, the *Bretwaldas* and the Origins of the *Gens Anglorum*', in *Ideal and Reality in Frankish and Anglo-Saxon Society: Studies presented to J.M. Wallace-Hadrill*, ed. Wormald et al. (Oxford, 1983), pp. 99–129.

Englishmen before 1066 were the same people as Englishmen after 1066';[45] and which has made philologists attempt to promote the term 'Old English' rather than 'Anglo-Saxon', at least as regards the language. But in popular consciousness at least the damage had been done. Pre-Conquest England seemed weird linguistically, even in its names; ultimately unsuccessful politically; at best half-German in its self-reference. The contrast with the extraordinary success of British arms and empire through the eighteenth and nineteenth centuries was too great to be borne, and it became normal to write the Anglo-Saxons off as a mere phase or component.

The point is half-conceded by Velma Bourgeois Richmond, who in her comment on the boys' writer G. A. Henty, the greatest propagandist for Empire and Imperial virtue, remarks that he 'does not exalt Anglo-Saxonism in simple terms'.[46] I would say rather, first, that it is striking that he devoted only two of his massive output of works to Anglo-Saxon themes, predictably enough on Alfred and on Harold; and second that he shows something like a *rejection* of 'Anglo-Saxonism' in favour of an 'Englishness' which will become 'Britishness'. In his Preface to *Wulf the Saxon: a Story of the Norman Conquest* (London, 1894), Henty wrote as follows, in a passage quoted by Richmond, to which I have however inserted my own sub-text or gloss in italics:

that admixture of Saxon, Danish and British races which had come to be known under the general name of English [*English is a unification title, just as British came to be later*] was in some respects behind the rest of Europe . . . The arrival however of the impetuous Norman race . . . quickened the intellect of the people [*the English like to regard themselves as stolid and phlegmatic*], raised their intelligence, was of inestimable value to the English, and played a most important part in raising England among the nations [*so the Conquest was not a defeat but a case of 'reculer pour mieux sauter'*]. Moreover [*and here the Imperial theme emerges*] it has helped to produce the race that has peopled North America, Australia and the South of Africa, holds possession of India, and stands forth as the greatest civilizer in the world. The Conquest of England by the Normans was achieved without even a shadow of right or justice [*anti-French feeling breaks out*]. It was at the time an unmixed curse to England; but now we can recognize the enormous benefits that accrued when in his turn the Englishman conquered the Norman [*defeat again reinterpreted as victory*], and the foreign invaders became

[45] Freeman, *The History of the Norman Conquest*, Preface to the 1st edition.
[46] Richmond, 'Historical Novels to Teach Anglo-Saxonism', p. 186.

an integral portion of the people they had overcome [*returning neatly to the theme of British assimilation and unity*].[47]

Henty's defensive stance shows the difficulties that had grown up by 1900 in taking a positive view of pre-Conquest England, at least for a popular audience: it is a difficulty and a prejudice we still labour under.

It may be said finally that one person perhaps had the chance, as he certainly had the talent, to reverse the trend and put Anglo-Saxondom in an imaginatively attractive setting, and that was J. R. R. Tolkien. Tolkien in several ways recalls his predecessors the Grimms, in Germany, and the Grundtvigs (father and son), in Denmark: all five were major philologists in their own right, all five were deeply attached to national themes and the creation of national spirit, and all in their different ways had genuine creative skill and daring. Awareness of the loss of English national story and national mythology was also clearly a motive for Tolkien's fictional work from a very early stage,[48] resulting eventually in the creation (in *The Lord of the Rings*, 1954–1955), of the two cultures of the Shire and the Mark. The Shire is obviously an idealized vision of the England of Tolkien's childhood, with very strong Anglo-Saxon elements in its name-system and its vestigial 'government' (Thain, Shirriffs, Shire-moot at Michel Delving, etc.). Meanwhile the Mark and its Riders are pure Anglo-Saxon from their poetry, rendered by Tolkien as correctly-scanned Sievers-style Five Types alliterative verse, to their court behaviour and even their proverbial stock, all taken straight out of *Beowulf* with barely a change.

Yet the odd thing is that Tolkien denied that he was doing any of this. He declared in his Appendix F to *The Lord of the Rings* that the consistent use of Old English in their names and language 'does not imply that the Rohirrim closely resembled the ancient English otherwise . . . except in a general way'. As a result the work's millions of readers rarely recognize

---

[47] *Ibid.* I have expressed my debt to Dr Richmond in note 42 above, and acknowledge it again here. However I do note that (as with most Americans, see for instance my comment on Horsman on p. 230 above) English/Scottish/British distinctions do not seem significant to her. I understand but cannot fully agree with her remark in 'Historical Novels to Teach Anglo-Saxonism', p. 174, that Scott in *Ivanhoe* 'celebrates a new "Englishness"'; it is Britishness he has his eye on. William Morris meanwhile (pp. 174–5) is clearly of the 'Scandinavian' faction. Neither writer has much time for 'Anglo-Saxonism', though 'Teutonism' is a different matter.

[48] See T. A. Shippey, *The Road to Middle-Earth*, 2nd edn. (London, 1992), pp. 268–72.

that the Riddermark has anything to do with Anglo-Saxons at all. I have to conclude by saying that the currently available literary images of Anglo-Saxon England remain extraordinarily vague or limited. 'Wessex', to the literary mind, means only the lost and nostalgic countryside of Thomas Hardy. Tolkien's Mark, or 'Mercia', is preserved only in the again deliberately nostalgic childhood memories of Geoffrey Hill's *Mercian Hymns* (London, 1971).

Does any of this matter? It could be said that it is a sign of maturity not to need a national anthem, a flag, an origin myth, a narrowly exclusive version of history: in that case England is doing very well, and there is no need for any attempt to revive or keep in being any sense of the Anglo-Saxon past. On the other hand it does not take much persuasion for one to agree with Linda Colley that 'the factors that provided for the forging of a British nation in the past have largely ceased to operate'.[49] Both the United Kingdom, to a lesser degree, and England, to a greater degree, are suffering from a sort of identity crisis caused by the retreat from Empire, and showing itself in nationalist movements in Scotland and Wales, and a stifled nationalism in England which breaks out too often in football riots, exacerbated by the complacent non-recognition of officialdom. I have remarked elsewhere how strangely the sad history of the twentieth century was prefigured in philological disputes of the nineteenth century.[50] One might say, fancifully, that if agreement had been reached in about 1840 on what the word *deutsch* really meant, then the world would have been spared a great deal of hardship a hundred years later. In the same sort of way it seems to me that the population of England (and the United Kingdom outside it) needs to come to terms with its

[49] Colley, *Britons: Forging the Nation*, p. 374.

[50] See my review of Wawn, *Northern Antiquity: the Post-Medieval Reception of Edda and Saga*, and *Heritage and Prophecy: Grundtvig and the English-Speaking World*, ed. A. M. Allchin et al. (Norwich, 1994), in *London Review of Books*, 8 June 1995, pp. 16–17. For accounts of the philological *querelle* over Germanic classifications, see H. F. Nielsen, 'Jakob Grimm and the "German" Dialects', *The Grimm Brothers and the Germanic Past*, ed. E. H. Antonsen, et al. (Amsterdam and Philadelphia, 1990), pp. 25–32; S. A. J. Bradley, '"The First New-European Literature": N. F. S. Grundtvig's Reception of Anglo-Saxon Literature', *Heritage and Prophecy*, ed. Allchin, pp. 45–72; and (largely translating Stephens, but an important article for *Beowulf* studies), Gísli Brynjúlfsson, 'Oldengelsk og Oldnordisk: tildeels efter det Engelske', *Antikvarisk Tidsskrift* (1852–1854), pp. 81–143.

pre-Imperial and pre-Union history in order to adjust to a post-Imperial (and conceivably post-Union) situation. During the nineteenth century Walter Scott and a host of lesser figures created an image of co-operative British history which played a major part in reconciling contemporary Britons to British poliics and the English language. So far there have been only hints and fragments of a popular image of pre-Conquest or Anglo-Saxon history. It may be the case that this more-than-marginality needs now for other than literary reasons to be brought 'on to the page' and into clear focus.

# Index of Anglo-Saxons mentioned in the text

# Index of authors and works cited

# Index of authors and works cited

Lightning Source UK Ltd.
Milton Keynes UK
UKOW03f1410030217

293513UK00001BA/153/P